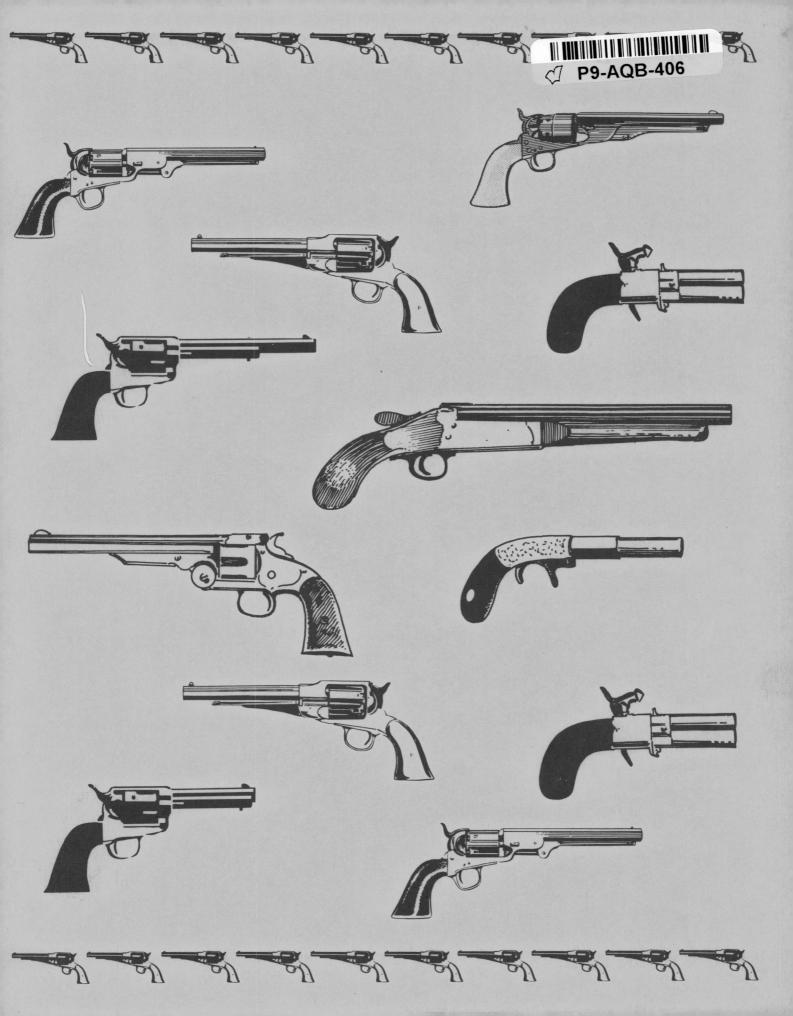

THE GUNFIGHTERS

THE
GUNFIGHTERS

BY DALE T. SCHOENBERGER

ILLUSTRATED BY ERNEST L. REEDSTROM

THE CAXTON PRINTERS, LTD.

CALDWELL, IDAHO

1983

First printing, December, 1971
Second printing, June, 1976
Third printing, May, 1983

International Standard Book Number 0-87004-207-6

Library of Congress Catalog Card No. 70-123583

Lithographed and bound in the United States of America by
The CAXTON PRINTERS, Ltd.
Caldwell, Idaho 83605
141150

TO MY PARENTS
Walter Thomas and Edna Walters Schoenberger

ACKNOWLEDGMENTS

MANY PERSONS AND THE STAFFS of several historical societies, libraries, and archives have given me valuable assistance in the preparation of this work. To all the people who have given their knowledge, time, and energy, I am deeply grateful.

I personally wish to express my indebtedness to Elmer O. Parker, Garry D. Ryan, and Miss Jane F. Smith and the staff at the National Archives; Glenn R. Sanderson and the staff at the Federal Records Center at Fort Worth, Tex.; James McGurrin, County Clerk and Clerk of the Supreme Court, N.Y.; the Office of the County Clerk of Herkimer, N.Y.; Gardner P. H. Foley, Professor of Dental History at the Baltimore College of Dental Surgery of the University of Maryland; Harold R. Manakee, Director of the Maryland Historical Society; Milt Hinkle, Kissimmee, Fla.; Mrs. Lilla M. Hawes, Director of the Georgia Historical Society and her staff; Carroll Hart, Director of the Department of Archives and History of Georgia; Isabel Erlich, the Atlanta Public Library; Margaret Ruckert, the New Orleans Public Library; Campbell H. Brown and the staff at the Tennessee State Library and Archives; Stanley J. Sieron, Jr., Chief of Detectives, East Saint Louis (Ill.) Police Department; the staffs at the Arkansas History Commission; the State Historical Society of Missouri, and the Missouri Historical Society; the University of Missouri Library; Joseph W. Snell, Curator of Manuscripts, and Don W. Wilson, Archivist, the Kansas State Historical Society; George R. Henrichs, Executive Director, the Boot Hill Museum

at Dodge City, Kans.; Robert E. Eagan, Dodge City; Ben L. Witherspoon and Donald C. Gisick, Deputy City Clerks, Wichita, Kans.; Public Health Department, Fort Worth, Tex.; Waldo E. Koop, Wichita; K. G. Bittle, City Manager, Abilene, Kans.; Stewart P. Verckler, Abilene; the Chamber of Commerce, Hays, Kans.; William F. Schmidt, Archivist, Nebraska State Historical Society; J. D. Haley, University of Oklahoma Library; James M. Day, former director of the Texas State Library and Archives, and his successor, Charles W. Corkran; Ronald A. Seeliger and Andrew M. Ruth, Newspaper Collection, University of Texas Library; Henry R. Small, Bureau of Records and Identification, Texas State Department of Correction; Mrs. Lucille A. Boykin, Dallas Public Library; Elsie Woosley, City Clerk, Austin, Tex.; O. T. Martin, Jr., District Court Clerk, and Eli Greer, Deputy District Court Clerk of Travis County, Tex.; Tom Hill, County and District Court Clerk of Hemphill County, Tex.; F. Stanley, Pep, Tex.; Ed Bartholomew, Fort Davis, Tex.; Ernest R. Archambeau, Amarillo, Tex.; W. W. Dennis, Jacksboro, Tex.; Lonnie Lee, Iowa Park, Tex.; the Chamber of Commerce, Pecos, Tex.; Mrs. Jane Rowley and the staff at the Austin Public Library; the Austin Police Department; Benecio López Padilla, General of the Division, Department of Archives, and J. Ignacio Rubio Mañé, Director of Special Correspondence of the National Archives, Republic of Mexico; Dr. David T. Carr of the Mayo Clinic; Mrs. Alys H. Freeze, Head of the Western History Department, Denver Public Library; Gilbert Garcia, Deputy District Clerk, Las Animas, Colo.; Mrs. Laura Allyn Ekstrom, Mrs. Luisa Arps, and Mrs. Enid T. Thompson, the State Historical Society of Colorado; Mrs. Velma Churchill of the Colorado State Archives and Public Records Center; Mrs. Katherine Halverson, the Wyoming State Archives and Historical Department; Mrs. J. K. Shishkin and Ruth E. Rambo, the Museum of New Mexico; Mrs. Dorotha M. Bradley, the New Mexico State Records Center and Archives; Frank Pfeiffer, publisher, the *Raton* (New Mex.) *Daily Range;* Phil Cooke, Santa Fe, N. Mex.; Margaret J. Sparks, Arizona Pioneers' Historical Society; Mrs. Marguerite B. Cooley, Director of the Arizona State Library and Archives; Mrs. Zelma B. Locker, San Diego Public Library; Mrs. Virginia Rust, the Henry E. Huntington Library and Art Gallery; John D. Gilchriese, field historian, the University of Arizona; T. F. Hobble, Needles, Calif.; the Office of the County Clerk and Clerk of the Superior Court, County of Los Angeles; T. Morton of the Los Angeles Police Department; the Office of the County Recorder, San Bernardino, Calif.; the Office of the County Recorder, Los Angeles, Calif.; Emil A. Pavone, Vice-President of the Bourbon Institute; the Royal Naval Library of Great Britain; Michael Godfrey of the Public Record Office of Great Britain; and Alan G. Merz of St. Louis, a firearms buff, for bringing a certain item to the author's attention.

Special thanks should go to Mrs. Mary Ann Schoenberger for her kind and generous help in several matters concerning the manuscript. To her, and all of the others, go my sincere thanks.

D. T. S.

The Crow's Nest

CONTENTS

ILLUSTRATIONS

INTRODUCTION

THE WESTERN GUNFIGHTER (or "man-killer" as he was more commonly called) undoubtedly was the single most colorful individual that the wild American West ever produced. He—and he alone —can stand as a personification of that great era in which he lived, and oftentimes killed. The Western gunfighter—his legendary quick-draw, his mythical marksmanship— has whetted the appetites of Western buffs and fast-draw enthusiasts for more than a century, and has made the gunfighter a fable in both song and legend.

For many years there has been a lack of a painstaking and exhaustive study of the lives of several of the more famous Western gunfighters which would result in the most accurate and definitive analysis of these particular men. I hope that I have suc-ceeded in producing this definitive study. Such a study has not been an easy task under the existing handicap of limited contemporary records, many of which are vague and conflicting, but nonetheless, are the bread and butter of any historian.

However, in writing this work (the research has taken sixteen years) I have relied quite heavily on the contemporary records (newspapers, police and court records, municipal and county records, federal documents, diaries, old manuscripts, and, where verifiable, old-timers' recollections) to tell the stories of the famous Western gunfighters *as their contemporaries saw them.* One rule which I have tried to maintain throughout this work was to keep rumor and legend from being intermingled with the facts. Rumor and legend have no place in a historical work. On several occasions, however, I have quoted a rumor or legend to show by documentation that a well-known incident in a gunfighter's life did not happen, or that there may be reasonable doubt that such an incident occurred, or to bring to the reader's attention the possibility of such an incident actually having occurred. But I have endeavored to refrain from including all rumors and legends in this work because the reader would be eventually overwhelmed by them and would not know just where truth stopped and legend began. I have tried to write a work of truth; not one of truth interwoven with legend. In total, I have strived to separate the Western gunfighter from his bigger-than-life legend.

The men whose biographies appear in this work were the famous gunfighters per se. They weren't outlaws and murderers (in the sense that they were hunted down by the law for murder). They killed; were arrested and tried for their killings except in isolated incidents. In every instance except one, they were either acquitted or fined for their shootings and killings. In the lone exception, the man involved (Ben Thompson) served two years in prison. Men such as John Wesley Hardin, Johnny Ringo, and Wild Bill Longley were famous gunfighters, but I have excluded them from this work. Hardin was a hunted fugitive who was imprisoned for more than fifteen years, and Longley was hanged for murder. And for the most part, the reputations of Hardin and Longley were made in Texas, whereas the other men in this work made their reputations in various parts of the American West. I would have included Ringo in this work, but unfortunately Ringo's complete life story has not yet come to light.

I have written this work in the overall hope that the reader may have a better understanding of a way of life that is gone forever, and of an extinct breed of men whom history has chosen to call "The Gunfighters."

DALE T. SCHOENBERGER

The Crow's Nest
St. Louis, Missouri
January 6, 1971

THE GUNFIGHTERS

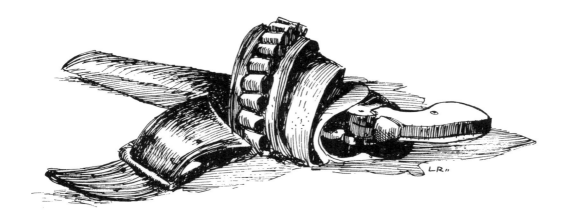

1.

CLAY ALLISON

(1840-1887)

ROBERT A. CLAY ALLISON was born to John Allison (1801-1845) and Nancy McCullough Lemmond (1798-1864)[1] near Waynesboro, in Wayne County, Tennessee, in the year 1840. For the first twenty-one years of his life Clay eked out an existence laboring on his parents' farm. It was the War Between the States which ultimately took Allison from the obscure life of a Tennessee dirt farmer and cast him into the role of one of the most feared gunfighters on the Western frontier. When his native Tennessee seceded from the Union in 1861, Clay exchanged the family plow for a Confederate uniform.

Tennessee at the time of the war was divided into two political factions: a pro-Unionist group located principally in eastern Tennessee and a strong Confederate and pro-slavery group throughout the remainder of the state. As with most Southerners, Clay Allison felt a deep sense of loyalty to his native state. It was Tennessee for which he fought. To Clay's way of thinking, anything else would have been treason.

The war gave Allison his first taste of human blood, and the shedding of human blood was something which he came to enjoy. His war record is sketchy at best. It is known that on October 15, 1861, he enlisted in the Tennessee Light Artillery in Hardin County for a period of one year,[2] but his enlistment was short-lived because of a mental condition and he was discharged on January 15, 1862, at Bowling Green, Kentucky.[3] Allison's medical discharge was dated January 10[4] and it read in part:

. . . Incapable of performing the duties of a soldier because of a blow received many years ago, producing no doubt a [illegible] of the skull, since which time [illegible], emotional or physical excitement produces paroxysmal of a mixed character, partly epileptic and partly maniacal. He is suffering from such a paroxysmal caused by an attack of [illegible] during which he manifested an exact [illegible] to commit suicide. . . .[5]

Clay Allison, however, was always something of a paradox, both in personality and physical stature. His body was athletic in build. He stood six feet two inches in height and weighed about 175 pounds. He had wavy black hair and fierce-looking blue eyes. His right eye was slightly cocked. He was clean-shaven, but in later life he grew thin chin whiskers and sometimes wore a mustache. His only physical deformity, probably a birth defect, was a crippled right foot which caused him to limp. Some old-timers who knew him say Allison's foot was clubbed. Subsequently, he shot himself accidentally in the foot[6] and the compounded injuries forced him to use a cane in later life. While not in his cups (which wasn't often), Allison was mild-mannered, sober-minded, and congenial, but when drinking he became surly and destructive, his bloodlust reaching a fever pitch. After these frequent drinking bouts he was usually embarrassed at what he had done. It would seem, therefore, that Allison suffered from manic-depressive psychosis, one of the more common forms of mental illness.

It has been said that while Clay was recuperating from his illness at the family farm in March, 1862, he shot and killed a corporal of the Third Illinois Cavalry for breaking one of his mother's favorite serving pitchers during a raid on the Allison place. Many Union soldiers lost their lives on raids of Tennessee farms and it is impossible to know who killed every one, but if Clay Allison did kill a Union soldier for offending his mother, then it would have been entirely in keeping with his character.

Allison enlisted in Company F, Nineteenth Tennessee Cavalry (commonly referred to as the Ninth Regiment Tennessee Cavalry) on September 22, 1862, at Leatherwood, Tennessee, for a period of two years.[7] Later he was reassigned to Company C of the same regiment.[8] Little is known of Allison's individual war activities from the date of his second enlistment until the end of the war, although by his own admission he served as a scout for fellow Tennessean, Lieutenant General Nathan B. Forrest,[9] probably sometime between November 17, 1864, and May 4, 1865, when his regiment surrendered to Union forces at Citronelle, Alabama.[10] (Forrest commanded a cavalry corps of the Army of Tennessee at this time.)

The words "scout" and "spy" were interchangeable and indistinguishable during the War Between the States. The duties of a scout were to pinpoint enemy troop movements and locate enemy supply depots, oftentimes by disguising one's self as an enemy soldier and penetrating enemy lines. A scout's duties (which usually befell privates) had nothing to do with the work of an intelligence agent per se, but it was almost as dangerous. Allison's work as a scout for General Forrest, therefore, was not that of a spy per se.

One of the more publicized stories about Clay Allison's war activities is that he was captured behind enemy lines in a Union uniform and sentenced to death as an intelligence agent. According to the story, Clay

Clay Allison as he looked at age twenty-six, shortly after the War Between the States when he went west across the Missouri.

records also show that Clay was *paroled* as a private from military confinement by Federal authorities at Gainesville, Alabama.[12]

Soon after the war, countless young men began to leave their shattered, war-torn homes in the South to seek a new life west of the Missouri. They were restless, adventurous men with a lust for betterment. Such a man was Clay Allison. As best it can be determined Clay, together with two of his brothers, John W. and Monroe (or Munroe), and a sister, S. A. Mary, and her husband, Lewis G. Coleman, left their homes in Tennessee and traveled west to Texas in the fall of 1865.

While the Allison-Coleman party was en route to the Brazos River country of Texas, Clay and a ferryman named Zachery Colbert had a dispute over the party's being ferried across the Red River into Texas. The dispute erupted into a fistfight and Colbert was severely beaten by Allison. After the fight, Clay ferried his relatives into Texas. The site of Allison's fight with the ferryman was about eight miles below the old city of Preston, Texas (now inundated by Lake Texoma), on what is now the Oklahoma side of the Red River. Denison, Texas, is located about five miles south of the site.

In the Brazos country, Clay hired out trailing herd for Oliver Loving and his partner, Charles Goodnight. It was while riding for Loving and Goodnight that Clay saw the territory of New Mexico for the first time in 1866.[13] It is not known whether Allison was among the eighteen trail hands who accompanied Loving and Goodnight on their historic drive from near Fort Belknap, Texas, to the Pecos River at Horsehead Crossing, on up the Pecos to Fort Sumner, New Mex-

escaped at Johnson Island, in Sandusky Bay off Lake Erie, on the eve of his scheduled execution by killing a guard and swimming to shore, later returning safely to his lines. The War Department, however, has no record of Allison ever being a prisoner of war at Johnson Island. The Union Army, which kept extensive prisoner of war records, has a record of Allison being a prisoner only from May 4-10, 1865, in Alabama.[11] The ico, where Goodnight stopped and Loving drove to the mouth of Crow Creek on the South Platte, seventy-five miles north of Denver, during the summer of 1866. The route became known as the Loving-Goodnight Trail.

The roster of the cowhands on this famous drive has been lost, but several drovers who later worked for Allison were of the opinion that Clay was with Loving and Goodnight.[14] Allison was at Las Vegas, New Mexico, in 1866, where the only known photograph of him was taken,[15] so it is conceivable that he was on the historic drive.

Clay also wrangled for M. L. Dalton, formerly of Tennessee.[16] Later, when his brother-in-law and another man, Isaac W. Lacy, formed a cattle partnership, Clay became their trail boss.

The early-day Texas career of Clay Allison, except for his wrangling activities, is extremely sketchy. There is the often-told story that one day in 1866 Clay rode into the west Texas town of Canadian completely in the nude, except for sombrero, gun belt and boots, firing his revolver. The story goes that when the town marshal attempted to arrest Clay for indecent exposure and general all-around cursedness, the big Tennessean turned his pistol in the direction of the startled peace officer, marched him to a nearby saloon, and forced him to buy a drink.

The town of Canadian was not founded until July 4, 1887,[17] and Clay had been dead three days by that time.[18] John A. Chambers, a friend of Allison, said that the now famous ride in the nude actually occurred at Mobeetie, Texas,[19] sometime between February, 1880, and October, 1883, when Allison ranched in the Texas Panhandle. Ac-

cording to Chambers, Clay called the ride into Mobeetie his "Chief Mogul" ride.[20] Regardless, however, of where and when the ride took place, there seems to be little doubt that it occurred.

There is the story that Allison was forced to leave Texas, circa 1870, after he had killed a west Texas cattle rancher named Johnson in a knife duel fought with both men stripped naked in an open grave which had been dug by the adversaries. The strange duel allegedly was fought over the ownership of a certain water hole that was adjacent to both men's property. Allison's relatives know nothing of this particular fight.[21] Also, there is no record of Allison owning land in Texas prior to 1880. A search of the old records in the Hemphill County courthouse at Canadian also failed to turn up any documentary evidence of the knife fight.[22]

What might have been the real story about Allison's alleged fight in the open grave is this, according to Mrs. T. Y. Moorhead and Francis J. Kraus, Sr., two old-time residents of Pecos, Texas. Shortly before his death in July, 1887, Clay was feuding with a cattle rancher in Lincoln County, New Mexico, where Allison had established his last ranch. The name of this other rancher was forgotten by Kraus and Mrs. Moorhead, but he and Clay had been quarreling for some time. They agreed to a duel and to dig a grave for the loser's cadaver. At the time of Allison's accidental death, the grave had not been finished, but the two men had hauled an unmarked headstone to the grave site, to be used as a marker for the fallen victim.[23] Allison was a frequent visitor to Pecos. He went there often to pick up supplies for his ranch. He knew many of the

Pecos residents, and Mrs. Moorhead remembered attending Allison's funeral as a youngster.[24] If this story is true, Allison's death probably saved a human life.

For whatever the reason, by the summer of 1870 Clay Allison had taken up residence in Colfax County, New Mexico, a country he had probably seen and fallen in love with when he trailed herd for Goodnight. Lacy and Coleman located a ranch in Colfax County near the Vermejo River. Coleman persuaded Clay to trail the Lacy-Coleman herd to the Vermejo country for a payoff at the end of the trail in cattle.[25] After reaching the Vermejo, Clay received three hundred head of cattle as his payment.[26] He purchased a ranch near Ponil Creek, not far from the town of Cimarron. Allison eventually built his spread into one of the finest ranches in the county.

It was in New Mexico where Clay Allison actually became a legend in his own time. His first known New Mexico exploit involved a man named Charles Kennedy who lived near Elizabethtown. One night in September 1870, Allison and some of his cowboy friends, including a Texas hardcase with the famous name of David Crockett, were drinking in a saloon at Elizabethtown when the wife of Kennedy entered and told them that her husband had murdered their infant daughter. She also informed them that her husband had murdered several persons who had stopped at their cabin.

Allison, Crockett, and the others went to the Kennedy cabin only to find him too drunk to answer questions. There was no visible evidence of foul play, so Clay and his friends brought the drunken man to Elizabethtown and jailed him. Judge Benjamin F. Houx of Elizabethtown ordered an extensive search of the Kennedy cabin and the surrounding property in the hope of discovering what he had done with the remains of his alleged victims. The investigation turned up enough assorted bones to fill two sacks, but five medical men could not agree whether there were any human bones among them.[27] Judge Houx ordered Kennedy held for trial pending further examination of the evidence.[28]

The bones were conclusive evidence of Kennedy's guilt as far as Clay Allison and Davy Crockett were concerned. With several others, Allison and Crockett broke into the jail, took Kennedy to the town slaughterhouse,[29] and dispatched him with a rope on October 7, 1870.[30] In a fit of maniacal rage Allison is reported to have decapitated Kennedy, placed the head on a pike, and displayed the gruesome object in Henri Lambert's saloon at Cimarron,[31] his favorite haunt.

Clay Allison's reputation as a man-killer dates from January 7, 1874, when he killed a man at Tom Stockton's Clifton House, an inn and supply store located near the Canadian River crossing in Colfax County along the old Barlow and Sanderson stage route. The man Allison killed was "Chunk" Colbert (sometimes erroneously spelled Tolbert), a west Texas gunman and nephew of Zack Colbert, the ferryman who was bested by Allison several years before.

Chunk Colbert was a noted desperado who allegedly killed seven men.[32] One of Chunk's victims was said to have been Charles Morris who allegedly was killed at Cimarron in 1871 or 1872 for trifling with the affections of Colbert's wife.[33] Colbert's last victim was Walter Waller[34] (or Walled) who was said to have been killed at Trinidad, Colorado. Waller might have been a friend of Porter Stockton (who was no relation to Tom Stockton),[35] a Colorado hardcase and acquaintance of Clay Allison.[36]

Chunk Colbert, for some reason,[37] decided that Clay Allison would be his next victim. He sent Clay a message daring Allison to meet him in a horse race at the Clifton House. Clay saw through Colbert's challenge and agreed to meet the Texas gunman. The race was held on Tom Stockton's quarter-mile track and settled nothing. The judges declared it a dead heat.

After the race Colbert invited Allison to eat with him in the main dining room of the Clifton House.[38] Chunk also asked his friend Charles Cooper to witness the occasion. Allison and Colbert had finished their meal and were drinking coffee when the shooting occurred. Colbert reached for another cup of coffee with one hand while he slowly drew his pistol above the table with the other. Allison saw Colbert's move and went for his own weapon. The muzzle of Chunk's revolver had not quite cleared the top of the table in his anxiety to fire. As a result, the muzzle was not leveled at Allison. The bullet struck the tabletop and deflected away. Allison then fired, hitting Colbert directly above the right eye,[39] killing him instantly. The startled Cooper, who earlier in the day had been accidentally wounded in the hand by Colbert,[40] made no motion to draw his pistol.

Chunk Colbert was buried on the hill in the rear of the Clifton House, where a makeshift cemetery had sprung up.[41] The old Clifton House was abandoned in 1879 and is now in ruins. Colbert's grave is obliterated. Western buffs invariably enjoy re-

peating the often-told story about what Clay Allison reportedly said when asked why he sat down to dinner with a man whom he intended to kill. According to the story, Allison replied soberly, "Because I didn't want to send a man to hell on an empty stomach."

Charles Cooper disappeared mysteriously on or about January 19, 1874,[42] and was never seen again, at least in New Mexico Territory. The last time Cooper was seen, he was riding in the direction of Cimarron with Clay Allison. Allison never said one way or the other what happened to Cooper, if, indeed, he knew. Some people suspected that Clay had killed Cooper somewhere along the trail to Cimarron and buried his body. For the time being the fate of Charles Cooper remained a closed matter.

Except for an occasional incident, such as his semi-nude dance with Mason T. Bowman,[43] Allison turned his attention to his cattle ranch and Colfax County politics. The dance with Bowman is one of the few escapades of Allison which can be substantiated.

Mace Bowman had nerves of steel and was noted for his gameness under fire. He knew of Allison's reputation and Clay knew that Bowman was a man not to be trifled with. The first time the two men met, they were in their cups. Some say that Bowman originally sought out Allison because Clay had killed "Buck" Bowman, Mace's nephew, at Cimarron. This is erroneous. There is no record of Allison's killing any Bowman.

Clay and Mace Bowman wanted to see who was the quicker in drawing his pistol. Witnesses said that Bowman beat Allison to the draw almost every time. Tiring of this game, the two men stripped down to their underwear and began dancing with each other. Finally, they took turns shooting at each other's feet to see who was the better dancer. The whole affair ended without any tragedy,[44] but for a while it looked as if someone would be killed.

There is the often-told story of Bowman's shooting Clay Allison at Tascosa, Texas. The story goes that Clay was on one of his drinking sprees when he and some of his cowhands rode in to shoot up Tascosa and were confronted by Bowman. Allison then rode out of pistol range and began firing his revolver in the air. Bowman stepped into a nearby saloon and got a rifle. He returned to the street and fired at Allison. The bullet struck Clay in the chest and he toppled from his mount. According to the story, it was several weeks before Clay was up and around again.[45]

Controlling politics in Colfax County during the 1870s were men who were affiliated with the political faction at Santa Fe, the territorial capital. The Santa Fe clique, or "Ring" as it was commonly referred to, was attempting to exert political control throughout the territory, even at the lowest levels in the counties and communities. Clay Allison was a frequent critic of the "Yankee monopoly at Santa Fe." He sternly believed that the citizens of Colfax County should be left alone to work out their own destinies.

One of the most outspoken critics of the political ring at Santa Fe was the Reverend F. J. Tolby, a Methodist minister, whose church was at Cimarron. The Reverend Mr. Tolby was murdered on September 20, 1875,[46] by "person or persons unknown" as he was riding back to Cimarron from Eliza-

bethtown where on Sunday he had conducted church services for the miners in that area.

Mr. Tolby's fellow churchman, the Reverend Mr. Oscar P. McMains, suspected Cruz Vega, a Mexican mail carrier, of having murdered Tolby. Since the Reverend Mr. Tolby had not been robbed, Mr. McMains was convinced that Vega had been hired by the ring at Santa Fe to silence the minister. Pressure was put on the authorities to have Vega taken into custody. The Mexican was arrested, but he denied killing the minister and was released for lack of evidence.

Mr. McMains convinced Allison that the way to get at the truth was to seize Vega and force him to talk. Allison, Mr. McMains, and several others seized Vega on October 30 and took him to a telegraph pole near Ponil Creek. Vega was threatened with lynching if he didn't tell who had killed Mr. Tolby. The frightened Mexican, as he was being hoisted upward, confessed that it was another Mexican, Manuel Cardenas, who had killed the minister. The confession did not save Vega's life. He was left dangling from the telegraph pole.[47] To hasten his death, someone put a bullet in the back of the Mexican as he dangled from the pole.[48] Allison, obviously overwrought, later tied the lynch rope to his saddle pommel and dragged Vega's corpse through the greasewood.[49]

The death of Cruz Vega had historic repercussions for Clay Allison. Vega had been a friend or relative of Francisco (Pancho) Griego. Griego had the reputation in Colfax County as being a *pistolero*. Vega had been a mail carrier in the employ of Florencio Donahue, Griego's business part-

Francisco ("Pancho") Griego sought to avenge the death of a friend but was killed by Clay Allison in a gun battle in Henri Lambert's saloon in Cimarron in 1875. Griego had a local reputation as a *pistolero*.

ner. Pancho Griego was noted for his courage and his ability to kill. Griego killed and wounded three soldiers of the Sixth U.S. Cavalry on May 30, 1875, in a wild fight at Lambert's saloon,[50] which was housed in the St. James Hotel at Cimarron. Pancho let it be known that he was going to avenge

Vega's death and that he blamed Allison for Vega's hanging.

Clay met Pancho in front of the St. James Hotel on November 1, 1875, in the company of Luis L. Griego, Pancho's eighteen-year-old son, and Donahue. *The Daily New Mexican* of November 5 carried an account of the meeting:

On the night of the 1st inst., Francisco Griego was shot and killed by R. C. Allison. Both parties met at the door of the St. James Hotel, entered with some friends, took a drink, when the two walked into the corner of the room and had some conversation, when Allison drew his revolver and shot Griego three times; the lights were all extinguished, and Griego was not found until next morning. Francisco Griego was well known in Santa Fe where his mother resides. He has killed a great many men, and was considered a dangerous man; few regret his loss.

More bloodshed followed.

Mr. McMains now thought that Griego and Donahue had hired Vega and Cardenas to murder Mr. Tolby. Mr. McMains claimed that Griego and Donahue were cattle rustlers and had been caught in the act by some Americans, and a gunfight had resulted. The fight between the two parties allegedly was witnessed by Mr. Tolby. Mr. McMains was now convinced that Griego and Donahue had wanted the minister dead for that reason.

Manuel Cardenas was arrested on November 10 and examined before a judge and then bound over to await trial. Mr. McMains and his vigilantes (Clay Allison was not among them) seized Cardenas and extracted a confession that he and Vega had killed Mr. Tolby and that Donahue, Melvin W. Mills, a Cimarron attorney, and Dr. R. H. Longwell, also of Cimarron, had hired

Cimarron, New Mexico Territory, as it appeared in 1875 when Allison and Pancho Griego faced each other. Lambert's saloon, where the shooting took place, is the middle building in the right background. At the far right is the courthouse to which Sheriff Isaac Rinehart brought Allison on a murder charge several months later, following more killings.

them to commit the murder. Mills and Longwell were said to have been associated with the Santa Fe ring. Cardenas was released by the vigilantes, but he was quickly rearrested and jailed because of his confession. Cardenas denied his confession upon being jailed. Later on the night of November 10, a group of masked men seized Cardenas, overpowered his guards, and shot him through the head, killing him instantly.[51]

Mr. McMains was charged with the death of Vega. He denied that he and his group had any intention of lynching Vega. He blamed the Mexican's death entirely on the fanatic Allison and some of his less stable followers who got carried away in a frenzy of excitement.[52] Mr. McMains was tried for

Vega's death in 1877 at Mora, New Mexico, on a change of venue. He was found guilty in the fifth degree and fined three hundred dollars. The judge, however, threw out the verdict because it did not state of what the churchman had been guilty. Another trial was held in 1878 at Taos, New Mexico, on another change of venue, but the case was dismissed.[53]

Most Colfax County citizens feared Allison and deplored his maniacal rages, but Clay was a desperate man and few desired to confront him. His wild antics were a common occurrence and no one was immune to his particular brand of enmity. He quarreled with his brother-in-law, L. G. Coleman. Clay felt his in-law needed killing and said as much. The pleading of Mrs. Coleman probably saved her husband's life.[54]

The citizens of Cimarron were singled out particularly for Allison's enmity. Allison and some of his cowboy friends raided a mule corral at a ranch on Crow Creek, south of Red River, New Mexico. The mules were being quartered temporarily at the ranch by the military, and when the soldiers heard the would-be rustlers, they came running toward the corral. In the confusion to escape, Allison accidentally shot himself in the foot. Allison later sent for Dr. Longwell at Cimarron to treat his wound. Longwell delayed in coming out of fear and Clay's friend, Davy Crockett, ridiculed the doctor about his delay in treating a wounded man. The remark offended Longwell; he said it was Allison's fault in the first place for not behaving himself. Longwell's remark angered Allison and Clay promised he would deal with the doctor after his foot healed. Clay also manhandled Colfax County court clerk Lee, whom he flung against a door and pinned there with a knife in his coat sleeve. He threw a knife at attorney Melvin Mills, pinning the lawyer's coat sleeve to a wall. Lee and Mills had made the mistake of voicing publicly that they thought Allison needed killing. Another man, James Wilson, who had a drunken argument with Allison, and said later that he would have killed Clay had the latter not been drunk, fled Cimarron when he sobered up and learned that Allison was looking for him.

Allison's political enemies at Cimarron pressured Governor Samuel B. Axtell into issuing a proclamation on February 21, 1876, offering a reward of five hundred dollars for his arrest in the death of Charles Cooper.[55] But out of fear, local law authorities made no move to arrest Allison.

To what extent Allison was feared at Cimarron is best shown by his maniacal destruction of the *Cimarron News and Press* on January 19, 1876. When the *News and Press* became caustic in an editorial, Clay and some of his friends in a drunken rage invaded the newspaper's editorial office and took the paper's type cases and printing press, dumping them into the Cimarron River. The first page of the paper's next edition had already been printed, so Allison and his friends appropriated the blank side of the newspaper sheets and marked every one "Clay Allison's Edition." Clay then sold the papers on the streets of Cimarron at twenty-five cents a copy.[56] The next day, when he was sober, Clay returned to the editorial office of the *News and Press* and paid Mrs. William R. Morley, wife of one of the owners of the paper, two hundred dollars in damages for the destroyed printing equipment.[57] Somewhere between the maniacal destruction of a printing press and the making of restitution for a wrong act lies the real Clay Allison.

Sheriff Isaac Rinehart of Colfax County knew of the reward proclamation for the arrest of Clay Allison, but he made no move to do so. The night of March 24, 1876, was to provide Rinehart with the necessary assistance that he needed to apprehend Allison. Three Negro soldiers walked into Lambert's saloon and were instantly shot dead. *The Daily New Mexican* carried an account of the triple slaying in its issue of March 25:

> A Cimarron dispatch dated today says: Last night after taps at 9 p.m. as 3 of the colored soldiers belonging to the detachment under Captain [Francis] Moore stationed at this place, were entering Lambert's saloon, they were fired upon by a party of cowboys, names unknown and killed instantly. From what we can gather from the bartender there was no provocation made, but the guilty parties are being searched for.

The three murdered Negro soldiers were Privates Anthony Harvey, John Hanson, and George Small of Company L of the Ninth U.S. Cavalry.[58]

Rinehart suspected Allison of having aired his vehement hatred of Negroes by killing the three soldiers. Rinehart requested a detachment of cavalry to assist him in arresting Allison. Even Clay Allison couldn't confront the United States Army. The sheriff and a detachment of Negro cavalry under the command of a white officer found Allison at the ranch of his former employer, I. W. Lacy, on March 30.[59] Clay refused to submit to arrest unless he was allowed to keep his firearms. Rinehart agreed reluctantly. The following day Allison was taken on a change of venue to

Taos by Rinehart and a detachment of colored troops. It must have galled Allison to be escorted by the Negroes. En route to Taos, Clay swiped Rinehart's *sombrero*, used it for a spittoon, and then returned it to the sheriff's head.[60] At Taos Allison was not charged with the killing of the Negro soldiers.[61] It was later discovered that at least two of Allison's friends, Davy Crockett and Augustus (Gus) Hefron, alias "Heifner" had killed the three soldiers.[62] Another man, Henry Goodman, was said to have been implicated in the triple slaying.[63] No one seemed to know for certain whether Allison was present in the saloon at the time of the killings.

Prosecuting attorney William G. Ritch, later governor of New Mexico, tried to indict Allison on several charges, including three for first-degree murder in the deaths of Chunk Colbert, Charles Cooper, and Francisco Griego. Clay was defended by a young attorney named Frank W. Springer.[64] The hearing was held in May or early June, 1876.[65] It soon became obvious that Ritch was going to have difficulty in presenting convincing evidence against Allison. The prosecution's mainstay was Luis Griego, an extremely biased witness. Ritch could not produce any witnesses to the Colbert killing nor could he produce conclusive evidence that Cooper was dead, much less that Allison had killed him. Luis Griego testified that his father had been shot in the back by Allison, but the jury refused to return an indictment and Allison was released for lack of evidence. Ritch's major mistake had been in trying to indict Allison mainly on his reputation rather than with specific facts.

The reward proclamation for his arrest

Clay Allison and his brother John were celebrating the 1876 Christmas season at Las Animas, Colorado Territory, when local law officers went to quell a disturbance. John was wounded and Clay killed Deputy Sheriff Charles Faber in a battle at the Olympic Dance Hall.

angered Allison. He intercepted a stage carrying Governor Axtell a few miles from Cimarron on June 3, 1876.[66] During the brief ride to Cimarron, Clay told the governor what he thought about the proclamation.

The year 1876 was a difficult one for Clay Allison. On December 21, he killed a peace officer during one of his drinking sprees at Las Animas, Colorado. Clay and his brother John were at Las Animas, a frequent haunt of the brothers, celebrating the Christmas season. The Allisons were patronizing the Olympic Dance Hall on that evening. The dance hall was owned by

Frank Fagley, a friend and business associate of Clay Allison.

Bent County Sheriff John Spiers and his deputy and constable, Charles Faber, were "posted" that Clay Allison and his brother were in town bent on hell-raising. Sheriff Spiers thought it best to leave the Allisons alone unless they got too far out of hand. Faber decided to ask the brothers to check their weapons[67] which they refused to do. The Allisons were soon in their cups and creating a disturbance at the dance hall. At least one person said the Allisons were insulting people and intentionally tramping on the feet of others as they danced with the girls, hoping to incite a fight.[68] Faber was notified of the disturbance and armed himself with a borrowed shotgun.[69] He also enlisted the aid of two special deputies.[70]

When Faber and his deputies reached the Olympic, Clay was standing at the bar with his back to the entrance.[71] John Allison was dancing a quadrille at the end of the hall.[72] As Faber entered, he leveled the shotgun at John (probably mistaking him for the more dangerous Clay). Faber fired at John just as someone cried, "Look out!"[73] John turned at the shout and was struck in the chest and shoulder by Faber's blast.[74] Clay, even in his drunken stupor, realized what had happened. He whirled, drew, and fired four shots in rapid succession at Faber.[75] Clay's first bullet struck the peace officer in the chest,[76] killing him almost instantly. Allison's remaining shots went wild. As Faber fell, he dropped his shotgun and its second load discharged when it struck the floor, wounding John Allison in the leg.[77] The two special deputies who had accompanied Faber fled when they saw him fall. Clay chased after them, firing from the steps of the Olympic.[78]

As Faber lay dead or dying, Clay dragged the officer over to where his brother had fallen. Bending over John, Clay repeatedly told him that he had killed Faber.[79] Clay was visibly overwrought by his brother's being shot, and he seemed to take comfort in giving John assurances that Faber was dead and that vengeance had been carried out in typical Allison fashion.

While John was being carried over to the Vandiver House, where the Allisons had rented rooms,[80] Sheriff Spiers was notified of his deputy's death. Spiers went to the Vandiver House and arrested the brothers. Clay was deeply concerned about his broth-

er, but he surrendered without argument. The Allisons were lodged in the new stone jail.[81] John was confined on the second floor,[82] which housed the jail's infirmary.[83]

On December 22 the coroner's jury returned the following verdict:

Charles Faber came to his death by pistol shots fired by the hands of Clay and John Allison, while Charles Faber, constable and deputy sheriff, was in the performance of his official duty, and that it was premeditated by John and Clay Allison.[84]

Clay and John Allison were given a preliminary hearing at Pueblo before Judge John H. Jay. Jay ordered Clay held for trial and John released temporarily for medical treatment.

Clay Allison went before Judge John W. Henry in the District Court at Pueblo on January 8, 1877, and was charged with manslaughter.[85] Bail was set at $10,000[86] and later raised.[87] Clay retained Denver attorney Thomas Macon to defend him.[88] John Allison recovered eventually from his wounds and the murder charge against him was dismissed for lack of evidence at Pueblo on February 3, 1877, by Judge Jay.[89] Fearing conviction, Clay transferred all of his property in Colfax County to John.[90] It is interesting to note that Colorado authorities permitted Clay to accompany his brother to New Mexico after John's release.[91]

Clay went before Judge Henry in the District Court at Las Animas in mid-March, 1877. He was ordered released from custody on the ground that no bill had been found against him.[92] The state could produce no witnesses to testify against Allison. One cannot help but wonder whether it was Allison's money or his reputation as a man-killer which kept witnesses from appearing.

The Allison brothers were taken to Pueblo, Colorado, for a preliminary hearing on the Faber killing. They were later released for lack of evidence. This is how Pueblo looked at the time the brothers were held there.

For more than a year after the Faber killing, Clay Allison remained relatively free of trouble. Most of this time his activities were devoted almost entirely to his cattle ranch. During the summer of 1878, he took a herd of cattle to the National Stockyards at East Saint Louis and sold the herd to Robert D. Hunter, president of the St. Louis Beef Canning Company. Hunter was a veteran Missouri stockman and cattleman. He had had extensive interests in Texas cattle herds for several years. In 1872 he had been superintendent of the stockyards at Ellsworth, Kansas, reputed to have been the largest in the state at that time. During his trip east, Clay became involved in the now famous "East St. Louis scrimmage."

The *Missouri Republican* of St. Louis, in its issue of July 25, 1878, carried an account of "the scrimmage":

A lively encounter occurred at the Green Tree House yesterday afternoon between Alexander Kessinger and a Texas drover from the St. Louis National stock yards. It appears that the Texan, who gives his name as Allison, had made some inquiries concerning Kessinger and stated that if he found him he intended to kick him. He did not know Kessinger by sight, but by reputation, and desired to meet him. The latter was informed of this by his friends, and the Texan was pointed out to him. They met in the bar-room, Kessinger had the advantage of being posted. He approached the Texan and engaged him in conversation, and finally asked him if he was looking for a man named Kessinger. The latter replied that he was.

"I understand that you have some difficulty to settle with him."

"Yes, I want to meet him; he is said to pride himself on being brave and a good fighter, and I want to see for myself, and when I meet him he will hear and feel me."

"I know Kessinger and he is not going to allow anyone to get the drop on him."

"Oh, I understand that he is handy with weapons, I am a shootist also."

With this last remark the Texan made a motion towards his pistol pocket, as if to draw a weapon, and Kessinger, who thought that the Texan who pretended not to know him actually did know him, and that he was about to commence shooting, hauled off and struck the Texan, who measured about 6 feet 2 inches in his stocking feet, knocking him down and afterwards pounded him fearfully until he cried for quarter.[93]

A year and a half later, on February 26, 1880, Allison wrote the *Ford County Globe* of Dodge City explaining his version of the East Saint Louis incident. Clay's report of the affair was published in the newspaper's March 2 issue:

About the 26th of July there appeared in one of the St. Louis papers an account of an altercation between myself and one Tisinger, in East St. Louis, in which account there appeared several gross misrepresentations which I desire to correct.

1st, It was alleged that I was a murderer of fifteen men.[94] In answer to this assertion I will say that it is entirely false, and that I stand ready at all times and places for an open inspection, and anyone who wishes to learn of my past record can make inquiries of any of the leading citizens of Wayne County, Tennessee, where I was born and raised, or of officers of the late rebellion on either side. I served in the the Tennessee Regiment, Co. F, and the last two years of the service was a scout for Ben McCulloch[95] and Gen. Forrest. Since the war I have resided in Mexico,[96] Texas and Kansas, principally on the frontier, and will refer to any of the tax payers and prominent men in either of the localities where I have resided. I have at all times tried to use my influence toward protecting the property holders and substantial men of the country from thieves, outlaws and murderers, among whom I do not care to be classed.

2nd, It was also charged that I endeavored to use a gun on the occasion of the St. Louis difficulty, which is untrue, and can be proven by either Col. Hunter, of St. Louis, or the clerk of Irwin, Allen & Co. It was also stated that I got the worst of the fight. In regard to this I also refer to Col. Hunter. I do not claim to be a prize fighter, but as an evidence of the correct result of this fight, I will only say that I was somewhat hurt but did not squeal, as did my three opponents.

My present residence is on the Washita in Hemphill County, Texas, where I am open for inspection and can be seen at any time.

Clay Allison

Dodge City, Feb. 26, 1880
St. Louis and other papers please copy

As Clay Allison passed through Dodge City, Kansas, on his way home from East St. Louis, he learned that George R. Hoyt (sometimes spelled Hoy), a young Texas cowboy, had been shot by certain members of the Dodge City police force on July 26 during a disturbance outside of the Comique Theater. Hoyt died of blood poisoning on August 21. Hoyt's death reportedly brought Allison back to Dodge because the young cowboy is said to have worked for Clay at one time.

Clay came to Dodge City accompanied by his friend, Bill Carr.[97] Allison wanted to see Ford County Sheriff W. B. (Bat) Masterson and Assistant Marshal Wyatt Earp, according to the generally accepted story. (Earp and policeman James P. Masterson, younger brother of Bat, were the two officers who had fired at Hoyt.)[98] Allison and Carr arrived at Dodge City on September 5, 1878, and there are at least four versions as to what happened.

One version has Wyatt Earp and Clay Allison tangling as if rowdy schoolboys in the middle of Front Street, with the whole town looking on behind closed doors, and Wyatt forcing Allison to back down and leave town. Another version, usually championed by pro-Masterson enthusiasts, has Bat, rather than risk a fight with Allison in which bystanders might be shot, deciding that it was best to keep a watch on Clay from a dis-

Rustic Front Street of tough Dodge City, Kansas, lived up to the legends in the 1870s when Wyatt Earp, Bat Masterson, and other legendary heroes tromped its boarded walks to "keep the peace." The famous Dodge House is seen plainly at right center. Clay Allison came to Dodge looking for Bat Masterson. Allison met both Masterson and Wyatt, for reasons unknown, but it was all very congenial, despite stories to the contrary.

tance.[99] Still another version has the Dodge City peace officers hunting their hiding places while Allison, backed by twenty-odd cowhands, was in town looking for them.[100] The fourth version, told by Thomas Masterson, Jr., the younger brother of Bat and Jim, has officer Jim Masterson arresting and jailing Clay for being drunk and disorderly.[101] However, there is no record of Clay Allison ever being arrested, jailed, or fined at Dodge City for any reason.[102]

It is of interest to note that a study of the Dodge City police court dockets for 1878 shows that policeman Jim Masterson made arrests on August 29 and September 7. City Marshal Charles E. Bassett, who was also undersheriff of Ford County, is listed as having made city arrests on September 1 and 4. Assistant Marshal Wyatt Earp is listed as having made an arrest on September 6.[103] No arrests are recorded as being made on September 5, the day on which Clay Allison visited Dodge City. (Sheriff Bat Masterson and his only deputy sheriff,

William Duffey, were county officers and did not make city arrests.)

What really happened when Clay Allison came to Dodge City on September 5 is as follows, according to George T. Hinkle, the bartender in ex-Mayor George M. Hoover's saloon and later sheriff of Ford County. Allison entered Dodge quietly without showing off. He stopped at Hoover's saloon and asked Hinkle where he might find Bat Masterson and Wyatt Earp, saying only that he had been looking for them but couldn't locate them. He did tell Hinkle that he had been to Charlie Bassett's house in the hope of finding Masterson and Earp. Bassett sent word eventually to Bat and Wyatt through William M. Tilghman, Jr., that Clay wished to talk with them. Tilghman then arranged a meeting for the three men.[104] The meeting was a congenial one and Earp and Allison were particularly friendly before Clay left town.[105]

Had Clay Allison been looking for any peace officers to kill, or if he had been involved in any incidents while in Dodge City, then the *Ford County Globe* and the *Dodge City Times* would have most certainly made mention of it in their news reports because Allison was such a well-known figure on the frontier that just his arrival in Dodge City was enough to warrant its being reported in the local newspapers. Whatever the reason that Allison had for wishing to talk with Earp and Masterson, it was for some purpose other than wanting to kill them.

By 1879 Clay Allison had sold his lucrative holdings in Colfax County and taken up residence at Hays City, Kansas, where he operated as a cattle broker.[106] But by Feb-

Courtesy Oklahoma State Historical Society
Bill Tilghman, peace officer and friend of Bat Masterson and Wyatt Earp, set up the meeting with Clay Allison in Dodge City.

ruary, 1880, he had established a cattle ranch on the Washita River in Hemphill County, Texas.[107] A year later Clay married Miss Dora McCullough (who was no relation to his mother) of the Vermejo River country.[108] Their place of marriage is not known; possibly it was somewhere in west Texas. John Allison had married Dora's sister, Betty, in Colfax County in 1878.[109] From his marriage Clay fathered two daughters. Patsy, the elder child, was born crippled.[110] The younger child was named Clay in honor of her father[111] and was born after his death.[112]

Marriage and fatherhood seemed to have

had a sobering effect upon Clay Allison. His wild antics gradually tapered off after he had assumed the responsibilities of a wife and family. His reputation, however, was enough to warrant him the sobriquet of "Wild Wolf of the Washita" when he resided in Hemphill County. Age had not mellowed Allison's character. He rode several miles out of his way on one occasion to confront one Jen Clayton at Pecos, Texas, for dropping a remark about his fighting ability. Later in New Mexico, friends talked him out of the idea of killing two of his young cowhands for making a cryptic observation about him.

By May, 1886, Allison had established his last ranch in the Seven Rivers country of Lincoln County, New Mexico.[113] Age had so crippled his right foot by this time that he was forced to walk with a cane. To avoid unnecessary walking, he rode more. In June, 1886, Clay drove a herd of one thou-

Wyoming Stockgrower's Association Collection, University of Wyoming Western History Research Center, Laramie
Cheyenne, Wyoming, was a bustling Western town when Clay Allison arrived in 1886 after driving a large herd of cattle from his ranch in New Mexico. Suffering from a toothache, he sought out a Cheyenne dentist who drilled the wrong tooth. Allison evened the score by extracting one of the dentist's teeth as "fair exchange."

sand, five hundred half and three-quarters bred steers to Rock Creek, Wyoming Territory,[114] near Cheyenne. While there Clay developed a toothache. He went to a Cheyenne dentist,[115] either Dr. Rees Williams or Dr. F. L. Warner,[116] to have the tooth extracted. The dentist didn't extract the aching tooth. Instead he began drilling a good tooth (or what Allison thought was a good tooth) and part of it broke off. Allison went to the other Cheyenne dentist and had the damage to his teeth repaired at a cost of twenty-five dollars. Then Clay returned to the first dentist and extracted one of the doctor's teeth with a pair of forceps. He began to extract another molar and part of the dentist's upper lip when the screams of the unfortunate man attracted a crowd and Allison stopped.[117]

The end came rather ingloriously on July 1, 1887.[118] Clay loaded supplies for his ranch on a borrowed wagon[119] at Pecos, Texas, and started north to his ranch. About forty miles from Pecos a sack of grain fell from the wagon, and as Clay reached for it, he fell[120] beneath the wagon. One of the rear wheels rolled over his neck. He lived about forty-five minutes in great agony.[121] His body was brought to Pecos and buried in the old cemetery there. Many of the graves in this cemetery are sunken and of the few remaining headstones, only one has any visible markings. Allison's grave, if there, is unmarked. (There is a report that Dora Allison had Clay's remains removed to Fort Worth.[122] Dora later married J. Lee Johnson, a lumber merchant, at Pecos.[123] Later, the Johnsons moved to Fort Worth,[124] where Dora Allison Johnson died in 1939.[125]

A contemporary newspaper gave Clay Allison what might be the ultimate summing up when it said:

. . . Clay Allison . . . knew no fear. . . . To incur his enmity was about equivalent to a death sentence. He contended always that he never killed a man willingly; but that the necessity in every instance had been thrust upon him. He was expert with his revolver, and never failed to come out first best in a deadly encounter. Whether this brave, genteel border man was in truth a villain or a gentleman is a question that many who knew him never settled to their own satisfaction. Certain it is that many of his stern deeds were for the right as he understood that right to be.[126]

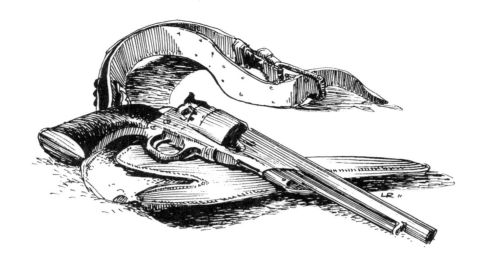

2.

WYATT EARP

(1848-1929)

WYATT BERRY STAPP EARP was born to Nicholas Porter Earp (1813-1907)[1] and Virginia Ann Cooksey (1823[2]-1893[3]) at Monmouth, Warren County, Illinois, on March 19, 1848. The early years of Wyatt Earp were spent on the family homestead near Pella, Iowa, except for sojourns in Missouri and California. About 1869, Nicholas Earp moved his family to Missouri for the second time. The Earps settled at Lamar, in Barton County, where young Earp took the initial step on the long road to becoming one of the most controversial men in Western history.

Little is know about Wyatt's life at Lamar. He married Miss Irilla (or Urilla) H. Sutherland there on January 10, 1870.[4] Nicholas Earp, as justice of the peace, performed the wedding ceremony.[5] The mar-

riage was short-lived. Less than a year later, Wyatt's wife was dead,[6] perhaps of typhoid fever.

Wyatt was elected constable at Lamar on or about April 4, 1870. He defeated his older half brother, Newton J. Earp, for the position by a vote margin of 137 to 108[7]. Less than a year later Wyatt resigned as constable and left Lamar. Rumors are that he had trouble with his late wife's family.[8] There is also the story that he had difficulty with two brothers named Brummett (or Brummer). There may be some truth in the latter story, for on June 13, 1870, Wyatt arrested two brothers who were drunk and disorderly.[9]

The life at Lamar had little meaning to Wyatt Earp, except for his brief marriage to Irilla Sutherland, and the fact that it was

Wyatt Earp, most famous of Western law officers, was thirty-eight when this photograph was taken in 1886. He appears far different from motion-picture and television portrayals of later times.

there where he first became a peace officer —an occupation which later brought him much notoriety and controversy.

After leaving Lamar, Wyatt drifted south into the Cherokee Nation (what is now part of the state of Oklahoma). There, on March 28, 1871, he and two companions, Edward Kennedy and John Shown, stole two horses belonging to a William Keys. The theft occurred on the Arkansas River near Fort Gibson. An elaborate escape plan was conceived by the three men. Shown took the stolen horses to a rendezvous point fifty miles north of Fort Gibson. At the meeting place Earp, Kennedy, and Shown's wife met

Shown with a hack and two other horses. The two stolen horses were put in the hack and the other two mounts were given to Shown. The party made for the Kansas border, traveling only at night. They were overtaken by a posse led by James M. Keys on or about April 1 before they had reached Kansas. Keys placed the thieves under citizen's arrest, taking them to Fort Gibson. The men were jailed in the post stockade to await the arrival of Deputy U.S. Marshal J. G. Owen of the Western District of Arkansas (to which the Cherokee Nation was attached for judicial purposes). Earp and Kennedy warned Shown not to turn state's evidence.[10] (Evidently Shown had been merely a pawn in the scheme and was not fully trusted by Earp and Kennedy.)

Deputy Owen arrived at Fort Gibson on April 6 and escorted the three prisoners to Van Buren, Arkansas. At Van Buren the three men were charged on April 13 with horse stealing. They were held for a preliminary hearing, but waived examination, and bail was set at five hundred dollars each. Only Kennedy did not raise his bail. Earp, Kennedy and Shown were indicted for horse stealing on May 8, 1871, by the grand jury at Fort Smith, Arkansas. Trial was set for June 8 with Judge Henry C. Caldwell initially presiding. Later Judge William Story was assigned to hear the case. Earp and Shown fled jurisdiction of the court. Kennedy was tried and acquitted for his part in the theft.[11] Wyatt escaped to Kansas where he remained in almost complete obscurity for three years. He had evaded the dubious distinction of becoming one of the first men tried in the famous criminal court at Fort Smith.[12]

In Kansas Wyatt Earp turned his atten-

Wyatt Earp and two companions were apprehended by a posse in 1871 for stealing horses along the Arkansas River and were brought to nearby Fort Gibson. Officers' quarters for the fort are shown. Later, the men were indicted at Fort Smith. Earp jumped bail and fled back to Kansas.

tion to the trail towns, which during the 1870s and 1880s were the major receivers of Texas beeves. In the cowtowns Earp became a professional gambler. These towns were havens for gamblers and saloon "hangers-on" such as Earp, for the cowhands coming from Texas were flush at the end of the trail. Kansas led the country as a railhead for Texas cattle and Wichita led Kansas

from 1872 through 1876 in cattle shipments, shipping a total of 223,373 head.[13] Wichita's single biggest year was 1872 when it shipped about 70,600 head.[14]

Wyatt Earp was at Hays City during the early days. The father of a Hays City resident remembered Earp there as a gambler.[15] Wyatt was also at Ellsworth, Kansas, during that city's cowtown era.[16] By 1874 Earp was

Courtesy Kansas State Historical Society, Topeka
Wyatt Earp, the gambler, arrived in Wichita, Kansas, in 1874 when the cow town appeared as in this photograph, taken at the intersection of Main and Douglas streets. Gambling was illegal, so Earp spent much of his time across the river in "West Wichita." His brother James tended bar in Wichita. During the cattle seasons, the town was wide open.

at Wichita. Gambling became illegal in Wichita proper. But across the Arkansas River was "Delano," or what was commonly called "West Wichita," a separate community which had no law of its own. It was Wyatt Earp's favorite haunt during his sojourn at Wichita.

James C. Earp, Wyatt's older brother, was also at Wichita in 1874 tending bar in W. W. (Whitey) Rupp's Keno House and driving a hack part time. Jim's wife (or mistress), Bessie Earp, was operating a bordello in Wichita's red-light district. Wichita was overrun with the lawless element. Gunfighter Ben Thompson, late of Abilene

and Ellsworth, was dealing monte and faro at the Keno House. Kate Elder, who later became famous as the mistress of Doc Holliday, was an inmate at Bessie Earp's house of ill fame. The notorious frontier hardcase, William A. (Hurricane Bill) Martin, appeared in 1874. Bat Masterson was in and out during the first part of that year between buffalo hunts, trips to Dodge City, and scouting for the Army. The Masterson homestead was near Wichita. Ida May, the well-known "soiled dove" and then the mistress of gambler and part-time Army scout Mike Gordon (who was later killed by Doc Holliday), was there. And briefly, during the cattle season of 1874, at least two of the Clements brothers, Emanuel (Mannen) and James—who were cousins of the Texas killer and outlaw John Wesley Hardin—were in town.

Wichita was wide open during the cattle season of 1874 and again in 1875. A sign outside of Wichita read: "Everything Goes In Wichita." The cowhands took this message literally and the local police force had its hands full as a result. A good index of the level of lawlessness in 1874 is the total amount of fines assessed by Police Judge E. B. Jewett—more than $5,600 during the cattle season.[17] The regular police force of City Marshal William (Billy) Smith, Assistant Marshal Daniel F. Parks, Policemen James Cairns, William Dibbs, John Behrens, Joseph T. Hooker, and Samuel Botts was weak. Only Cairns (who later married the sister of Bat Masterson), Behrens and Parks were first-rate peace officers, although the integrity of Behrens left much to be desired. Into this bevy of frontier riffraff came Wyatt Earp in 1874.

In October, 1874, M. R. Moser, of Wichita, sold a new wagon to some trail hands of B. F. Higgenbottom. They left town without paying for the wagon and Moser hired Policeman Behrens to go after the drovers. Behrens enlisted the aid of Earp, and the two men caught up with the hands about seventy-five miles south of Wichita near the Kansas border. Earp and Behrens collected $146 at gunpoint from trail boss McGill in payment for the stolen wagon.[18] This was Earp's first connection with law enforcement at Wichita.[19]

In Wichita's municipal election, held on April 5, 1875, veteran police officer Michael Meagher was elected city marshal.[20] Beh-

rens was appointed assistant marshal and Cairns and Earp were appointed city policemen on April 21.[21] Later in the month John M. Martin was added to the force as a policeman.[22] Wyatt's salary was sixty dollars per month.[23]

There is much latter-day controversy surrounding Wyatt Earp's career as a Wichita police officer. As an old man in 1928, he tried desperately to recall the old days on the frontier, but, somewhat inevitably, age had distorted his memory to the extent that many of his recollections were erroneous. He thought he had been a police officer at Wichita from 1874 to 1876, but the city records show that he was on the police force there only in 1875 and 1876. He also thought that he and his fellow officers had arrested more than eight hundred persons while he was on the police force at Wichita. The reports of the police judge for the period that Earp was an officer at Wichita show that 366 persons were fined.[24] The reports for 1875, however, are not complete.

Those for June, July and December of that year are missing or destroyed. These reports do not include those persons found not guilty, nor do they give the names of the arresting officers, nor are the offenses listed.[25] Also missing from the police judge reports are the names of several prominent men whom Earp is said to have arrested or had trouble with at Wichita: Mannen, Jim, Joseph, and John G. (Gip) Clements; Corporal Melvin A. King, Fourth U.S. Cavalry; Texas gambler George Peshaur; cowhand Ed Morrison; and Texas cattleman Abel H. (Shanghai) Pierce.[26] Mannen and Jim Clements and J. W. Glover were charged with a lawsuit resulting from a defaulted payment of $137 for new clothing in September 1874.[27] This, of course, was a civil suit.

More than a half century later Charles Hatton, who was city attorney at Wichita in 1874, and Jimmy Cairns offered testimony that Wyatt pistol-whipped Corporal King, physically beat George Peshaur, and backed down Mannen Clements, his brothers, and several of their friends.[28] Their testimony, however, is not substantiated by contemporary records, police judge reports, or newspaper accounts.

Sam Jones, a Negro whose grandmother was a cook in Bessie Earp's house of prostitution, said that his grandmother told him that Wyatt once shouldered Gip Clements and his cousin Simpson Dixon off the sidewalk at Wichita. Clements and Dixon were unarmed at the time, but knew Wyatt to be, so they let him pass without incident. According to Jones, Gip later told his three older brothers about the sidewalk jostling and the four Clements went to Bessie's place looking for Wyatt. Wyatt hid in the kitchen and Bessie told Mannen Clements that Wyatt wasn't there. She pointed to boot marks across her yard, saying that Wyatt had made them shortly before their arrival. Jones said that Bessie Earp had made the tracks with Wyatt's boots to throw the Clements off his trail.[29] This story is, of course, hearsay, told by an old man who had to recall a story he heard second hand more than eighty years before.

Old age had obviously warped the memories of Hatton and Cairns in trying to recall Wyatt Earp's days at Wichita. Wyatt himself was not immune to such difficulties. On September 10, 1928, he wrote his cousin George W. Earp, then living at Wichita, requesting specific information about the

Courtesy Kansas State Historical Society, Topeka
A landmark of old Wichita was this post office where the famous and infamous of the West received their mail. In 1928, unable to recall life in Wichita in the 1870s, Wyatt Earp wrote to his cousin, George, who lived there, asking for details.

town during the years 1874 to 1876. One of the things Wyatt wanted to know was who had been city marshal during that period. He said, however, that he knew the information he was seeking, but only wished to have it verified.[30]

Earp's police career at Wichita can only be judged by the contemporary newspapers since the police court records are incomplete. Wyatt arrested W. W. Compton, a livestock thief, on May 4, 1875.[31] Later that month he may or may not have been one of the unnamed police officers who chased a drunken cowhand, who had fired his pistol in the street, to the city limits.[32] On December 8 of that year he arrested a drunk who had $500 in his possession.[33] And on January 9, 1876, Wyatt's revolver slipped from its holster, discharged, and nearly shot him.[34] When he wasn't policing Wichita, Earp collected "fines" from prostitutes and gambled in Delano or in the back room of Charles Schattner's Custom House Saloon.[35] A portion of the fines Wyatt kept without knowledge of city authorities. Assistant Marshal Behrens did the same. Another of Earp's duties, as well as that of Wichita police officers, was the inglorious task of repairing the thoroughfares and sidewalks of Wichita.

In the spring of 1876 Wyatt Earp became involved in a political dispute which resulted in his dismissal from the police force. Former marshal Billy Smith was a candidate for the office of city marshal against incumbent Mike Meagher. Earp backed Meagher for reelection. For some reason, Smith turned the election into an anti-Earp campaign. He accused Meagher of sending for Wyatt's brothers to put them on the police force,[36] if reelected. On April 2 Wyatt broke into Smith's room while he and Meagher were having a political discussion. Earp accosted Smith and physically beat him as Meagher stood witness. Wyatt was arrested for disturbing the peace. He was fined thirty dollars by Judge J. M. Attwood on April 3.[37] Wyatt was also assessed two dollars court costs.[38] He was then ordered dismissed from the police force.[39] Wyatt was allowed, however, to remain on the force until his successor could be appointed by the newly-elected city council.[40] Rumors in Wichita were that Meagher had Earp beat Smith so he couldn't campaign effectively.[41] At any rate, the election

was held on April 5 and Meagher won by a vote margin of 477 to 249 for Smith.[42]

The *Wichita Weekly Beacon,* in its issue of April 5, came to Earp's defense when it reported in part, ". . . It is but justice to Earp to say he has made an excellent officer, and hitherto his conduct has been unexceptionable."

More than one person in Wichita thought that Wyatt Earp was an efficient officer. When the police force was reduced to a marshal, assistant marshal, and one policeman for financial reasons in August 1875, the city council dismissed policemen Cairns and Martin and retained Earp.[43] On April 19 the new city council voted twice on whether to reinstate Earp as a policeman. The first vote was two for and six against reinstating Earp. The second vote ended in a four-four deadlock, after which the matter of reinstatement was tabled. The council then appointed R. C. Richey and ex-Assistant Marshal Dan Parks as policemen.[44] Wyatt was officially dismissed from the Wichita police force on April 20.[45]

The Wichita city officials, however, were not through with Wyatt Earp. The police committee on May 10 recommended that Marshal Meagher enforce the vagrancy act against Wyatt and Morgan S. Earp, Wyatt's younger brother, and that the salaries of Wyatt and Assistant Marshal John Behrens be withheld until all money collected by them be turned over to the city treasurer.[46] The city council sanctioned the recommendations of the police committee on May 22.[47] By this time, however, Wyatt and Morgan Earp had left Wichita.

The record left behind in Wichita by Wyatt Earp, although somewhat tainted by

Dismissed from the police force, Wyatt Earp left Wichita from this railroad station in the spring of 1876, heading for Dodge City. In preelection activities, Earp beat up the opponent of the man he was backing and was arrested for disturbing the peace.

his abrupt dismissal from the police force and his dishonesty in keeping money he had collected for the city, seems to have been a good one as far as some of his contemporaries were concerned. In November 1881, several citizens of Wichita signed a testimonial which read in part:

"... We ... certify that ... Wyatt S. Earp was a good and efficient officer and was well known for his honesty and integrity; that his character while here was of the best, and that no fault was ever found in him as an officer or as a man."

Among the signees of the testimonial were Jimmy Cairns, then city marshal at Wichita; former mayor George E. Harris; and ex-city councilmen C. M. Garrison and M. Zummerly.[48] Attorney Charles Hatton notarized the testimonial.[49]

After leaving Wichita Earp went to Dodge City, Wichita's sister railhead to the west and soon the boss cowtown in Kansas. Sometime between May 17-24, 1876, Earp was placed on the police force at Dodge City[50] by Mayor George M. Hoover through the intercession of Bill Tilghman.[51] Wyatt was appointed as a seventy-five dollar a month deputy city marshal under 307-pound City Marshal Lawrence E. (Larry) Deger.[52] As a bonus Wyatt received two dollars for the court conviction of each person whom he arrested, As far as is known, only Deger and Earp comprised the police force at Dodge City until April, 1877. Latter-day writers have taken Wyatt Earp to task because in his later years, he allegedly recalled that he was "chief deputy marshal" under Deger and that Deger was marshal in "name only." Considering that Wyatt was Deger's only deputy of record and that Deger's weight greatly hampered his mobility, Wyatt would not have been too wrong in his statements.

By June 1876, Morgan Earp was at Dodge City serving as a deputy sheriff of Ford County under Sheriff Charlie Bassett.[53] Morgan had probably come to Dodge City with Wyatt.

In 1876 Dodge City had not yet passed Wichita as the leading end-of-trail railhead in Kansas. That year Wichita shipped 14,643 head on the Santa Fe line as compared to 9,540 head from Dodge City.[54] Dodge had shipped a mere 5,826 head in 1875.[55] The U.S. government estimated that 321,928 head were driven north to Dodge City and Ellis, Kansas, in 1876.[56] In 1877 Dodge City shipped 22,940 head of cattle.[57]

Courtesy Kansas State Historical Society, Topeka
Dodge City was rapidly becoming Queen of the Cow Towns when Wyatt Earp took up residence there: The scene along Front Street grew familiar to him, especially that part south of the railroad tracks and the Dead Line. The famous Long Branch Saloon may be located in the photograph just left of center. Earp's favorite hangout, however, was the Beatty & Kelley Saloon, behind the barber pole at the far right. The Dead Line was at the extreme lower left.

Western History Collections, University of Oklahoma Library
Morgan Earp was also in Dodge, serving as a deputy sher-
iff. He may have arrived at the same time as his brother.
He became a dealer at the Long Branch Saloon.

The following year, the city freighted 16,237
head;[58] an estimated 20,000 head were
shipped in 1879; 17,957 head in 1880[59]; and
33,564 head loaded in 1881.[60] Most of the
cattle were pushed over the Western Trail
and the Jones and Plummer Trail to Dodge
City, grazed there, and then driven to other
points. From 1875 to 1884 Dodge shipped
an estimated total of 349,097 head of cattle,[61] a record for a Kansas cowtown. During seven of those years, Dodge City led all
Kansas railheads in total shipments.

Wyatt Earp at this time was a picturesque
figure. He stood six feet two inches in
height, weighed about 185 pounds, and had
cold, hard blue eyes, ash blond hair and a
thick mustache which he allowed to droop
profusely in later life. His spare time was
spent gambling at Peter L. Beatty's and
James H. (Dog) Kelley's Alhambra Saloon
on Front Street.

Front Street was the main thoroughfare
in Dodge City. It was divided by the tracks
of the Atchison, Topeka and Santa Fe Railroad. South of the tracks were the houses of
prostitution, the dance halls, and most of
the saloons. Dodge City residents referred
to south of the tracks as "across the Dead
Line." Contrary to what has been written,
across the Dead Line offered no sanctuary
from the law for those wishing to carry le-
thal weapons on their person within the city
limits. City Ordinance Number 4, Section
7, passed on December 24, 1875, stated:

> No person shall in the city of Dodge City carry
> concealed about his or her persons any pistol,
> bowie knife, sling shot, or other dangerous or
> deadly weapons except United States, County,
> Township, or City Officers and any person con-
> victed of a violation of this section shall be fined
> not less than three nor more than twenty-five dol-
> lars.[62]

And contrary to another popular belief, it
was not the cowhands who were the big
troublemakers in Dodge City, although they
certainly did their share of hell-raising.
George Hinkle, the bartender at G. M. Hoover's saloon, said "the cowboys were over-
drawn; it was the drifters and the railroad
men who caused more trouble than the cowboys."[63] Dr. Samuel J. Crumbine, who came
to Dodge City during the 1880s and later
became secretary of the Kansas State Board
of Health, said that the cowboys "had no intention to harm anyone. . . . The real street
fights . . . were chiefly between gamblers,
sportsmen, and their 'hangers-on.' Or be-

tween the town marshal and the gamblers of their kind. . . . "[64]

Little is known about Wyatt Earp's first tenure as a Dodge City police officer, which ended on or about April 1, 1877.[65] It is known, however, that while at Dodge City he became an intimate friend of fellow gambler Bat Masterson. Bat had been in Dodge City off and on since the cow camp's founding in 1872. Earp said many years later he first met Masterson at Wichita.[66] Bat once wrote that he had known Earp since the early 1870s.[67] Since Bat's parents had a farm near Wichita, the two men had probably known each other casually during Earp's sojourn at Wichita. At any rate, their friendship was an enduring one and lasted until Masterson's death many years later.

It is known that on July 1, 1876, Earp signed a complaint against Ford County Deputy Sheriff Edward O. Hogue, a former peace officer at Ellsworth, Kansas, for fighting in the street.[68] Two months later Wyatt was involved in a fight at the famous Long Branch Saloon. The fight occurred on September 4, and Wyatt's opponent was a huge cowboy named Patrick (Red) Sweeney. Earp and Sweeney fought over the affections of a local dance hall girl. The girl is said to have favored Sweeney and Earp allegedly threatened her because of it.[69]

Wyatt and the cowhand exchanged blows and Sweeney, who stood six feet six inches and weighed 245 pounds, literally mauled Earp. Sweeney and his girl then fled town. Mayor Hoover questioned two of Sweeney's cowhand friends, J-Bob Lee and Wooley Bates, concerning the whereabouts of Sweeney and the girl. Hoover told Lee and Bates to report to him again on the following day for further questioning. The next day the two cowhands reported to Hoover and he sent them to the police court. They were ordered jailed while a search was made for Sweeney and his girl. The search proved futile. Two days later Lee and Bates were given their release.[70]

Red Sweeney vowed to kill Wyatt Earp on the next drive north, but he was trampled to death in a stampede the following year while on a drive to Dodge City. He was killed fifty-five miles north of the present town of Iowa Park, Texas.[71]

The great lack of contemporary sources makes it exceedingly difficult for Western historians to evaluate properly Wyatt Earp's first tenure as a Dodge City police officer. The police court dockets for this period are now lost or destroyed. There are only three issues of the *Dodge City Times* in the newspaper collection of the Kansas State Historical Society at Topeka that cover the period of Earp's first tenure.[72]

From the stories that have been written about him, one would imagine that Wyatt Earp filled Dodge City's famous Boot Hill all by himself. As late as 1967 the Associated Press stated that the peacefulness of Dodge City attests to Wyatt Earp.[73] Of the thirty-three cadavers which were originally removed from Dodge City's Boot Hill in 1879,[74] only one is generally accredited to Wyatt Earp's six-gun.

With a lack of contemporary records, historians must turn to some of Earp's contemporaries for an assessment of his efficiency as a police officer at Dodge City for the period of 1876 to 1877. Bat Masterson, who probably knew Earp better than anyone in Dodge, said that Wyatt "on a great many occasions, at the risk of his life, rendered valuable service in upholding the . . . law.

U.S. Signal Corps Photo, National Archives
In the summer of 1877, Wyatt Earp left Dodge for the "gambling circuit" into Texas, hitting many of the Army posts. Among them was Fort Davis. In was on this trip, which lasted ten months, that Wyatt met Doc Holliday and the pair became fast friends.

. . . While he invariably went armed, he seldom had occasion to do any shooting in Dodge City. . . . "[75] Tom Masterson, Bat's brother, called Earp "a courageous, square, and likeable man."[76] Bob C. Vandenberg, who was city marshal at Dodge City in 1881, called Earp a shrewd, courageous peace officer with a sense of duty, but who had shortcomings.[77] George Hinkle, who had reason to dislike Earp, called Wyatt "a big blow"[78] and said that his veracity could always be doubted.[79] Hinkle also called Earp "a fighting pimp."[80] Cowboy Pink Simms, who knew Earp and disliked him, said that Wyatt was an intelligent, efficient police officer who didn't like to work alone, and invariably surrounded himself with a group of killers.[81]

Frank A. Hobble, who came to Dodge City as a youngster in 1879, remembered Wyatt Earp. Hobble's father owned the Iowa House Hotel at Dodge City and young Frank remembered that Earp was a frequent visitor to the hotel. Frank Hobble remembered that Wyatt was a man who handled his own affairs, or those of people whom he represented, with the most advantageous results.[82]

The *Tombstone Nugget*, in its issue of November 18, 1881, published a testimonial to Wyatt Earp which was signed by sixty citizens of Dodge City. It can be concluded that Wyatt Earp was an efficient officer and was well liked by the majority of his contemporaries at Dodge.

After resigning as deputy marshal at Dodge City, Wyatt sojourned into the Black Hills in what is now the state of South Dakota. He returned to Dodge City by July 1, 1877. That month he and Frankie Bell, a dance hall girl, collided on Front Street. She cursed him and Wyatt slapped her. He was arrested and fined one dollar. Frankie was jailed and fined twenty dollars and costs.[83] Shortly after this incident, Wyatt again left Dodge City and drifted down into Texas.

Prior to his departure the *Dodge City Times* of July 7 had commented on Wyatt's return and gave a brief insight on his ability as a peace officer:

Wyatt Earp, who was on our city police force last summer, is in town again. We hope he will accept a position on the force once more. He had a quiet way of taking the most desperate charac-

ters into custody which invariably gave one the impression that the city was able to enforce her mandates and preserve her dignity. It wasn't considered policy to draw a gun on Wyatt unless you got the drop and meant to burn powder without any preliminary talk.

For the next ten months—from July, 1877, to May 1878—Wyatt followed the gambling circuit in Texas: from Sweetwater (later changed to Mobeetie), to Fort Worth, Jacksboro, Fort Griffin, Fort Davis, Fort Clark, and back to Fort Worth. Sometime during 1877 Wyatt met Doc Holliday, the professional gambler and dentist, at Fort Griffin. Doc Holliday became Wyatt Earp's most intimate friend and associate. No one has ever fully explained the strange bond that existed between these two men, but exist it did. Writing many years later of Holliday's devotion to Earp, Bat Masterson, who knew both men intimately, said that Doc's *"whole heart and soul were wrapped up in Wyatt Earp and he was always ready to stake his life in defense of any cause in which Wyatt was interested."*[84]

With Wyatt Earp at Fort Griffin was a young woman named Matilda (Mattie) Blaylock. Somewhere along the way, Wyatt had picked up the young girl as a mistress (or wife). On May 8, 1878, Wyatt returned to Dodge City.[85] Mattie Blaylock came with him. The *Dodge City Times* of May 11 commented on Earp's return:

Mr. Wyatt Earp, who has during the past served with credit on the police [force] arrived in this city from Texas last Wednesday. We predict that his services as an officer will again be required this summer.

Within a week Wyatt was appointed assistant marshal[86] under City Marshal Char-

U.S. Signal Corps Photo National Archives
Another stop on Earp's gambling trek to Texas was Fort Clark. This view shows troops drilling on the parade grounds. In the spring of 1878 Wyatt returned to Dodge with a young woman, either wife or mistress, and resumed his police duties.

lie Bassett at a salary of seventy-five dollars a month[87] plus the two dollars arrest fee for the court conviction of each person whom he arrested.

The *Ford County Globe,* in its issue of May 14, commented on Wyatt's appointment:

Wyatt Earp, one of the most efficient officers Dodge ever had, has just returned from Fort Worth, Texas. He was immediately appointed Asst. Marshal, by our City dads, much to their credit.

There is little doubt that Wyatt Earp was a popular police officer at Dodge City. The *Ford County Globe* of June 18 commented that "Wyatt Earp is doing his duty as Ass't Marshal in a very creditable manner.—Add-

ing new laurels to his splendid record every day."

In addition to Marshal Bassett and Assistant Marshal Earp the regular Dodge City Police force consisted of Policemen Jim Masterson and John Brown during the summer of 1878. Brown, however, was dismissed in August of that year.[88]

Across the Dead Line was the toughest section of town. It was there where the majority of trail hands hung out. The saloon and dance hall owners had their hands full trying to keep order in their establishments. Earp made deals with many of these owners whereby he maintained law and order in their places for monthly protection money. Bob Vandenberg, when asked about Earp's protection racket, said he had no knowledge of it.[89] In addition to his "interest" across the Dead Line Wyatt had a small percentage of the gaming tables at the Long Branch Saloon, co-owned by Gambler William H. Harris and Chalkley M. (Chalk) Beeson, and first opened by Charlie Bassett in 1873. He also held a small interest in the Alhambra Saloon. While Morgan Earp looked out for his brother's interest as a dealer at the Long Branch, Wyatt made his gambling headquarters at the Alhambra. One of the principal owners of the Alhambra was Mayor Jim (Dog) Kelley. Kelley was elected mayor of Dodge City four consecutive years (1877-1880) on what has been termed the "saloon ticket." It was Kelley who had appointed Earp as assistant marshal.

Wyatt Earp's only gunfight at Dodge City which resulted in a death occurred on the early morning of July 26, 1878. George R. Hoyt (some sources spell it Hoy), a young cowboy who was free on a $1,500 bond on a charge of cattle rustling,[90] and another cowhand left the Comique Theater after an argument with Ben Springer,[91] one of the owners of the Comique. Hoyt and his companion were drunk. As they rode by the rear of the theater, they fired several shots into the thin-walled building. Wyatt Earp and Jim Masterson were standing outside of the Comique when Hoyt and his companion triggered their guns. The two police officers gave chase on foot as the assailants fled down Bridge Street toward the toll bridge over the Arkansas River. Hoyt and his companion exchanged several shots with Earp and Masterson.[92] Several citizens also joined in shooting at the two cowhands.[93] One of the many bullets struck Hoyt in the arm and he fell from his mount. His companion made good his escape.[94] The bullet

and the fall broke Hoyt's arm in two places. He said that he had nothing to do with shooting up the Comique,[95] and a study of the Dodge City police court dockets show that Hoyt was not arrested.

Hoyt's wound became worse and Assistant Surgeon William S. Tremaine, post surgeon at Fort Dodge, amputated the arm on August 21. Hoyt never rallied after the operation, dying that same day. Later in the day he was buried on Boot Hill,[96] becoming one of the last persons interred there.

Earp and his fellow peace officers had a difficult time with the cowhands across the Dead Line. The police were involved in a fight with several trail hands at the Comique Theatre on August 17, 1878. The fight resulted from a dispute between one of the cowhands and a bartender. Several shots were fired and several trail hands were pistol-whipped by the police but no one was shot.[97] The only trail hand arrested was James W. (Spike) Kenedy[98] who had started the melee. Wyatt Earp had arrested Kenedy the previous July 29 for carrying a pistol.[99]

In early October, 1878, Wyatt Earp was a member of Sheriff Bat Masterson's posse which wounded and captured Jim Kenedy for the killing of variety actress Fannie Keenan, who was also known as Dora Hand, in Dodge City.[100] Nothing of any consequence happened to Wyatt, except an off-season cut in salary to fifty dollars per month on December 3, 1878,[101] and a subsequent raise to one hundred dollars per month on April 9, 1879,[102] until his near assassination by "three unruly Missourians from Clay County" on May 5, 1879. Earp was rescued by his friend Bat Masterson who later averted as-

One of Wyatt's Dodge friends was fellow gambler "Mysterious Dave" Mather. The pair traveled to Texas together and were run out of town for attempting a swindle.

son. The three men who caused the difficulty the night before, assembled in the rear of a store building, Tuesday night, and sent word by a colored boy that a man wished to see him. The Negro "smelt a mouse," and put the sheriff on guard. Officer Duffey shortly afterwards arrested one of them. These fellows remarked that they "had run things in Missouri," and that they were no match for Dodge City officers. Dodge City is hard "to take." The pistol brigands find in it a "warm berth."

Who the three Missourians were is not known. Romanticists might believe that Earp and Masterson tangled with the infamous Missouri outlaws Frank and Jesse James. The exact whereabouts of the James brothers at this time is something of a mystery,[103] although the brothers were probably in Tennessee in May 1879. The Dodge City police court dockets list no arrests for May 5, but on May 6 there were two arrests recorded by Wyatt Earp, that of Henry Kaufman and Tom E. Ewen for carrying pistols.[104]

On May 21 Wyatt and Jim Masterson faced down seven trail hands at gunpoint on Duck Creek and collected a debt for a colored man.[105] And on June 9 Wyatt Earp may have been one of the peace officers who was involved in a gunfight with several cowhands refusing to check their firearms in accordance with the city ordinance and electing to shoot it out with the police officers. One cowboy was wounded in the leg and the others fled town.[106] The wounded cowboy was not arrested, for no arrests are recorded for June, 1879, until the seventeenth of the month.[107]

In September, 1879, Wyatt decided to resign as assistant marshal. He turned in his badge to city officials on September 4.[108] Two days later George Hinkle, who was run-

sassination by the same unruly Missourians.

The *Dodge City Times* of May 10 reported the attempted assassinations:

There was a little brush Monday evening, which however, terminated with a few bruised heads. Three movers on their way to Leadville from Clay County, Mo., under the influence of bad whiskey, undertook to "take the town." While Assistant Marshal Earp was attempting to disarm [them] and [was] leading an unruly cuss off by the ear, another one of the party told his chum to "throw lead," and endeavored to resist the officer. Sheriff Bat Masterson soon happened on the scene and belabored the irate Missourian, using the broadside of his revolver over his head. The party was disarmed and placed in the cooler. Tuesday night an attempt was made to assassinate Sheriff Master-

Tombstone was wild and woolly at the time the Earp brothers were there, and they added fuel to the fire. The town was set against the raw hills of southern Arizona in rich mining country. Wyatt Earp arrived late in 1879 for what became, in legend, the most colorful part of his checkered career.

ning for the office of Ford County sheriff against incumbent Bat Masterson,[109] ejected the latter from Hoover's saloon for being an obnoxious drunk. On September 7 Earp went to Hoover's looking to fight Hinkle, but the latter forced Wyatt to leave.[110] Shortly after this incident, Wyatt and Mattie Blaylock left Dodge City for Las Vegas, New Mexico Territory.[111]

Perhaps it would be well to discuss the police record of Wyatt Earp at Dodge City for the period of July 4, 1878, to September 4, 1879. (The police court dockets prior to July 4, 1878, are no longer available for study.[112] During this period Wyatt Earp made a total of thirty-two arrests and may or may not have shot two cowboys, one of whom died. Only two others cowboys were

shot (one of whom died) by a member of the Dodge City police force. The only other police officer whose arrest record approaches that of Earp is Jim Masterson's total of twenty-nine arrests for the same period.[113] While Wyatt never made a great many arrests while a police officer at Dodge City, he nonetheless made *more* arrests for the time that he was assistant marshal there than any other officer.[114] And missing from the police court dockets are the names of such well-known men as cowhands Tobe Driskill, Ed Morrison, and Tom Owens,[115] and leading citizen Robert M. Wright, whom Earp is said to have arrested. Despite the exaggerated claims Wyatt Earp may have inadvertently attributed to himself or that writers advertently attributed to

Wyatt and Morgan Earp rode shotgun for Wells, Fargo & Co. after arriving in Tombstone, Arizona Territory. A stagecoach robbery triggered events climaxed by the so-called "Battle at the O. K. Corral."

him, he was an exceptionally efficient police officer on the whole at both Wichita and Dodge City. The fact that he was a member of the saloon crowd (from which most police officers were drawn in that era) did not detract from his proficiency as a policeman.

En route to Las Vegas, Earp went to Fort Worth and visited an old Wichita crony, John Behrens.[116] Later in the month Wyatt was at Mobeetie, Texas, with "Mysterious Dave" Mather, a professional gambler he had known at Dodge City. At Mobeetie Earp and Mather were run out of town by Deputy Sheriff James McIntire (a hardcase himself) of Wheeler County for trying to swindle several persons with a "gold brick" hoax.[117] By the end of September, 1879, Earp was at Las Vegas.[118]

Wyatt and Mattie Blaylock left Las Vegas and arrived at Tombstone, Arizona Territory, on December 1, 1879.[119] En route to Tombstone Wyatt stopped at Prescott, Arizona, and talked his older brother, Virgil W. Earp, into going to Tombstone. (Virgil Earp had been appointed a deputy U.S. marshal for Yavapai County, Arizona, on November 27, 1879.[120]) Jim and Morgan Earp also followed Wyatt to Tombstone. Baxter Warren Earp, the youngest brother, later came to Tombstone from the family home at Colton, California.

At Tombstone Wyatt invested in several mining operations,[121] one of which he and his partner Harry Finaty of Dodge City sold for $30,000 in March 1880.[122] Wyatt also wrangled a job with the Tombstone office of Wells, Fargo and Company as a shotgun messenger[123] under Agent Marshall Williams. He resigned in October, 1880, to accept a job as a deputy under Sheriff Charles A. Shibell[124] when Tombstone was still part of Pima County. Morgan Earp was appointed shotgun messenger in his brother's place.[125]

As deputy sheriff Wyatt pistol-whipped and jailed the notorious Arizona rustler William Graham, alias "Curly Bill Brocius," on October 28, 1880, after the latter had fatally shot City Marshal Fred White. Wyatt, with the aid of his brothers Virgil and Morgan, then jailed several of Curly Bill's companions.[126]

Arizona State Library and Archives, Phoenix
The Earps worked from this unglamorous adobe Wells, Fargo Express office at Tombstone as shotgun messengers

Virgil Earp joined his brothers at Tombstone and was appointed city marshal after being twice defeated at the ballot box. Warren Earp, a younger brother, also came there.

With Marshal White dead, the city officials of Tombstone appointed Virgil Earp assistant marshal on or about November 1, 1880. He resigned this position on November 15, two days after he was defeated in a special election for interim city marshal by Ben Sippy.[127] Tombstone's first municipal election was held on January 4, 1881, and Sippy again defeated Earp for the office of city marshal.[128] On June 6, 1881, Virgil was appointed city marshal by Mayor John Phillip Clum (formerly the Indian Agent at the San Carlos Apache Reservation) and his city council, after Sippy had left Tombstone and never returned.[129]

Meanwhile, Wyatt Earp was having his own troubles. Shibell dismissed him as deputy sheriff and appointed John H. Behan, a former sheriff of Yavapai County, in his place.[130] When Cochise County was formed from part of Pima County in January 1881, Wyatt Earp and Johnny Behan were applicants for the office of sheriff of Cochise County. The famous explorer-politician-soldier, ex-Major General John C. Frémont, the territorial governor of Arizona, appointed Behan to the position.[131]

Earp and Behan became bitter enemies and the bitterness increased when Johnny's

Johnny Behan

John H. Behan was appointed sheriff of Cochise County over Wyatt Earp, the other candidate, by Governor John C. Frémont. The pair became bitter enemies.

The Oriental Saloon in Tombstone was a lively social center for the mining town. Wyatt Earp purchased a part interest in the gambling concession. His brothers, plus Doc Holliday and Luke Short, were dealers here at various times. On the eve of the O. K. Corral fight, the participants quarreled here.

young mistress, Josephine Sarah Marcus, left him for Wyatt. Wyatt, however, continued to live with Mattie Blaylock while he pursued an illicit relationship with the Marcus girl.

Wyatt soon bought a percentage of the gambling interest at the Oriental Saloon which was owned by gambler Milton E. (Mike) Joyce. At one time Wyatt installed his brother Morgan, Doc Holliday, and ex-Dodge citizens Bat Masterson and Luke Short as dealers at the Oriental. The association between the Earp faction and Joyce and his gambling colleagues was not a cordial one, and on one occasion Wyatt slapped

Joyce. Wyatt's spare time was spent reading the area newspapers in the hope of finding his name. He and his brother also farmed themselves out as part-time possemen for U.S. Marshal Crawley P. Dake of Arizona.

The year 1881 saw a chain of events happen to Wyatt, Virgil, and Morgan Earp, and Doc Holliday which culminated later that year in a now famous street fight at Tombstone and a bloody feud in 1882. The first incident involved the theft of six U.S. government mules. First Lieutenant Joseph H. Hurst and a detail of four troopers were assigned to recover mules stolen from Camp Rucker, Arizona. Hurst enlisted the aid of

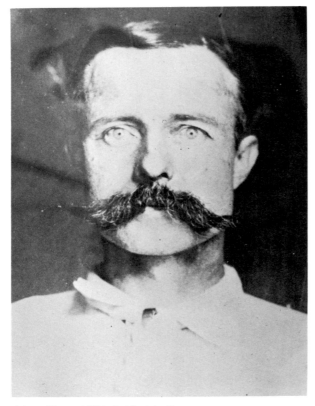

"Buckskin Frank" Leslie was bartender and bouncer at the Oriental Saloon. He joined the posse tracking road agents of the Benson stage as a scout.

Deputy U.S. Marshal Virgil Earp and his brothers, Wyatt and Morgan. The government posse tracked the stolen mules to Charleston, a town about eight or nine miles southwest of Tombstone. There the posse learned that the mules were at the ranch of Thomas and Robert F. (Frank) McLaury. The posse went to the McLaury ranch, but the two brothers refused to step from their house or to give up the stolen mules which were in their corral. Frank Patterson, a McLaury associate came outside at the Mc-Laury's request and said the brothers would give up the mules if the Earps went back to Tombstone. Hurst agreed and the Earps returned to Tombstone, but the McLaurys did not keep their part of the deal. Instead, they

made threats against the Earps. Several weeks later Wyatt Earp met the McLaurys at Charleston and they tried to start a fight with him. When Wyatt refused they threatened to kill him if he ever crossed them again.[132]

An event occurred on the night of March 15, 1881, which was to have severe repercussions for the Earps and Doc Holliday and eventually triggered the bloody fight history has erroneously chosen to call "the battle at the O. K. Corral." That night the Benson stage was about a mile from Contention City, near Tombstone, when a masked man stepped from the east side of the road and called, "Halt!" Several other men then made their appearance. One of the men fired a shot which struck the driver, Eli (Budd) Philpot. Philpot toppled dead from the box and the horses bolted. Robert H. Paul, the Wells, Fargo & Company's shotgun messenger, fired at the bandits as the coach raced away. The bandits shot back, fatally wounding Peter Roering, one of eight passengers. The robbers failed to get a reported $26,000 that was on the stage.[133]

Benson authorities wired Agent Williams about the attempted holdup. A large posse was organized consisting, among others, of Sheriff Behan, the Earps, Bat Masterson, and N. F. (Buckskin Frank) Leslie, the congenial bartender at the Oriental Saloon. Leslie acted as scout and tracker, having had scouting experience for the Army. From the scene of the holdup the posse tracked the robbers to the Redfield ranch. In the Redfield corral were two horses belonging to the holdup men. Also at the ranch was Luther King who admitted that he had held the horses during the holdup attempt. King named three other accomplices: Bill Leonard, Harry Head, and Jim Crane. King was taken to Tombstone and jailed. By March 19 King had escaped from jail and was never apprehended. King's escape was never fully explained; he simply stepped out the back door and mounted a horse that someone had waiting for him. Undersheriff Harry M. Woods and two other men were present at the jail during King's move to freedom.[134]

Circumstantial evidence pointed to Doc Holliday as one of the men who had been involved in the attempted holdup of the Benson stage. It was a well-known fact that Bill Leonard, one of the men implicated by King, was a friend of Holliday. Doc had known Leonard at Las Vegas, New Mexico. Under oath at the preliminary hearing that followed the famous street fight at Tombstone, Joseph Isaac Clanton testified that Holliday had admitted to him that he had killed Philpot. Clanton also testified that Leonard later told him the same thing. Ike and his teenage brother, William, and the McLaury brothers also said that they had seen Holliday in the holdup area the night of March 15. (The Clantons and McLaurys were notoriously anti-Holliday.) A man named Russell was stringing telegraph wire between Charleston and Tombstone that night when he heard a rifle shot. A few minutes later Russell said he saw Holliday riding toward Tombstone.[135] While en route to Tombstone, Holliday was seen by John H. Slaughter, a rancher who later became sheriff of Cochise County. Doc was easily identifiable because he had rented a blaze-faced roan from John Dunbar's livery stable at Tombstone. The Dunbar horse was well known in Cochise County because of

Courtesy New-York Historical Society   *Photo by Camillus S. Fly*
Ike Clanton testified against Doc Holliday in the Benson stage hearing and carried on a feud with the Earps.

its speed.[136] Witnesses saw Holliday at Charleston at 8:30 P.M. on the night of the holdup attempt. He was also seen between ten and eleven o'clock the same night at Tombstone with a flagged-out horse. (Charleston was less than ten miles from Tombstone and the Dunbar horse was known for its endurance.)

The most damaging piece of evidence against Holliday was an affidavit signed by Doc's mistress, Kate Elder, on or about June 5. The affidavit stated that Holliday was implicated in the murder of Philpot. Kate had signed the document after she and Doc had quarreled. Behan arrested Holliday on June 5, but Doc was released on a $5,000 bond.[137] Wyatt Earp persuaded Kate to swear that the affiidavit was false, that Behan had got her drunk, and that she did not know what she had signed. Years later Kate signed a deposition stating that Holliday was involved in the murder of Philpot,[138] but she also lied in the same deposition when she swore that she had been married to Holliday. Doc was released on July 9 for lack of evidence.

Many persons in Tombstone believed that the Earps and Agent Williams were responsible for the several stagecoach holdups in Cochise County. Many suspected that Williams was tipping off the Earps and their accomplices on what stages to rob and when. At the preliminary hearing that followed Tombstone's famous street fight, Ike Clanton testified that Virgil Earp told him he did not want to capture the robbers of the Benson stage because he was afraid they would talk, if captured, and involve his friends. Ike also stated that Morgan Earp told him that Wyatt had given $1,400 to Doc Holliday and Bill Leonard several days before the Benson holdup and that Wyatt had given $29,000 to an unnamed source.

At the same hearing Wyatt Earp testified that he offered Ike Clanton and Frank McLaury the $3,000 reward for the capture of Leonard, Head, and Crane if they aided him in finding the three men, who were friends of the Clantons and McLaurys. Ike Clanton attested that he turned down Wyatt's offer. Earp said that he wanted the credit of capturing the three bandits, but the glory of apprehending them escaped him with the violent deaths of the men at

Courtesy New-York Historical Society
Frank McLaury, considered the best gunfighter in the Clanton-McLaury crowd, backed Ike Clanton. He threatened Morgan Earp with his life.

the hands of others. Leonard and Head were killed in an attempted holdup in June 1881 at Eureka, New Mexico.[139] Crane was killed by Mexicans in August of that year in New Mexico.[140]

Incidents between the Earps and the Clantons and McLaurys continued to inflame both sides. Wyatt Earp and Billy Clanton exchanged heated remarks over the ownership of a horse which Wyatt said belonged to him. On the night of September 8, 1881, the Bisbee stage was robbed of $3,100 by Cochise County Deputy Sheriff Frank C. Stilwell, the younger brother of the celebrated Army Scout Simpson E. (Comanche Jack) Stilwell of Beecher's Island

Courtesy New-York Historical Society
Tom McLaury sat in a poker game on the eve of the O. K.
Corral battle. The game ended in a heated argument. The
next afternoon Tom was killed by Doc Holliday.

when Marshall Williams, in a moment of
drunken byplay, accused Ike Clanton of
"selling out" his friends, Leonard, Head and
Crane. Clanton confronted Wyatt Earp, ac-
cusing him of telling Doc Holliday about
the offer to "sell out" Leonard, Head, and
Crane. Wyatt denied that he had told Holliday about the offer. Ike said that Holliday
had told him as much.[142] Doc denied this,
however.

On the night of October 25 Wyatt and
Morgan Earp and Doc Holliday confronted
Ike Clanton. Holliday goaded Clanton
three times to fight and Morgan Earp also
tried to incite Ike into action. Clanton demurred, saying he was unarmed and had
not threatened the Earps. The abuse he
had taken from Holliday and Morgan Earp
angered Ike. He armed himself and later
that evening, confronted Wyatt, telling him
that he was armed and would be ready for
a fight in the morning.[143] Then Ike Clanton
sat in a poker game with Virgil Earp, Johnny Behan, and Tom McLaury. After the
game Ike and Virgil exchanged heated remarks.

Next day the showdown came. On the
morning of Wednesday, October 26, 1881,
Virgil Earp pistol-whipped and arrested Ike
Clanton for carrying weapons within the
city limits. Virgil and Morgan took Ike to
the police court where he was fined twenty-
five dollars plus two dollars and fifty cents
court costs. At the police court Clanton and
Morgan exchanged heated remarks and
Morgan offered Ike a gun. Third parties
came between the two men and separated
them.

Meanwhile, Tom McLaury had come to
the police court to aid Ike Clanton. As Mc-
Laury was leaving the courthouse, he col-

fame, and Peter Spence. A sheriff's posse
led by Deputy Sheriffs William M. Breakenridge and David Neagle arrested Stilwell
and Spence at Bisbee and took them to
Tombstone. Wyatt and Morgan Earp, Marshall Williams, and Frederick J. Dodge, a
Wells, Fargo detective, arrived at Bisbee
after the arrests had been made and aided
the posse in escorting Stilwell and Spence
to Tombstone. Stilwell and Spence were
friends of Ike Clanton and Frank McLaury.
Later, McLaury confronted Morgan Earp
and threatened his life and those of his
brothers because they had aided in the arrest of Stilwell and Spence.[141]

The whole bitter feud reached a climax

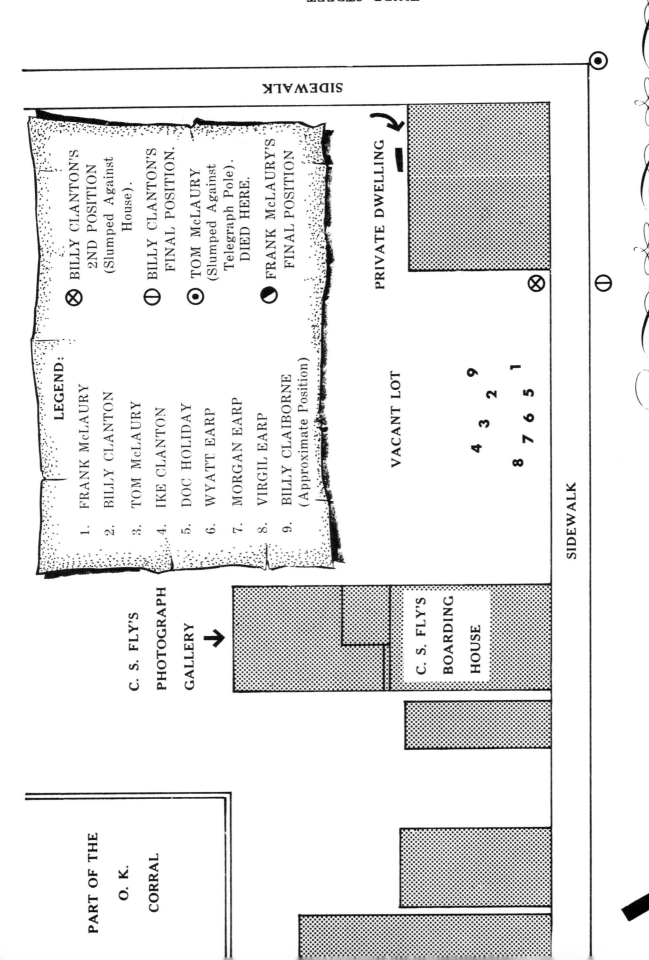

OK CORRAL GUNFIGHT 1881

THIRD STREET

SIDEWALK

LEGEND:

BILLY CLANTON'S 2ND POSITION (Slumped Against House).

BILLY CLANTON'S FINAL POSITION.

TOM McLAURY (Slumped Against Telegraph Pole). DIED HERE.

FRANK McLAURY'S FINAL POSITION

1. FRANK McLAURY
2. BILLY CLANTON
3. TOM McLAURY
4. IKE CLANTON
5. DOC HOLIDAY
6. WYATT EARP
7. MORGAN EARP
8. VIRGIL EARP
9. BILLY CLAIBORNE (Approximate Position)

PRIVATE DWELLING

VACANT LOT

4 3 2 9

8 7 6 5 1

C. S. FLY'S PHOTOGRAPH GALLERY

C. S. FLY'S BOARDING HOUSE

PART OF THE O. K. CORRAL

SIDEWALK

FREMONT STREET

NORTH

Map Data by Dale T. Schoenberger
The most celebrated gunfight in the saga of the West occurred in the streets of Tombstone, not inside the O. K. Corral as legends and novelists have portrayed it. The map shows the positions of the Clanton and Earp parties at the outset of the fight, October 26, 1881.

lided with Wyatt who was entering. Wyatt became angry; he slapped McLaury with one hand and pistol whipped him with the other. Later in the day Wyatt and Frank McLaury had a verbal fight when Wyatt led McLaury's mare from the sidewalk back into the street.

About 2:30 in the afternoon the Earps and Doc Holliday decided to force a showdown with the Clantons and McLaurys. One witness, B. H. Fallahy, testified that he heard Virgil Earp tell Sheriff Behan, "I will not arrest them, but will kill them on sight."[144] Behan made an effort to thwart a fight between the two groups. He pleaded with Virgil only to disarm the Clantons and McLaurys, not to start any shooting. Virgil demurred, saying that he would give them a chance to fight.

Behan went to the Clantons and McLaurys and asked them to give up their weapons. Frank McLaury and Billy Clanton refused. Tom McLaury threw open the lapels of his coat and said he was unarmed. (Some say that McLaury had a pistol in his waistband.) Behan felt the waist of Ike Clanton for weapons but found none. (Ike's weapons were at the saloon of J. H. Allman. He was not armed during the ensuing fight. This was substantiated by Wyatt Earp in his written testimony at the hearing which followed the street fight and which appeared in the *Tombstone Nugget* of November 17, 1881.) William F. Claiborne (or Claibourne), a friend of Frank McLaury, may or may not have been armed, but told Behan that he was not a member of the Clanton-McLaury group.

Behan returned to the Earps and Holliday and asked them not to force a fight, but they brushed him aside. Behan knew that it was too late. The time for talk had passed. The showdown was only minutes away.

The Earp-Holliday party confronted the Clantons and McLaurys on the south side of Fremont Street, a short distance east of Third Street. Here is where the fight occurred. *It did not take place in the O. K. Corral.* The Clantons, McLaurys, and Billy Claiborne were standing in a vacant lot between photographer Camillus S. Fly's boardinghouse and a private dwelling. The lot had open stalls which were used in connection with the O. K. Corral stable. When the Earp party got within a few yards of the Clantons and McLaurys, Virgil Earp called out, "Throw up your hands!" Frank McLaury and Billy Clanton immediately cocked the hammers of their revolvers. Doc Holliday drew and aimed his revolver, as he walked within a few feet of Frank McLaury.

"Hold! I don't mean that," Virgil Earp cried, as he raised his right hand in the air. (He had been carrying Doc Holliday's cane hooked on his right wrist, and as he raised his hand, it slipped down his forearm to the elbow. Evidently Holliday had intended to do some shooting and he didn't want to be incumbered by the cane.)

"You sonofabitches have been looking for a fight; now you can have one!" interrupted Wyatt Earp. He reached into his right overcoat pocket for his pistol.[145]

"We will!" cried Frank McLaury.

"Let them have it!" said Morgan Earp.

"All right!" added Doc Holliday.

Billy Claiborne, who was standing a short distance to the rear of the Clantons and McLaurys broke and ran toward Fly's boardinghouse, missing a chance to be like his recently deceased idol, Billy the Kid. The

Interior of the O. K. Corral as it appeared years later, apparently in disuse and a depository for junk. It was just outside the corral that the gun battle took place. It lasted only thirty seconds.

grandson of one eyewitness said eighty-five years later that Claiborne handed the unarmed Tom McLaury a pistol as he fled the scene.

There are two versions of what happened next. Less than a month after the fight, Wyatt Earp testified that the first two shots were fired by him and Billy Clanton at almost the same time. Virgil Earp also testified that one of the first two shots was fired by Billy Clanton. Wyatt said he shot at Frank McLaury (Frank had the reputation of being the best gunfighter among the Clanton-McLaury party) and that Billy Clanton fired at him. Behan, a witness to the fight, alleged that at least the first two shots, and possibly the next three, came

from the Earp party. Ike Clanton, Claiborne, and Wesley Fuller, a gambler and friend of the Clantons and McLaurys, each testified that the first two shots were fired by the Earp-Holliday party. At any rate, there were several shots and three men died as a result.

Frank McLaury was struck in the abdomen by Wyatt Earp's first bullet and fatally wounded. McLaury's rearing mount (he was holding the reins) bolted and carried him into the middle of Fremont Street. Tom McLaury made a leap for the Winchester rifle slung in the boot on his brother's mount as the animal bolted, but missed by a split second. Holliday shot McLaury in the chest and the right side with the sawed-off shotgun he brandished from beneath his overcoat, as Tom reached for the Winchester. McLaury pitched dead near a telegraph pole at the corner of Third and Fremont.

Before Billy Claiborne reached Fly's in safety, a spent bullet ricocheted across his knee. Meanwhile, Ike Clanton had grabbed Wyatt Earp by the gun arm and momentarily pinned him against Fly's boardinghouse. Billy Clanton reeled backwards against the private dwelling from a bullet in the chest from the pistol of Morgan Earp.[146] Another bullet from Virgil Earp's pistol broke Billy's right wrist; the bullet entered the outside of the wrist and passed through it and struck Billy in the stomach. (Pro-Earp enthusiasts claim that the nature of Billy Clanton's wrist wound proves that he did not have his hands raised when shot. They claim that had Clanton had his hands raised then the bullet would have entered the wrist from the inside, which would have been facing the Earp party. This argument, however, is not valid. Billy Clanton could have had his hands raised when first shot, then dropped them when hit, and received his wrist wound with his hands down.) As Ike Clanton clung to Wyatt Earp, Wyatt fired a shot. Wyatt then threw off Clanton. Ike darted into Fly's boardinghouse as Doc Holliday put two wild shots after him.

The Earps and Holliday backed into Fremont Street during the fusillade. Young Billy Clanton, slumped against the private dwelling, began fighting back despite his mortal wounds. Using his left hand, he fired his pistol, hitting Morgan Earp[147] near the base of the neck; the bullet entered the right shoulder blade, shattered off a piece of a vertebra, and passed out through the left

shoulder blade.[148] Morgan was felled by the wound. Meanwhile, two shots burst on the Earp-Holliday party from a window in Fly's. Holliday returned the fire. Frank McLaury and Doc Holliday then exchanged shots. McLaury's bullet ricocheted off Doc's holster and ripped across his back. Morgan Earp shot Frank McLaury in the head a split second after McLaury and Holliday had exchanged shots. Morgan's bullet struck McLaury near the right temple, behind the ear, killing him instantly. Ike Clanton darted from the boardinghouse into Fly's photograph gallery. Two more wild shots were fired at him.

Billy Clanton gamely continued to fight as he crawled into Fremont Street. He shot Virgil Earp in the calf of the right leg; the bullet passed through the limb, but the wound did not fell Earp. Billy tried desperately to cock his pistol for another shot, but but C. S. Fly came out and took the weapon from Billy's hands. Behan then tried to place Wyatt Earp under arrest, but Wyatt refused to be arrested.

Within thirty seconds what has been called "the greatest face-to-face gun battle in the annals of Western history" was over. The McLaury brothers were dead. Billy Clanton was carried to a nearby house and given two injections of morphine.[149] Billy was mortally wounded and he died within the hour. The three dead men were dressed in fine clothes and placed in a window of a hardware store with a sign stating that they were murdered in the streets of Tombstone. They were buried on Boot Hill with the epitaph "Murdered In The Streets Of Tombstone" on their headstones.

One of the biggest controversies surrounding the street fight at Tombstone was

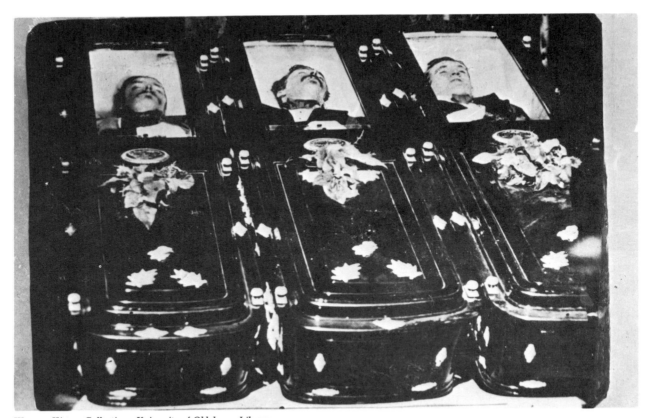

Western History Collections, University of Oklahoma Library
Bodies of Tom and Frank McLaury and of Billy Clanton were displayed in their coffins. They were buried on Tombstone's
Boot Hill where the graves are seen annually by thousands of tourists.

whether Tom McLaury was armed. R. F. Coleman, who witnessed the famous fight, stated that he saw "Tom McLaury fall first and then raise and fire *again* before he died."—*Tombstone Epitaph,* October 28, 1881. Wyatt Earp testified that he *believed* that Tom McLaury had fired two shots at his party before he was killed. Virgil Earp attested that McLaury had fired once or twice over the back of Frank McLaury's mare. Two other men, Albert C. Biliche and J. B. W. Gardiner, swore that on the afternoon of the fight they noticed Tom McLaury's flat right trouser pocket when he went into A. Bauer's meat market, but when McLaury came out of Bauer's the trouser pocket protruded as if it contained a pistol.

This of course was a *conclusion* on the part of both men.

Johnny Behan testified that he saw no weapons on McLaury only minutes before the fight. (Behan, however, was notoriously anti-Earp.) Andy Mehan, a bartender, signified that between one and two o'clock on the afternoon of the fight, Tom McLaury had left his pistol with him. Dr. H. M. Matthews, the Cochise County coroner, swore that a dozen buckshot entered Tom McLaury's chest—in the right side, near and together under the arm. The wounds of McLaury tend to indicate that he had his hands raised toward the rifle boot on his brother's mount when shot. Dr. Matthews also testified that he found no weapons on the body of Tom McLaury, adding further doubt that he was armed at any time during the fight. Billy Claiborne, who helped load the body of Tom McLaury into a wagon after the fight, testified, too, that he saw no weapons on McLaury's body.

The battle could hardly be called fair in two respects. At least one, and possibly two, of the Clanton-McLaury party were unarmed during the fight. The Clantons and McLaurys were obviously surprised by the heavily-armed Earp-Holliday party. Had the Clantons and McLaurys expected a fight, Ike Clanton and Tom McLaury would have most certainly armed themselves with the two Winchesters only a few feet away in the rifle boot on their brothers' mounts.

Murder warrants were issued for the arrest of the Earps and Holliday on October 29.[150] Because Virgil and Morgan Earp were bedridden with their wounds, the warrants were served only on Wyatt and Doc Holliday. Bail was set and raised at $10,000 each.[151] Despite the friendship between Mayor Clum and the Earps, the city council dismissed Virgil Earp as town marshal on October 29.[152] Wyatt and Doc were rearrested on November 7 after additional evidence was gathered against them. They were admitted to jail without bail. Their attorney Thomas Fitch had them released on November 20 on a writ of *habeas corpus*.[153] Bail was set and raised at $10,000 each for Wyatt Earp and Doc Holliday.[154]

On October 31 a preliminary hearing began before Justice of the Peace Wells Spicer. Testimony was heard from both sides, including Wyatt Earp, who read a written statement and presented the court with two written testimonials from the citizens of Wichita and Dodge City. The testimony

was conducted during most of the month, ending on November 30. The case then went to Judge Spicer for a ruling. On December 1, Judge Spicer ruled that Earp and Holliday be released from custody on the grounds "that the defendants were fully justified in committing these homicides."[155] In December the grand jury reviewed the evidence and refused to return an indictment against the Earps and Holliday.

Friends of the three dead men decided to take matters into their own hands on December 28. As Virgil Earp was crossing Allen Street in Tombstone, he was critically wounded in the back and the left arm by hidden marksmen. Virgil's arm was left partially crippled from the wound.

Ike Clanton tried another legal move against the Earps and Holliday at Contention. On February 10, 1882, he swore out murder warrants against Wyatt and Morgan Earp and Doc Holliday, charging them with the murder of his brother William Clanton. (Virgil Earp was still bedridden with the wounds he received on December 28.) The two Earp brothers and Holliday were arrested on February 10 and taken to Contention. They were released the next day because no new evidence had been brought against them. They were then taken back

By 1937 the O. K. Corral was in ruins. It has since been restored and is a major tourist attraction in Tombstone. Books, motion pictures, and a television series have revived interest in the historic town and the O. K. Corral fight.

to Tombstone and released from official custody on February 14.

There seems to have been some question as to the legal status of the Earps and Holliday during the fight. Virgil Earp, of course, was city marshal of Tombstone. Wyatt Earp testified that Morgan Earp had been a special policeman for six weeks prior to the fight and that he (Wyatt) had taken Virgil's place while the latter was at Tucson for the hearing of Frank Stilwell, and was still a police officer at the time of the fight. Wyatt also asserted that at the time of the fight Virgil had asked him, his brother Morgan, and Doc Holliday for assistance. Virgil Earp corroborated his brother's testimony, except to clarify that Wyatt's capacity as a policeman was to keep order in a saloon and make arrests, if necessary.

More bloodshed followed. . . .

On the night of March 18, 1882, Morgan Earp was assassinated and another man, George A. B. Berry, was wounded by hidden marksmen while Morgan played billiards with Robert S. Hatch in the latter's saloon and billiard hall. Wyatt Earp, who was watching the game, barely missed being assassinated himself. One bullet struck Morgan in the right side of the abdomen, bore through his spinal column, shattering it, and passed out through the left side, striking Berry in the thigh.[156] Berry died of heart failure following the shooting. A second bullet struck the wall a little above the head of Wyatt Earp, who sat watching the game.

On the testimony of Mrs. Marietta Spence, wife of Pete Spence, a coroner's jury ruled that Morgan Earp had been killed by Frank Stilwell; Pete Spence; Florentino (Indian Charlie) Cruz, a *Mestizo* woodcutter who worked for Spence; a faro dealer named Fries who dealt at the Oriental Saloon (Fries had replaced Morgan Earp as a faro dealer at the Oriental after Wyatt Earp had sold his interest there); and another Indian half-breed whose name was unknown. Mrs. Spence said that her husband had killed Morgan Earp and that the others were with him at the time. Mrs. Spence also testified that she and her husband had quarreled and that he had struck her. Morgan was Wyatt's favorite brother and as far as Wyatt was concerned, the coroner's verdict was a death sentence for Stilwell, Spence, and the others.

Wyatt and Warren Earp, Doc Holliday, and two Earp cronies, "Turkey Creek Jack" Johnson and Sherman McMasters, accompanied Virgil Earp and his wife and the body of Morgan Earp and his widow to Tucson via rail on March 20. The body of Morgan Earp was on its way for burial at the family home at Colton, California. While the steam cars were stopped at Tucson, Wyatt and Warren Earp, Holliday, Johnson and McMasters left the train. That evening the Earp party cornered Stilwell in the Tucson railroad yard and shot him to death. (Stilwell had been in Tucson for his trial on charges of robbing the Bisbee stage. Ike Clanton was also in Tucson at this time acting as a character witness for Stilwell.)

Stilwell was taken by surprise by the Earp party. His pistol was found undischarged. Four rifle bullets and two loads of buckshot had riddled his body. Both of his legs were shot through. A charge of buckshot had entered his chest and another charge had struck him in the left thigh.[157]

Murder warrants were issued at Tucson

Arizona Pioneers' Historical Society, Tucson
When Morgan Earp was killed by assassins, Wyatt Earp, his brother, Doc Holliday, and other companions went after the killers, as named by a coroner's jury. They caught up with Frank Stilwell, cornering him in the Tucson railroad yard (*above, left*), and riddled him with bullets.

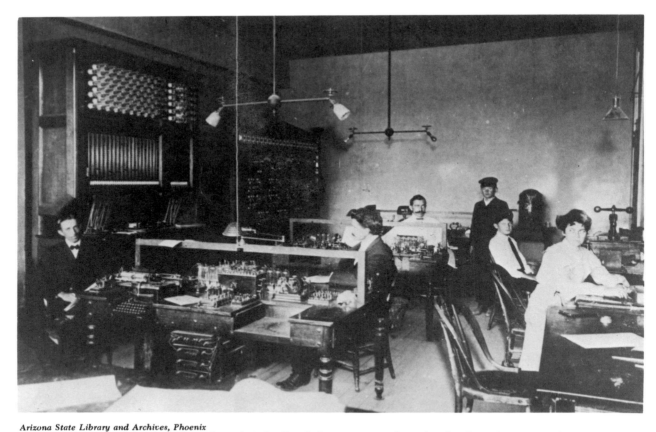

Warrants were issued for the killers of Frank Stilwell and they were wired to Sheriff John Behan at Tombstone from this Western Union office at Tucson, along with news of the shooting. A friendly telegrapher delayed contacting the sheriff, however, until the Earps and their friends could escape.

for the two Earps, Holliday, Johnson and McMasters. The Earp party returned to Tombstone on the evening of March 21. The murder warrants for Stilwell's death were wired to Sheriff Behan, but the telegraph manager was a friend of Earp and at Wyatt's request, he delayed giving Behan the warrants until the Earp party had time to pack their belongings.[158] As the Earp party, which now included Charlie Smith, Dan Tipton, and the others, was about to leave town, Behan came up and said he wanted to see Wyatt. Earp replied that he had seen Behan once too often. The Earp party then rode out of Tombstone.

On March 22 Wyatt and Warren Earp, Holliday, Johnson, McMasters, and another Earp crony, "Texas Jack" Vermillion, went to Pete Spence's wood camp near Tombstone looking for Spence. Spence was not there, but Indian Charlie Cruz was resting on the ground. The Earp party riddled the *Mestizo's* body with five bullets. Spence, fearing for his life, surrendered to Sheriff Behan for protective custody.[159] He was later given a hearing regarding the death of Morgan Earp and released.[160]

While the Earp party was galloping all over southern Arizona looking for Morgan's murderers, they came across four saddle tramps camped at a water hole in the Whettone Mountains. The four drifters, fearing the Earp party for some reason, fired on them, killing Texas Jack Vermillion's horse and shooting the pommel off Wyatt Earp's saddle. Earp dismounted and charged the drifters on foot, exchanging several shots with them. The rest of the Earp party fled to shelter.[161] No one, however, was hit during the brief encounter. The four drifters told the story of the fight to two residents of Tombstone, "Whistling Dick" Wright and Tony Kraker, who repeated the report to the *Tombstone Epitaph*.[162]

Wyatt Earp always claimed that he shotgunned to death Curly Bill Brocius, the outlaw for whom the Arizona Cattlemen's Association had offered a $1,000 reward,[163] in the Whetstone fight on March 26, 1882. Curly Bill's body, however, was never found. Several persons, including Bill's friend Jim Hughes; Judge James C. Hancock, who clerked in a store at Galeyville, Bill's favorite haunt; and Melvin W. Jones, a rancher, who also knew Curly, said that Bill left Arizona some time after he had been wounded in a dispute[164] by a man named Jim Wallace at Galeyville in May, 1881.[165] Fred Dodge, however, admitted to Stuart N. Lake, in letters dated October 8, 1928, and September 15, 1929, that a Wells, Fargo Company's investigation showed that Wyatt Earp killed Curly Bill, and that Ike Clanton admitted that Earp had killed Curly Bill.

Meanwhile, Arizona authorities were pressing the Stilwell murder warrants against the Earps and their cronies. Johnny

Arizona Pioneers' Historical Society, Tucson
This stately courthouse at Tucson was brand-new at the time of the Stilwell killing and might well have been the scene of the trial of Wyatt Earp and Doc Holliday for the murder. But the gunmen fled north into Colorado.

Wyatt and Warren Earp "hid out" amid the Rocky Mountains at Gunnison, Colorado, while Doc Holliday was in Pueblo. Arizona authorities tried to extradite Wyatt but a wealthy gambler pressured the Colorado governor not to sign the papers. Now a fugitive, Wyatt's career in Arizona was at an end.

Behan had a posse in the field chasing the Earp party, but it seemed reluctant to apprehend the Earps and their cronies. In April 1882, Wyatt and Warren fled to Gunnison, Colorado. Doc Holliday went to Pueblo, Colorado. Arizona authorities attempted to have Wyatt extradited, but Earp had a wealthy gambler with political influence persuade Governor F. W. Pitkin of Colorado not to sign the extradition papers.[166] While Wyatt was in Colorado, his mistress Mattie Blaylock was at Colton awaiting his return. Wyatt did not go to Colton, so she went back to Arizona. She died a tragic suicide at Pinal on July 3, 1888, from an overdose of laudanum.[167]

The Tombstone years were Wyatt Earp's salad years—the high-water mark of his frontier career. These years were also the most controversial of his life: the accusation of being a stage robber; the semi-travesty called "the battle at the O. K. Corral"; the brutal murders of Stilwell and Indian Charlie; the unsubstantiated claim of having killed Curly Bill; his fleeing Arizona on a murder charge; the death of his favorite brother; the hatred of his two mortal enemies, Ike Clanton and Johnny Behan.[168]

Between 1882 and 1906 Wyatt Earp led a checkered life of endless wandering in the West. During this time he was often in San Francisco, the home of his third wife or mistress, Josephine Marcus—the same one he had met at Tombstone. He was at Denver and Fort Worth, and in June 1883, he arrived back in Dodge City from Silverton, Colorado, to aid his friend Luke Short in some domestic trouble with city officials. Between February and September, 1884, Wyatt and his brother Jim were at Eagle

Wyatt Earp's remaining years on what was a fading frontier were spent wandering from town to town, mining camp to mining camp. At one time in the 1880s he was in Eagle City, a mining town near Murray, shown here, in Idaho's Shoshone County, where he had mining interests and operated a saloon with his brother Jim. But once again he got into trouble, this time for "claim jumping.'"

City, Idaho, where they and several associates had mining interests. In at least three instances, Wyatt, Jim and their associates were sued for "claim jumping" and found guilty on two of those occasions. Wyatt and Jim were also operating the White Elephant Saloon at Eagle City.[169]

Earp is said to have been wounded in the arm during a card game at Lake City, Colorado, on or shortly before September 14, 1884. The shooting cannot be substantiated. The Arizona Pioneers' Historical Society and the Arizona State Library and Archives searched their old newspaper files for September, 1884, and found nothing about the shooting.[170] A search of the *Lake City* (Colorado) *Mining Register* for September, 1884, found no mention of Earp.[171]

In 1889 and 1890 Wyatt Earp was living at San Diego, California.[172] At this time he was operating three gambling houses in San Diego. Josephine Marcus, listed as "Mrs. Wyatt Earp," was living there as early as 1886.[173] By December, 1896, Wyatt was at San Francisco where on December 2 of that year, he refereed the heavyweight fight between Robert Fitzsimmons and Tom Sharkey. He awarded the fight to Sharkey on a foul in the eighth round. Fitzsimmons was favored (he won the heavyweight championship of the world in 1897 by defeating James J. Corbett) and according to many ringside observers, Fitzsimmons was ahead when Earp stopped the bout. Wyatt's decision caused a tremendous uproar in San Francisco for weeks. Many persons believed that Wyatt had "thrown" the fight to Sharkey, since the latter had repeatedly

The "Last Frontier" for old-time Westerners was Alaska and the Yukon, scene of the final great gold strike near the turn of the century. Wyatt Earp joined the miners and opportunists bound for the northland. Falling back on the profession he knew best, he operated a saloon in Nome.

fouled Fitzsimmons. A court hearing was held to determine who was to receive the $10,000 fight purse. At the hearing Wyatt testified that he was almost destitute, owning no property, only the clothes he was wearing. At the time of the fight, Wyatt was leasing a stable of racing horses at Santa Rosa, California.[174] According to the *San Francisco Chronicle* of December 9, 1896, Wyatt was beside himself with joy over the notoriety that the fight had brought him.

Near the turn of the century Wyatt was at Nome, Alaska, operating a saloon. On one occasion he and United States Marshal Albert Lowe allegedly had a dispute and Lowe slapped him.[175] He also found time to lose fist-fights with Tom Mulqueen,[176] a professional fighter, and one Alfred Williams.[177] The early 1900s found Wyatt in the mining districts around Tonopah and Goldfield, Nevada. Later he had mining interests near Parker, Arizona.

Finally, Wyatt and Josephine settled at Los Angeles in 1906. Wyatt is said to have

been a special police officer for the Los Angeles police department in areas around the California-Mexican border, but Los Angeles police officials deny this, saying that he was never an officer or special policeman of their department.[178]

In July 1911 Wyatt and two other men were arrested and arraigned at Los Angeles on a charge of fleecing J. Y. Patterson out of $25,000 on an alleged bunco game. He was released on a $1,000 bond. His trial was set for July 27,[179] but a search of the felony criminal indices from 1886 to 1925 was made by the Office of the Clerk of the Superior Court of the County of Los Angeles, as well as the records of January 1, 1909 to December 31, 1914, and no record of Wyatt Earp was found.[180]

One of the last bits of notoriety Wyatt received before his death was when he testified at the estate trial of the famous theatrical personality Lotta Crabtree at Los Angeles in the spring of 1925. Miss Crabtree died at Boston in 1924, leaving an estate valued at several million dollars. She reportedly had visited her brother at Tombstone when the Earps were there.

Before his death Wyatt was thinking of having his life story written. He began gathering notes on his career. In 1928 he met journalist Stuart N. Lake and two years later, Lake wrote a series of controversial articles on the Kansas cow-town career of Earp for the *Saturday Evening Post*. And in 1931 Lake's controversial biography of Earp was published. Wyatt did not live to see Lake's book. Wyatt passed away at Los Angeles on January 13, 1929. Cause of death was given as "a chronic cystitis with a contributory [cancerous] prostate." His remains were cremated and his ashes buried in the Hills of Eternity Memorial Park at Colma, California, near San Francisco. Josephine survived him until 1944.[181]

Wyatt Earp, like many men, was a product of his times. He was not a friendly man by nature, consequently he had few friends. Many considered him a potential enemy. And many who met him disliked him, but few really knew him.

Courtesy Nevada State Museum
Tonopah and Goldfield (pictured above) in Nevada became the scene of Wyatt Earp's activities for a time in the early 1900s, after the Alaska rush was over. Earp finally settled in Los Angeles to live out the balance of his life.

3.

WILD BILL HICKOK

(1837-1876)

JAMES BUTLER HICKOK was born to William Alonzo Hickok (1801-1852) and Polly Butler (1809?-1878)[1] at Troy Grove, La Salle County, Illinois, on May 27, 1837. As a youngster Jim Hickok was fascinated by stories of the Western frontier, especially those about the famous Army scout, Christopher (Kit) Carson, his boyhood idol. He dreamed about going west. The opportunity came three years after his father's death.

Young Jim Hickok ran away from home in 1855 following a fistfight with a bully named Charles Hudson. Thinking he had killed Hudson, Jim fled Illinois. (Hudson survived the fight.) That year Jim—somewhere along the way he began calling himself Bill, his father's name which he admired —found his way to Johnson County, Kansas,

in what is now Monticello Township. There he hired out doing odd jobs.

Hickok had arrived in Kansas during the infamous Missouri-Kansas border wars that preceded the War Between the States, or the period known in history as "Bleeding Kansas." In 1854 Congress created the Kansas and Nebraska territories and authorized the people in those territories to determine whether they would be free-staters or slaveholders. The majority of Missourians were people who either held slaves or were from slave states in the South, and consequently they wanted to have Kansas as a slave territory. The slaveholders in western Missouri were those most concerned with the Kansas problem.

Antislavery organizations in the North promoted and financed migrations of anti-

Ed Bartholomew Collection, Toyahvale, Texas
James Butler Hickok adopted the name "Wild Bill" during a colorful career in the Old West. He was marshal of Abilene when this photograph was taken in 1871.

of "Free-Staters" under Jim Lane and served as one of Lane's personal bodyguards. He remained with Lane's army in 1857. Finally, Bill quit Lane and was elected constable of Monticello Township on March 22, 1858. His commission was signed by Acting Territorial Governor James W. Denver on April 21. It was Hickok's first job as a peace officer.

To supplement his income, Bill continued working at odd jobs. He also took up housekeeping (without benefit of preacher) with Miss Mary Jane Owen. Tiring of the dull life, Bill went to Leavenworth, Kansas, in 1859 or 1860 and secured a job as a teamster on the Santa Fe Trail. At Leavenworth Bill met a young teamster's whelp by the name of William Frederick Cody, who later became famous as "Buffalo Bill."[2] As a

Courtesy Kansas State Historical Society, Topeka
"Buffalo Bill" Cody was plain Bill Cody when Hickok first met him as a teamster at Leavenworth, Kansas. The pair's paths crossed later on the plains.

slavery settlers to Kansas. Newspapers in Missouri objected feverishly to such migrations. Irregular groups of so-called "Border Ruffians" from the Missouri border raided into Kansas committing acts of aggression, influencing elections, and intimidating the antislavery settlers. In retaliation groups of "Free-Staters" from Kansas under various leaders such as James H. Lane, later a brigadier general in the Union Army and United States senator from Kansas, Charles R. Jennison, James Montgomery, and the infamous John Brown, raided into Missouri and proslavery settlements in Kansas.

In 1856 Hickok joined the irregular army

teamster, Hickok trailed all the way to Santa Fe, New Mexico, where he met his hero, Kit Carson.

In March, 1861, Hickok went to work at the Pony Express and Overland Stage and Express station at Rock Creek in Jones County (now Jefferson County), Nebraska Territory. The famous express firm of Russell, Majors and Waddell was paying the station superintendent, David Colbert Mc-Canles, for the use of his property and buildings. McCanles, who was born in Iredell County, North Carolina, on November 30, 1828,[3] had settled at Rock Creek in 1859. He put Hickok to work as a stable hand.

From the very beginning McCanles

Sarah Shull was McCanles' mistress at Rock Creek, but she transferred her affections to Bill Hickok after he came there. This widened the rift between the two men.

David C. McCanles ran the Rock Creek stage station beside the Oregon Trail in Nebraska Territory and hired Bill Hickok to work for him. He came to dislike Hickok and teased him about his girlish features.

seemed to have disliked young Hickok. For one thing, McCanles taunted Bill about his feminine features and slender, girlish build. He went so far as to doubt publicly Hickok's sex by calling him a hermaphrodite. McCanles's insults did not stop there. Because Hickok's long, slender nose and protruding lower lip resembled that of a duck's bill, McCanles often taunted him by calling him "Duck Bill." McCanles's insults and insinuations only made Hickok simmer. He refused to fight McCanles, but on at least two occasions the older man cornered Hickok and "playfully" roughed him up, pretending it was all in good fun. Wild Bill knew better.

The more serious trouble between Hickok and McCanles was over the latter's mistress, Sarah Shull, whose real name is said to have been Katherine Shell. Sarah had been McCanles's paramour for at least two years before Wild Bill arrived at Rock Creek. In 1859 she came west with McCanles when he deserted his wife and family in North Carolina. That year McCanles and Sarah settled at Rock Creek. Later McCanles sent for his wife and family. They came to Nebraska with Dave's brother, James L. McCanles, and his family. Dave McCanles still kept Sarah Shull as his mistress and refused to let any other man near her. When Hickok arrived at Rock Creek, Sarah transferred her affections to Bill. This angered McCanles and he repeatedly warned Hickok to keep away from Sarah. Bill refused and McCanles fumed.

In April or early May, McCanles sold his property at Rock Creek to Russell, Majors and Waddell and moved to Johnson County where his brother was residing. Sarah Shull did not go with him. She moved into a cabin a few miles from Rock Creek. With McCanles gone, Russell, Majors and Waddell sent Horace Wellman and his wife (or mistress) to the Rock Creek station as superintendent.

The express firm, however, was delinquent in its first payment to McCanles for his property, and for some reason, he blamed Wellman for not receiving the compensation. On several occasions in June, McCanles went to the Rock Creek station and threatened Wellman because he hadn't gotten his money. In early July Wellman and William Monroe McCanles, the young son of Dave McCanles, traveled to Brownsville, Nebraska, the district headquarters of

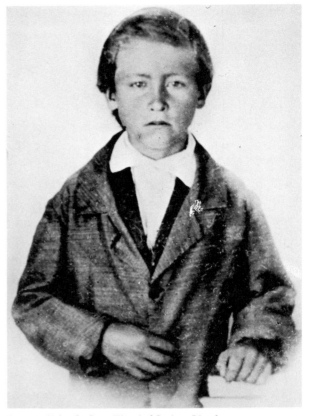

Courtesy Nebraska State Historical Society, Lincoln
William Monroe McCanles, young son of the stage station operator, witnessed the shoot-out at Rock Creek when Hickok fired on his father.

Russell, Majors and Waddell, to check on the delinquent payment. While Wellman was away, McCanles came to the station and threatened Mrs. Wellman about the overdue sum. Wellman and Monroe McCanles returned from Brownsville on July 11 without the money. The following day a bloody chapter in Western history was written with Wild Bill Hickok as the author.

On July 12, 1861, Dave and Monroe McCanles; James Woods, Dave's cousin; and James Gordon, a McCanles employee, came to the Rock Creek station. What McCanles really intended to do at the express station is still a matter of great controversy. McCanles told Sarah Shull that very morning that he was going "to clean up on the people at the station."[4] Whether he meant to kill them or merely to rough them up is open to speculation. Although Monroe McCanles always said that his father's party was unarmed when it went to the station, it has never been substantiated one way or the other. Men on the frontier seldom went unarmed. Some say if McCanles had expected trouble, he would not have allowed his young son to accompany him. This, too, is speculation, for youngsters on the frontier had a habit of maturing fast.

When the McCanles party arrived at the station, Woods and Gordon headed for the barn while the McCanleses went to the west door (kitchen door) of the two-room building where they met Horace Wellman. McCanles and Wellman argued about the delinquent payment. Wellman went back inside, while Mrs. Wellman came to the door and cursed McCanles. McCanles ignored the woman by saying that his business was with her husband. Hickok came to the door. His presence surprised McCanles.

"What the hell have you got to do with this?" McCanles asked.

"The station is my business," replied Hickok soberly.

"Well, then, if you want to take a hand, come out and we'll settle it like men," McCanles said.

Hickok didn't answer. He just stared coldly at McCanles.

McCanles broke the momentary silence. "We're friends, ain't we, Hickok?"

"I guess so," replied Hickok feebly.

"Well, send Wellman out here," replied McCanles in a half plea, "or I'll come in and get him."

Hickok didn't answer. He stepped back inside the station as if complying with McCanles's request. McCanles and his son went around to the south door (front door) where he had a better view of the two-room house. McCanles stepped to the doorway and asked for a drink of water. A water bucket was on a nearby table. Hickok handed him a dipper of water and quickly went behind a curtain that was the only partition between the two rooms. McCanles saw Hickok's move and called for him to come from behind the curtain. Hickok didn't answer. McCanles dropped the dipper of water and threatened to drag him out from behind the curtain.

"There will be one less sonofabitch when you try that," Hickok warned. Behind the curtain Bill had armed himself with a Hawken rifle, which ironically belonged to McCanles, left there when he sold the Rock Creek property.

McCanles started toward the curtain. Hickok fired through the partition. His bullet struck McCanles in the chest, fatally wounding him. McCanles staggered outside and collapsed in the yard. Monroe McCanles ran and bent over his dying father. Woods and Gordon heard the shot and came running from the barn toward the station. After shooting McCanles, Hickok put the rifle aside and armed himself with a pistol.

Woods reached the west door of the station and entered. He was instantly shot by Hickok and fatally wounded. Gordon entered the south door of the station only seconds after Hickok had shot Woods. Hickok turned and shot Gordon. Despite his wound, Gordon fled the station with Wild Bill in pursuit. Hickok shot him a second time, mortally wounding him. Gordon con-

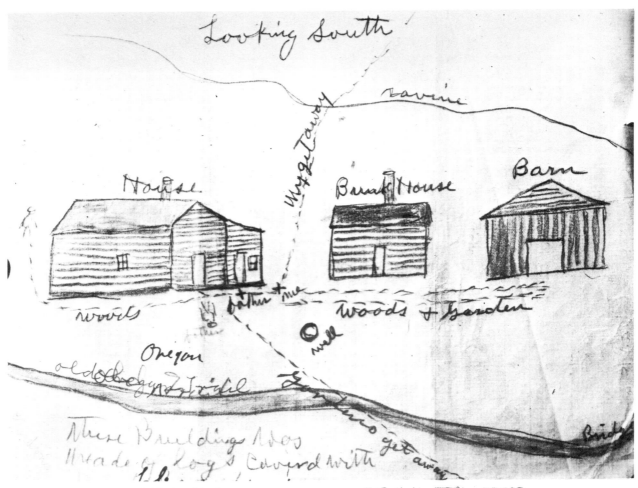

Looking South

ravine

Wagon Trail

House

Bunk House

Barn

woods

father + me

father

woods + garden

Oregon

well

old . . . Trail

. . . get away

These Buildings Was
Made of Logs Coverd with . . .

Monroe McCanles made this drawing depicting the gunplay at Rock Creek station. Bill Hickok was inside the house on the left. Monroe and his father were standing at the points marked X in the center of the drawing when Hickok's gun blazed. Dotted lines show trails of escape taken by Gordon, Woods, and Monroe when they fled to safety in a ravine.

tinued to run and Hickok emptied his pistol at him.

The mortally wounded Woods ran from the station around to the rear of the house, where he fell dying in a weed patch. Mrs. Wellman ran out screaming, "Come on! Let's kill all of the sonofabitches!" Either she or her husband (it has never been certain which one) picked up a heavy garden hoe and crushed Woods' skull as he lay dying. Then one of the Wellmans swung the hoe at Monroe McCanles's head while he was bending over his dying father. Fortunately, the blow missed the youngster and

he fled across a ravine to the south of the express station.

After emptying his pistol at Gordon, Hickok returned to the station. He threatened to kill Joe Baker, one of the stock tenders who was a friend of McCanles. Baker's stepdaughter, Sarah Kelsey, who had been in the station with Mrs. Wellman, pleaded with Wild Bill not to kill her stepfather. Hickok heeded the girl's pleas.

Hickok, Wellman and James W. (Doc) Brink, a Pony Express rider at the station, tracked Gordon into the underbrush with the aid of one of McCanles's hounds which had followed its master to the station. They found Gordon breathing his last under a large tree and there one of them (probably Brink) shotgunned the helpless man to death.

James L. McCanles swore out murder warrants against Hickok, Wellman and Brink on July 13 in Gage County (to which Jones County was attached for judicial purposes). Sheriff E. B. Hendee of Gage County arrested Wild Bill, Wellman and Brink on July 15. They were taken to Beatrice and given a preliminary hearing on July 18[5] before Justice of the Peace T. M. Coulter. Hickok employed two Marysville (Kansas) attorneys, Brumbaugh and Bolinger, to defend him.[6] Hickok, Wellman and Brink maintained that they were defending private property when they killed McCanles, Woods and Gordon. Judge Coulter ordered the prisoners released from custody on the grounds that the killings were done in self-defense.[7] Monroe McCanles, who died in 1934, was the only witness against the defendants, but for some reason, he was not called to testify. Sarah Shull also never testified. She left the Rock Creek area before the hearing. She was alive as late as 1925.

After the incident at Rock Creek, Wild Bill left Nebraska and went to Leavenworth. From Leavenworth he went to Sedalia, Missouri, where on October 30, 1861, he was enlisted by the Union Army as a civilian wagon master at one hundred dollars a month. He served in this capacity until February 28, 1862.[8]

Historians for more than a century have written of Wild Bill Hickok's exploits for the Union Army during the War Between the States. He is said to have been a civilian scout in the battles at Wilson's Creek, Missouri, on August 10, 1861,[9] and at Pea Ridge, Arkansas, on March 7-8, 1862. Hickok is erroneously reported by some writers to have killed Confederate Brigadier General Ben McCulloch at the Pea Ridge battle. Actually, eyewitnesses reported that Private Peter Pelican of the Thirty-Sixth Illinois Infantry killed McCulloch. Hickok is said to have scouted throughout Missouri and northern Arkansas for Major General Samuel R. Curtis during the early part of the war. He also was reported to have scouted for both Curtis, who was then the commanding general of the military district of southwest Missouri, and for Major General Alfred S. Pleasanton during Major General Sterling Price's invasion of Missouri and Kansas in September and October, 1864. Price, a former governor of Missouri, commanded the Confederate District of Arkansas. The military records of the Union Army, which are usually thorough, are skimpy when it comes to Hickok's services with the Union Army.

U.S. Provost Marshal General records of "Scouts, Guides and Spies" for the period of 1861-1866 contains a reference to Hickok's services as an unauthorized special military policeman. According to these Provost Marshal records, Wild Bill served in this capacity at Springfield, Missouri, in March, 1864, at sixty dollars per month. Hickok served from March 1-10 under First Lieutenant N. H. Burns, the Acting Provost Marshal of the District of Southwest Missouri at Springfield. From March 11-31 Hickok served under First Lieutenant W. H. McAdams, the Provost Marshal of the District of Southwest Missouri, at Springfield. Although Brigadier General John B. Sanborn, the commanding general in southwest Missouri, had approved Hickok's services as a special civilian policeman, Wild Bill was not paid for his services on a technicality. The Provost Marshal General of the Department of Missouri had not authorized his appointment.[10] In reality, Wild Bill had been employed as a civilian detective under Chief of Police S. R. Squires of Springfield and was attached to the Union Army's district headquarters at Springfield.[11] Herman Chapman and J. W. McLellan also served as policemen with Hickok in this capacity.[12]

We do know, however, that in February, 1865, Hickok was scouting (on verbal agreement) in southwest Missouri and northern Arkansas for General Sanborn because correspondence between Wild Bill and Sanborn to that effect is in the National Archives at Washington, D.C.[13] That Hickok did some scouting (obviously on verbal agreement only) for the Union Army during the war can also be attested by the editor of the *Springfield Weekly Patriot*, who on January 31, 1867, wrote in part on Wild Bill: "Except [for] . . . Tom Martin . . . Bill was the best scout, by far, in the Southwest."

By 1865 Hickok was a permanent resident of Springfield and was widely known as "Wild Bill." Years later he told Charles F. Gross, his friend at Abilene, Kansas, in 1871 that a woman in Missouri during the war had given him the name.[14] At Springfield Hickok was living with a red-haired woman named Susannah Moore, whom he had met during the war, and was earning his livelihood as a professional gambler.

It was at this time that Hickok had trouble with a twenty-six-year-old gambler from Yellville, Arkansas, by the name of Davis K. Tutt, Jr., formerly of the Twenty-Seventh

Courtesy Missouri Historical Society, Saint Louis
A sketch in *Harper's New Monthly Magazine* depicted the shooting of Dave Tutt by Bill Hickok in a street duel at Springfield, Missouri. Tutt and Hickok had quarreled over a gambling debt. Tutt had taken Hickok's watch. Wild Bill was tried and acquitted of the killing.

Regiment Arkansas Infantry. It is said that Tutt was a deserter from the Confederate Army, but his military service records are too incomplete to give a definite statement on the matter. Rumor has it that Hickok and Tutt knew each other at Yellville, where Wild Bill for a time lived with one of Dave's younger sisters, Dulcenia or Esther S. After the war the Tutt family moved to Springfield, and Bill and Miss Tutt are said to have resumed their illicit relationship to the dissatisfaction of Susannah Moore. Later Susannah took up with Dave Tutt, and he and Hickok quarreled over the matter.

More bad blood came between Hickok and Tutt over the payment of a gambling debt. In a card game in Bill's room at the Lyon House, Hickok lost considerable money to Tutt. Bill couldn't cover all of his losses and Tutt demanded payment. Hickok offered Tutt an I.O.U., but the latter refused

Photo by Dale T. Schoenberger
Dave Tutt was buried in Maple Park Cemetery, where his headstone may still be found.

it, taking Wild Bill's pocket watch which was lying on the table, as payment. Hickok objected, but Tutt refused to give back the timepiece. Wild Bill warned Tutt not to wear the watch or he would kill him. Tutt replied that he would kill Wild Bill if Hickok tried to stop him from wearing the watch.

On the evening of July 21, 1865, Hickok and Tutt faced each other across Springfield's huge public square. They walked toward each other and drew their pistols. Wild Bill placed the barrel of his pistol across his left forearm to level his shot. He and Tutt fired at almost the same time. Tutt's shot echoed harmlessly across the huge town square, but Wild Bill's bullet struck Tutt in the chest, killing him almost instantly.[15] Unofficial reports place the distance between Hickok and Tutt at approximately seventy-five yards when they fired. Hickok was arrested and tried for the killing. He retained ex-Brevet Brigadier General John S. Phelps, former U.S. military governor of Arkansas and later governor of Missouri, as his defense counsel. Bill was acquitted of the killing on August 5.[16]

In September, 1865, Lieutenant Colonel George Ward Nichols of the Union Army,[17] a correspondent of *Harper's New Monthly Magazine,* came to Springfield and met Wild Bill Hickok. Colonel Nichols became so fascinated with Hickok that he wrote a fictitious biography of Wild Bill which appeared in the February, 1867, issue of *Harper's.* The *Harper's* article made Wild Bill a living legend on the frontier. Needless to say, Wild Bill went overboard in supplying the "facts" to reporter Nichols.

Wild Bill decided to run for the office of Chief of Police at Springfield. The municipal election was held on September 13, 1865, and he ran a poor second in a field of five. Charles C. Moss was elected to office with 107 votes as against 63 for Hickok.[18]

Hickok remained in Springfield until February, 1866, when he again returned to Leavenworth. He later drifted to Fort Riley, Kansas, where his older brother Lorenzo B. Hickok was serving as a wagon master, scout and chief herder.[19] Wild Bill became a "hanger-on" at the fort. Contrary to popular belief, no record of Hickok having been a special deputy U.S. marshal for the Army at Fort Riley has been found.

At Fort Riley Hickok met the Custer family for the first time. By an Act of Congress on July 28, 1866, the famous Seventh U.S. Cavalry was created.[20] In the fall of that year the regiment was organized at Fort Riley. Brevet Major General George Armstrong Custer and his wife, Elizabeth (Libbie) Custer (nee Bacon), arrived that month at Fort Riley and General Custer

Fort Riley, Kansas, where Hickok's older brother was serving as a scout and wagon master, became another haunt of Wild Bill. Bill was said to have served there as a special deputy U.S. marshal, though no record has been found. Hickok spent his time gambling and tracking Army deserters for the rewards.

assumed eventually the duties of acting regimental commander (he was never official regimental commander) of the Seventh Cavalry.[21] Also at Fort Riley was General Custer's younger brother, First Lieutenant (later Captain) Thomas Ward Custer, acting regimental quartermaster and holder of two Congressional Medals of Honor,[22] who died with his famous brother at the Little Big Horn in 1876. The Custers became great admirers of Wild Bill, except Lieutenant Custer, who disliked Hickok for some reason. (Rumor says the two men later had trouble over a "soiled dove" at Hays City, Kansas, circa 1869.) The Custer brothers had an affinity for poker playing and Wild Bill, while he was at the fort, was a frequent player in their games. Hickok supplemented his gambling winnings by tracking Army deserters for their bounties.

General Custer persuaded Wild Bill to enlist at Fort Riley as a scout with the Seventh Cavalry on January 1, 1867. Wild Bill was not Custer's chief of scouts as has been popularly believed. This position was held in 1867 by William Comstock, a friend of Buffalo Bill Cody. Hickok served with the Seventh Cavalry until July 31, 1867, when his six-month enlistment expired. For the months of March and April, he was on special detailed assignment with the Seventh Cavalry as wagon master. During his tour of duty he was paid one hundred dollars per month.[23] When he could get leave from his scouting duties, Hickok spent much of his time gambling at Leavenworth. Many of Hickok's scouting duties with the Seventh Cavalry were done in connection with the peace-parley expedition of Major General Winfield S. Hancock (the commanding general of the Department of the Missouri and later the Democratic nominee for President) who in 1867 was seeking peace with the Plains tribes of the Southwest. The tribes refused to make peace and Hancock's expedition failed in the respect that it did not keep the Plains tribes from taking the warpath during the ensuing year in which nearly 130 persons were killed in Kansas by Indians.[24] Hancock returned to Fort Leav-

Courtesy Vincent R. Mercaldo Archives, Richmond Hill, N.Y.
Lieutenant Thomas W. Custer was acting regimental quartermaster at Fort Riley. He disliked Hickok. The pair was said to have quarreled over a woman.

Courtesy Kansas State Historical Society, Topeka
General George Armstrong Custer was stationed at Fort Riley when Hickok was there. Custer admired Hickok, played poker with him, and asked him to scout for the Seventh Cavalry.

enworth, leaving Custer to pursue and punish the hostiles.

Hickok might have been with Custer and five companies of Seventh Cavalry encamped on the north fork of the Republican River in Nebraska when at daylight on June 24, 1867, a large band of Oglala Sioux Indians under Pawnee Killer attempted to stampede the Seventh's mounts. The Indians failed, but one enlisted man was wounded in the raid.[25] Hickok and the Seventh had been en route to the Republican River from Fort McPherson, Nebraska, at the time of the attack. The skirmish was General Custer's first engagement with Indians. During most of General Hancock's expedition, Wild Bill served as a dispatch courier between various military posts and troop detachments in the field. When his hitch expired at the end of July, Bill decided temporarily to forego military life.

The highlights of Hickok's brief scouting career with Custer's Seventh Cavalry were his interviews in April and May, 1867, at Fort Harker, Kansas, with Henry M. Stanley,[26] then a war correspondent with the *New York Herald* and later famous as the explorer who found Dr. David Livingstone in Africa. In the April interview Wild Bill told the gullible Stanley that he had killed more than one hundred men.[27]

During the remainder of 1867, Wild Bill was often at Leavenworth. He was also a frequent visitor at Ellsworth, Kansas, which was less than a year old, having been established on the Union Pacific, Eastern Division Railroad (which in 1868 became the Kansas Pacific and later the Union Pacific) in January, 1867.[28] A few years hence Ellsworth was to become one of the wildest cow towns on the Kansas frontier. For a while in the latter half of 1867, Hickok lived at Ellsworth with a woman known only as "Indian Annie." Wild Bill made an attempt to be elected sheriff of Ellsworth County on November 5, 1867, but he and three other candidates were defeated by E. W. Kingsbury for the position. Bill polled 156 votes, all but one of which were cast in the town of Ellsworth itself.[29] Kingsbury received 213 votes.[30] By December 1867, Hickok was serving in the field as a deputy U.S. marshal under U.S. Marshal Charles C. Whiting.[31]

On March 30, 1868, Wild Bill, in his capacity as a deputy U.S. marshal, arrested eleven renegade soldiers who had been operating as horse thieves in the Solomon River country of Kansas. With the aid of Buffalo Bill Cody, Wild Bill brought his prisoners to Topeka, the state capital, and jailed them. The renegades had been operating as part of a larger band[32] which was menacing military posts throughout Kansas. About this time Hickok was engaged in a freighting venture at Hays City with his friend "Colorado Charlie" Utter to supplement his deputy marshal's income.

Hickok again was employed as a civilian scout for the Army. On August 18, 1868, he enlisted at Fort Hays with Brevet Major General Benjamin H. Grierson's Tenth U. S. Cavalry, a regiment of Negro "Buffalo Soldiers," whose officers were white. He served as a scout until August 31 and was paid $43.33 for his services.[33] During this time Hickok scouted for Captain George W. Graham and Company I of the Tenth Cavalry on Graham's scouting expedition to the Republican River. While detailed on special assignment from Graham's detachment, Hickok was wounded in the foot with a lance by some Indians in eastern Colorado as he carried a message for some beleaguered cattlemen who were under hostile attack.

Hickok again enlisted as a civilian scout with the Tenth Cavalry's headquarters detachment on September 1, 1868,[34] near Elkhorn Creek in present Lincoln County, Kansas.[35] He served until February 28, 1869, when his enlistment expired. He was paid the usual one hundred dollars per month for his services.[36] It is of interest to note that all through his scouting career, Hickok was paid $100 per month for his services. Only top-caliber scouts were paid such salaries.

Hickok's second tour of duty with the Tenth Cavalry took him to Fort Lyon, Colorado Territory. At Fort Lyon Bill was detached and assigned to duty as a scout for Brevet Brigadier General William H. Penrose of the Third U.S. Infantry.[37] His friend, Buffalo Bill Cody, was also at Fort Lyon at this time as chief of scouts for the Fifth U.S. Cavalry. On September 2, 1868, Wild Bill accompanied Captain George A. Armes and Company F of the Tenth Cavalry on a scout to Walnut Creek, Kansas. During September, 1868, Hickok scouted around Fort Dodge, Kansas.[38]

Hickok accompanied General Penrose, who left Fort Lyon on November 10, 1868, on his scout along the Cimarron River. The scout was part of General Philip Sheridan's stepped-up campaign against the hostiles of the Southern Plains. Penrose's detachment was joined by the detachment of Brevet Major General Eugene A. Carr of the Fifth U.S. Cavalry on Palo Duro Creek in the present Oklahoma Panhandle (most of Palo Duro Creek was in the Texas Panhandle) on December 21. The snow and bitter cold weather had severely plagued Penrose's command. When Carr's column caught Penrose (who had reached Palo Duro Creek about two weeks before Carr's arrival), the latter's detachment was on quarter rations and had lost about two hundred horses and mules because of starvation and the cold. Wild Bill's old friend Buffalo Bill was with Carr's column. Carr had difficulty in locating Penrose because of the drifting snow which had virtually obliterated the latter's trail. Cody, the exceptional scout that he was, struck Penrose's trail on high ground where the snow had been blown away. Carr's detachment knew it had struck the right trail when it discovered two Negro stragglers or deserters from Penrose's column.

Carr and Penrose had, however, prevented the Plains tribes from drifting west-

ward as Custer gained a major victory over the Southern Cheyennes at the Washita River in the Indian Territory on November 27 and Major Andrew W. Evans of the Third U.S. Cavalry scored a similar victory Christmas Day over the Comanches near the north fork of the Red River in Texas. The Carr-Penrose expedition met no Indians, and from December 28, 1868, to January 7, 1869, a portion of their detachment (including Hickok and Cody) was encamped on the south fork of the Canadian River in northern Texas. The expedition returned to its Palo Duro Creek supply base later in the month. At the supply base Wild Bill, Buffalo Bill, and some of the other American scouts were involved in a drunken free-for-all with some of Penrose's Mexican scouts. Cody admitted later that he and Hickok had been primarily responsible for the brawl. Carr had a fondness for Cody, so he let both men off with a verbal reprimand. Carr, however, had a low opinion of Hickok. Mrs. Mary Carr, wife of the general, considered Wild Bill a ruffian who boasted about killing his man.[39]

After his services with the Tenth Cavalry, Bill returned home to Troy Grove in the spring of 1869 to visit his family. It was the first time he had been home since 1855. While there Hickok had his wounded foot (received while scouting for Captain Graham) treated and dressed. By July, 1869, he was at Hays City on the Kansas Pacific Railroad. During Hickok's time Hays City (located less than ninety-five miles northeast of the Santa Fe Trail) was a major supply depot for travelers and freighters who were to trek the famous trail to various points west. Hays City was also the western terminus for military supplies

Hays City was a rough-and-tumble town on the Kansas Frontier, one which attracted the riffraff of the plains when this photograph was taken around 1878. The small building marked by an X, in the center of the photograph, was Tommy Drum's saloon, a favorite hangout for Bill Hickok.

shipped to Forts Hays, Larned, and Dodge.

While Hickok was at Hays City, it was the toughest town on the Kansas frontier. Although only two years old in 1869, it was a lusty, brawling little community with thirty-seven places licensed to sell liquor.[40] Added to the permanent population was a bevy of frontier riffraff, K. P. gandy dancers, freighters, and soldiers from nearby Fort Hays (the latter group was a particular source of trouble to the residents of Hays City).

Shootings were commonplace, although from June 1869 to June 1870, only three civilians were killed in the town,[41] two of them by Hickok. At least one soldier was killed there during the same period and the next month, Wild Bill killed another soldier. Mrs. Custer, who spent considerable time with her soldier-husband at Fort Hays, recalled that "every night in Hays sounded like the Fourth of July."[42] Mrs. Mary Carr

recalled Hays City as an "ungodly place" while she lived at Fort Hays with General Carr. When the city's old Boot Hill cemetery was razed, the workmen uncovered forty-five cadavers[43] (others were uncovered years later). The majority of those who had been buried there had met a violent death. Soldiers who were killed at Hays City were buried in the military cemetery at Fort Hays.

Several citizens of Hays City petitioned Governor James M. Harvey to appoint R. A. Eccles as acting sheriff of Ellis County,[44] in which Hays City was located, but he refused. In August 1869, a special election was held at Hays City and Wild Bill was elected interim sheriff.[45] His sheriff's commission was not signed by Governor Harvey,[46] but the county commissioners paid him seventy-five dollars per month.[47]

Hickok's law enforcement record at Hays City is sketchy at best. The early-day records are virtually nonexistent. It is known that Wild Bill spent much of his time playing cards in Tommy Drum's saloon on North Main Street while his only deputy of record, Peter Lanihan, did most of the leg and paper work. Hickok also spent considerable time visiting the "soiled doves" at Ida May's sporting house. Another famous visitor who frequented Ida's place when military duties permitted was Tom Custer.

Courtesy Kansas State Historical Society, Topeka
Grisly scenes like this were common in Hays City, which was described as an "ungodly place." The two dead troopers were from nearby Fort Hays. Note the boy standing at the right, surveying the bodies.

Shortly after his election as sheriff Wild Bill killed his first man at Hays City. He shot a man named Bill Mulrey (some sources say Mulvey) on August 24. Mulrey succumbed the next day.[48] The exact circumstances under which Mulrey died are not known. Rumor has it that he cornered Wild Bill and threatened to shoot him, but that Hickok looked beyond Mulrey and said, "Don't shoot him, boys, he's drunk!" When Mulrey turned to see who was behind, Wild Bill killed him.

A month later Wild Bill killed his second man at Hays City, a hardcased teamster named Samuel Strawhim (not Jack Strawhan). Strawhim and some of his friends were drunk and disorderly in a saloon on the night of September 27, 1869, when Hickok and Lanihan attempted to quell the disturbance. Strawhim objected to Hickok's interference and reached for his pistol, but Wild Bill was quicker and he shot the teamster dead.[49] It has been said that Hickok and Strawhim had had trouble at Ellsworth.

A little more than a month later, the regular Ellis County election was held. Hickok was a candidate to succeed himself as sheriff. He ran on the Independent ticket. His opponent was Pete Lanihan, who ran as a Democrat. Lanihan defeated Wild Bill in the election by a vote margin of 114 to 89.[50] Wild Bill was allowed to remain in office as interim sheriff until his term expired on January 11, 1870.[51] Before he could serve out his term in·office, Lanihan was shot and killed.[52]

Wild Bill remained off and on in Hays City until July, 1870 when he hastily departed after a bloody encounter with several members of the Seventh U.S. Cavalry. The fight occurred on July 17, 1870.[53] The newspapers of the day did not state what was the difficulty, but legend dictates that Lieutenant Tom Custer retaliated against Wild Bill for some personal injustice by leading the attack on the ex-scout with some enlisted men.

At least five soldiers attacked Wild Bill in Drum's saloon, knocked him to the floor and began kicking him. Hickok drew a brace of pistols and fatally shot twenty-four-year-old Private John Kile (alias "Kelly") and seriously wounded Private Jeremiah Lanigan[54] of Companies I and M. (Kile was actually listed on the muster roll of Captain Myles W. Keogh's Company I, but was on attached duty with Company M at the time of his death.[55] Kile died of his wounds in

the post hospital at Fort Hays on July 18.[56] Lanigan recovered from his wounds and returned to active duty on August 25, 1870.[57] The newspapers did not mention any officer (much less Tom Custer) as being a participant in the fight. Military records show that Tom Custer was the acting commanding officer of Company M at the time and this company was garrisoned at Camp Sturgis, near Fort Hays, from June 13 to August 8, 1870.[58] (At least it was a geographical possibility that Tom Custer led the attack on Hickok.[59])

Wild Bill was severely beaten by the soldiers. Soon after the brawl he boarded an eastbound locomotive. Many of the citizens of Hays City were up in arms against Wild

Kansas State Historical Society and Denver Public Library
After a saloon brawl with soldiers of the Seventh Cavalry, in which a trooper was killed, Wild Bill fled Hays City, swinging aboard an outbound locomotive at this railroad station. He hid out in Topeka and Ellsworth.

Abilene looks peaceful enough in this view, but at other times it was a roaring cattle town at the far end of the Chisholm Trail. For five seasons it was the foremost railroad shipping center on the Kansas plains, a tough place "owned" by the Texas trail hands. There were thirty-two saloons, sixty-four gambling joints, and numerous other deadfalls.

Bill,[60] and it has been erroneously reported by some writers that Lieutenant General Philip H. Sheridan, commanding general of the Division of the Missouri, ordered a military court of inquiry to look into the incident.[61] The character of the soldier whom Hickok killed left much to be desired. Captain Keogh, who later died at the Little Big Horn, in his written report dated August 16, 1870, to the Adjutant General's Office, which is preserved in the Old Military Records Division of the National Archives at Washington, D.C., stated that Kile was originally a deserter from Company M of the Seventh Cavalry and upon returning to duty with the regiment was assigned to Company I. After the fight, Bill traveled to Ellsworth to recuperate.[62] Later he went to Topeka.

Between the time of the fight and April, 1871, when he was sent for and appointed city marshal at Abilene, Kansas, Wild Bill seems to have spent much of that time hiding at Ellsworth and Topeka, as much as this was possible for a man of his nationally known reputation.

When Wild Bill came to Abilene at the personal invitation of Mayor Joseph G. McCoy, the city was only four years old, but the town already had had a brief and colorful history. Located on the Kansas Pacific line at the northernmost point of the historic Chisholm Trail, Abilene was the leading cattle-shipping town in Kansas for five seasons during the period 1867-1871. During that time Abilene freighted an estimated total of 306,500 head of Texas beeves. Newton, founded on the Santa Fe line in the spring of 1871, and Ellsworth on the K. P. line, hard-pressed Abilene as the leading railhead for Texas cattle in 1871. Because of the stiff competition, Abilene shipped only an estimated fifty thousand head in 1871, a pronounced decline from the peak year of 1870. Steers sold for an average twenty-five dollars a head in Abilene in 1871. This helped to make it a good market for Texas beeves that year.

Abilene in 1871 was a Texas trail hand's town. The city had thirty-two places licensed to sell liquor and sixty-four gambling establishments.[63] While Abilene was a Texan's town, only three men died violent deaths during the cattle-shipping season. Hickok accounted for two of those deaths and Texas' greatest man-killer, John Wesley Hardin, was credited with the other.

Wild Bill Hickok was a name to be reckoned with on the frontier. The noted ex-sheriff at Hays City, where his fast gun had snuffed out the lives of three men, was appointed city marshal at Abilene on April 15, 1871, at a salary of $150 per month[64] by Mayor McCoy and his city council. As an added bonus, Hickok was to receive one-fourth of all fines assessed against persons whom he arrested.[65] Later, on June 28 the city council authorized the city treasurer to pay Wild Bill fifty cents for each unlicensed dog that he killed.[66] In addition to his title as city marshal, Hickok was also Abilene's street commissioner (at no extra pay) and was responsible for keeping the city streets clear of any obstructions.

Some citizens of Abilene were anti-Texas cattle trade because they considered it the seed of the city's lawlessness. Among them were Theodore C. Henry, who had been chairman of Abilene's board of trustees in 1870 (which was equivalent to mayor that year), and Vear P. Wilson, the vitriolic editor of the *Abilene Chronicle,* the town's only newspaper. They were against hiring killers such as Hickok for city marshal. Henry and Wilson preferred the iron-handed rule

Tom ("Bear River") Smith was Chief of Police at Abilene and Wild Bill's predecessor. Smith was killed in the line of duty.

of Thomas James (Bear River) Smith, late chief of police of Abilene who had been killed in the line of duty on November 2, 1870,[67] or tolerated Patrick Hand, local gunsmith, who was unsuccessful as a part-time marshal.

Mayor McCoy has been dubbed as the "father of the Texas Cattle Trade" by Western historians. He came from Springfield, Illinois, and had been instrumental in bringing the first Texas herds to Abilene in 1867. But McCoy was a businessman first and a civic-minded resident second. He preferred to patronize and accommodate the visiting Texans. McCoy also favored a man such as Hickok for city marshal because of his reputation as a man-killer. He had sent his friend and business associate, Charles F.

Gross, to Fort Harker, near Ellsworth, with an offer to become Abilene's city marshal. Hickok had been at the fort scrounging for a scouting assignment. At Springfield, Illinois, Gross had been a classmate of Robert T. Lincoln, eldest son of Abraham Lincoln, and had worked as a civilian employee for General Philip Sheridan.[68] He later became Hickok's most intimate friend during the latter's stay in Abilene.

The city council gave Wild Bill several deputies to do his bidding. James Gainsford, a deputy U.S. marshal,[69] served as Hickok's deputy from June 16[70] to September 2, 1871.[71] Against the protest of Mayor McCoy, J. H. McDonald was also appointed as Wild Bill's deputy on June 16.[72] McDonald, an incompetent police officer who had deserted Tom Smith in his hour of need, was dismissed on September 2.[73] Tom Carson, reportedly a nephew of the famous Kit Carson, had been appointed a temporary deputy of Wild Bill on June 14,[74] but nine days later Carson's appointment was made permanent.[75] Carson resigned his position by August, 1871.[76] On November 4 of that year Carson and John W. ("Brocky Jack") Norton were appointed deputy city marshals under Hickok,[77] but both were dismissed on November 27.[78]

With several deputies to do his leg and paper work, Wild Bill whiled away his time playing cards at his favorite haunt, the Alamo Saloon on Cedar Street, and consorting with the ladies of the night. Abilene's strumpets seem to have occupied as much of Wild Bill's time as card playing. His favorite mistress was Jessie Hazel, whom he kept in a room at the three-story, eighty-four-room Drover's Cottage on South Main.[79] Later in the summer Jessie was employed as a semi-nude dancer at Billy Mitchell's Novelty Theater. Hickok kept two other women in a small cabin down in "McCoy's Addition" (Abilene's red-light district which was formerly called the "Devil's Half Acre"). These two women were Susannah Moore, his old flame, who had come to Abilene from Springfield, Missouri, and Nan Ross, a local prostitute.

Charlie Gross remembered Wild Bill and his many women:

The many talks I had with Bill I do not now recall any remarks or reference to any woman other than those he made to the one he lived with in the small house and he did not ever show before me any special affection for her. . . . He always had a mistress. I knew two or three of them, one a former mistress of his was an inmate of a cottage in McCoy's Addition. . . . She [Susannah Moore] came to Abilene to try and make up with Bill. He gave her $25, and made her move on. There was Nan Ross but Bill told her he was through with her. She moved on. . . .[80]

When Mrs. Agnes Mersman Lake and her traveling "Hippo-Olympiad and Mammoth Circus" came to Abilene during the summer of 1871, Wild Bill courted Mrs. Lake, a widow eleven years his senior, whom he married five years later.

Hickok's law enforcement record was poor. He made few arrests. The city council prodded him constantly to leave the games at the Alamo and enforce various city ordinances.[81] Many of Abilene's citizens had mixed feelings about Wild Bill's efficiency as a police officer. Mayor McCoy obviously tolerated Hickok as city marshal. The Henry-Wilson faction was a leading critic of both McCoy's city administration and city marshal Hickok. Editor Wilson published an editorial in the *Chronicle* of September 14, 1871, deriding Hickok when he wrote in part:

". . . It affords us no pleasure to write a word of censure against a sworn officer of the law—but when officers themselves violate [the law], and permit its violation, it becomes the duty of the press to stand up for the law and the rights of the people. . . ."

Stuart O. Henry, the younger brother of T. C. Henry, wrote years later that Abilene simmered with lawlessness while Hickok sat in the Alamo playing cards.[82] Citizen J. B. Edwards thought Hickok poor in comparison to Tom ("Bear River") Smith, and Wilson bitterly complained that Hickok and McCoy's city administration allowed Abilene to be overrun with gamblers, con men, prostitutes, and pimps.[83]

While in Abilene Wild Bill was quite a picturesque figure. He stood six feet two inches in height and weighed about one hundred and sixty-five pounds. He had a thick, shaggy mustache which he allowed to droop. At various times he wore a goatee. He wore his curly blond hair long, falling to the shoulders. Romanticists say his blue eyes were as piercing as cold steel. His mental state, however, left much to be desired. Unfortunately for Wild Bill's peace of mind, his nationally known reputation caused many men to be jealous of him; consequently, he was invariably on guard against possible assassination by some envious fanatic.

Hickok took great pains to avoid being bushwhacked. He seldom walked on the sidewalks in Abilene for fear some would-be assassin was lurking in an alley or doorway. He always entered a building by the

Courtesy Kansas State Historical Society, Topeka
Wild Bill Hickok, suave in his fancy duds and shoulder-length hair, tried to keep the peace in Abilene but was subject to much criticism. By then he had a national reputation, which didn't help matters with the local citizenry.

back door or a side entrance. Once inside, he would step to one side and study the faces of the men. He refused to sit with his back to a door or window and never allowed a friend or stranger to stand or sit behind him. At night he secured all the doors and windows of his room or cabin. His bed was never in the direct line of fire of a door or window. He usually put crumpled newspaper all around the floor of his bedroom so he could hear anyone prowling about the room. He was up several times during the night rechecking the security of his living quarters. He never fully trusted the various women who shared his bed, and invariably had his pistol within easy reach.

While he was marshal at Abilene, there were at least eight men who would have liked to see Wild Bill dead. These men were Ben and Billy Thompson; Wes Hardin; the latter's cousins, Mannen, Jim, Joe, and Gip Clements; and Philip Haddox Coe, Jr.—Texans all. Ben Thompson and Phil Coe were partners in the storied Bull's

Western History Collections, University of Oklahoma Library
Mannen Clements and his brothers came with Wes Hardin to Abilene in the 1871 trail drives. Hickok was said to have arrested Clements for killing some trail hands, then turning him loose at Hardin's request.

Head Saloon and Gambling House on Texas Street. (Coe's license to operate the Bull's Head was transferred to Thomas Sheran, an Abilene businessman, on August 2, 1871.)[84] Thompson had no license to operate the Bull's Head, but he was Coe's financial partner in the saloon. Billy Thompson was retained by his brother Ben as a house gambler. The teen-aged Hardin and the Clements brothers arrived at various times in Abilene during the cattle shipping season of 1871.

Joe Clements came to Abilene in early May, 1871, arriving with the trail herd of Columbus Carrol, the first bunch to reach

Western History Collections, University of Oklahoma Library
John Wesley Hardin, another famous Western gunman, tangled with Wild Bill in Abilene. Hardin later claimed he got the drop on the lawman.

Abilene that season.[85] Hardin and Jim and Gip Clements came with a herd to Abilene a few weeks later. Mannen Clements came still later with another trail drive. Rumor has it that Hardin and the Clements left a bloody path behind them from Texas. Hardin's trail herd was said to have been attacked by Osage Indians just across the Kansas state line. Near the present site of Newton, Wes and Jim Clements are alleged to have shot and killed six Mexican cowhands. Just across the Texas state line, in the Indian Territory, Mannen Clements is said to have done in two of his trail hands, Joseph and Adolph Shadden, in a dispute over work. The Indian Territory was under federal jurisdiction and by killing the Shadden brothers (if he really did) Mannen Clements had committed an alleged offense. Many writers claim that Clements was arrested by Wild Bill Hickok at Abilene for the Shadden killings, and that Bill turned Clements loose after Wes Hardin asked for Mannen's release. Other writers say that Clements later stood trial for the killings and was acquitted. A search of the existing federal records of the U.S. District Court, Western District of Arkansas (which had judicial jurisdiction over the Indian Territory), failed to turn up any records pertaining to Emanuel (Mannen) Clements.[86]

Wes Hardin wrote many years after Hickok's death that on one occasion Wild Bill tried to make him check his weapons in accordance with the city ordinance prohibiting the carrying of firearms. Hardin said he handed Wild Bill his revolvers butts forward but kept his fingers on the triggers. When Hickok reached for the pistols, Hardin worked the "border shift" by spinning the butts of the revolvers back into the palms of his hands, getting the drop on Hickok.[87] Despite Hardin's statement, no eyewitness to the incident has ever substantiated Wes's claim. It seems extremely doubtful that Hickok, a fanatic at personal security, would have reached openhanded toward a man with two pistols in his hands. Hickok did not enforce the firearms ordinance or any other city ordinance except at the urging of the city council.

Hardin, in his autobiography, stated that Ben Thompson tried to prejudice him against Hickok. Thompson asked him to kill Wild Bill, Hardin wrote. When Hardin asked Thompson why he didn't kill Hickok, if Bill needed killing, Thompson replied only that he would rather have someone else do the job.

Hardin was involved in two killings during his brief stay in Abilene. William M. Cohron, the popular trail boss of Oliver W. Wheeler,[88] was dispatched by a disgruntled Mexican cowhand named Juan Bideno on the Cottonwood (in Kansas) on July 5, 1871. Cohron was a friend of Hardin and the Clements. Hardin trailed Bideno to a cafe at Bluff Creek, Kansas, on July 7 and killed the Mexican herder.[89] The day Wes left Abilene for good, July 6, he killed a man named Charles Couger.[90]

Hickok's real trouble at Abilene was with Phil Coe and Ben Thompson. The first clash of personalities came when the city council instructed Wild Bill to inform partners Thompson and Coe that the obscene painting of a bull outside their establishment would have to be altered (the painting depicted a bull in full masculinity). Hickok ordered Thompson to alter the painting, but Ben refused. Bill then hired two painters who blotted out its vulgarity. Thompson

One of Wild Bill's equalizers was this English-made Deane, Adams five-shot .45-caliber pistol.

and Coe made no move to interrupt the painters.

The trouble over the painting started a bitter feud between Hickok and Coe. Coe accused Wild Bill of arresting Texans on false charges so he could collect his portion of their fines. Hickok retaliated by saying that Coe ran crooked games at the Bull's Head. Evidently the city council believed Bill's charges against Coe because the latter was forced to sell his interest in the Bull's Head. Coe however remained in Abilene as a free-lance gambler.

The feud between Hickok and Coe came to a bloody climax over Jessie Hazel, Wild Bill's favorite mistress. Coe had been living with a woman named Alice Chambers. He became interested in Jessie and deserted Miss Chambers. Women found him attractive. Coe was a handsome, well-built man. He wore a full blond beard and stood six feet five inches in height and weighed about 235 pounds. Jessie Hazel was also enamored with Coe and left Wild Bill to become his mistress. Hickok became infuriated. One night he accosted Jessie and Phil in a *tête-á-tête* in the Gulf House Hotel. Bill kicked Jessie in the face with his boot and Coe severely beat him for it. Later Coe made repeated threats to kill Wild Bill.

The climax of the feud came to a tragic end on the evening of October 5, 1871. Coe was celebrating the end of Abilene's cattle-shipping season with several of his Texas friends. On this particular occasion Coe was armed. Although he was known as a brawler and occasional troublemaker (he once threatened to kill Texas cattleman George W. Littlefield[91]), Coe was not known as a gunman. (Ben Thompson at this time was at Kansas City.) Coe and his Texas pals were making the rounds of all the saloons, and Wild Bill was "posted" that the Texans might cause trouble since this was their last night in Abilene. Earlier in the evening, the Texans had hoisted residents on their shoulders, carried them into saloons and asked them to buy a round of drinks. The "victims" usually obliged. The Lone Star boys had sought out Wild Bill for similar treatment, but he declined to participate in the frivolity. He told the Texans to treat themselves at his expense, but cautioned them to behave.[92]

When the Texas party neared the front of the Alamo Saloon, a vicious dog attempted to bite Coe and he fired a wild shot at the animal. Hickok was standing before the Novelty Theater talking with his friend Mike Williams, a special policeman hired to keep order there. (Because of its semi-nude shows, the Novelty Theater was the most popular establishment among Texans, consequently Hickok had stationed himself near the Novelty for possible trouble.) He rushed to the front of the Alamo, confronting Coe and several friends. Coe was holding his pistol in his hand, only eight feet from Hickok.

Hickok asked who had fired the shot. Coe replied that he had aimed at a dog. Instantly, Wild Bill drew two pistols and fired at Coe. Coe immediately returned Hickok's shots. One of Coe's bullets tore through Bill's coat. Mike Williams rushed around the corner to aid Hickok. Wild Bill turned and fired two quick shot at Williams, killing him instantly. He thought he had shot one of Coe's friends. He didn't realize until afterward that he had mistakingly killed his friend Williams. Hickok and Coe ex-

changed several shots until one of Bill's bullets struck Coe in the lower abdomen, fatally wounding him. One or two others in the crowd were grazed by flying bullets. Coe lived in great agony until October 8.[93] Coe was a Presbyterian and Wild Bill scouted up a Presbyterian minister to be with Coe at the end.[94] He also paid for the funeral arrangements of Mike Williams and to have the body shipped to the latter's home in Kansas City.[95]

For some time after Coe's death, Hickok received various reports from Texas that Coe's friends were planning to assassinate him. One such report came from Austin and stated that $11,000 had been offered to five men to kill him.[96] The five would-be assassins arrived at Abilene in late November. Wild Bill was "posted" that they were in town. He and a friend boarded the train for Topeka (where he intended to go for a brief vacation). The hired assassins also swung aboard and kept close watch on Hickok. Bill's friend informed Hickok that several suspicious men were watching him and that he should be on guard. When the train reached Topeka, Hickok confronted the men and told them that he would kill them if they left the train at Topeka. The men heeded Hickok's advice.[97]

The citizens of Dickinson County, led by T. C. Henry and the Farmers' Protective Association, decided they had had enough of the rowdy Texans and their cattle trade. In February, 1872, they voted to bar the Texas cattle trade from their county.[98] With this thought in mind, they did not need a man such as Hickok to enforce the law. On December 13, 1871 the Abilene city council issued the following resolution:

"Be it resolved . . . that J. B. Hickok be

discharged from his official position as city marshal for the reason that the City is no longer in need of his services. . . ."[99]

Abilene was the high-water mark in Wild Bill Hickok's life. He never really recovered from the killing of Mike Williams, and the remaining five years of his life were spent in aimless wandering. From 1872 on, Wild Bill was a man waiting to die.

After leaving Abilene, Hickok's wandering took him to many parts of the United States. The *Saline County* (Kansas) *Journal* of Salina, in its issue of January 18, 1872, reported that he was at Boston. In January 1872, Hickok was reported being a member of the Royal Buffalo Hunt[100] held in honor of the Grand Duke Alexis Aleksandrovich Romanov of Russia,[101] the third son of Czar Alexander II. Hickok might have met the Grand Duke's party in Kansas prior to the hunt. The Grand Duke's party included many Western notables: Generals P. H. Sheridan, G. A. Custer, and Edward O. C. Ord, commanding brigadier general of the Department of the Platte; Brevet Brigadier General Innis N. Palmer of the Second U.S. Cavalry; and Brevet Brigadier General George A. (Sandy) Forsyth of Beecher's Island fame, and his older brother, Brevet Brigadier General James W. (Tony) Forsyth, later regimental commander of the Seventh U.S. Cavalry; Brevet Brigadier General Nelson B. Sweitzer; Lieutenant Colonel Michael V. Sheridan, General Sheridan's younger brother; and Assistant Surgeon Morris J. Asch of the U.S. Medical Department. The hunting party also included Buffalo Bill Cody who acted as guide and the well-known Brulé Sioux Chief and diplomat Spotted Tail (Sinte Galeska). The Royal Hunt was held in Nebraska in mid-January and several bison were killed.[102]

Hickok was off and on at Kansas City from 1872 to 1875. In the early part of 1872, Hickok was reported at Georgetown, a Colorado mining camp, gambling for his livelihood. He appeared (of all places) in Sidney Barnett's Wild West Show at Niagara Falls in late August and early September, 1872.[103] Bill was also at Ellsworth in 1872 where he lived in a shack on North Main Street with a woman named Emma Williams, who had formerly been the mistress of Billy Thompson, brother of Ben. (The Thompson brothers were at Ellsworth in 1872 and 1873 operating as free-lance gamblers.) In March 1873, Bill spent some time visiting old friends at Springfield, Missouri.[104]

In 1873 Wild Bill was between careers. Against his better judgment he allowed Buffalo Bill to persuade him to take up stage acting. Cody had made his stage debut at Chicago on December 18, 1872, in the play "The Scouts of the Prairie," which had been written by the famous dime novelist Ned Buntline (Edward Z. C. Judson). Wild Bill made his debut at Williamsport, Pennsylvania, on September 8, 1873,[105] in Fred G. Maeder's "The Scouts of the Plains." Bill received third billing behind Cody and John B. ("Texas Jack") Omohundro, an ex-Army scout turned actor. The Cody-Hickok troupe also played Titusville, Pennsylvania, in November[106] and Portland, Maine, in late January 1874.[107] In March 1874, the troupe played Rochester, New York, where Wild Bill renewed his friendship with Mrs. Agnes Lake, his future wife. On March 14 Hickok left Cody's troupe.[108]

No one really knows why Wild Bill quit

stage acting, but it must have pained him greatly—a man with a legitimate claim to Western fame—standing on a stage before Eastern audiences uttering words that someone had written for him. Somehow Wild Bill must have known that he was out of place and character.

After leaving Cody's show, Hickok visited New York City. From there he went back to Kansas City. Later he was in Denver and Cheyenne, Wyoming. For a while in 1875 Bill was at Sidney, Nebraska, the "jumping off" point to the Dakota Territory. At Sidney he made his gambling headquarters in Tim Dyer's saloon and dance hall.

At this stage in his life Wild Bill was neither his picturesque self nor in good health. He was balding and this gave him an appearance of one much older in years. He was going blind; probably he had contracted the veneral disease of gonorrhea and it had affected his eyesight, causing *gonorrheal opthalmia*. Rumor has it that he had his eyes examined by military doctors at Camp Carlin, Wyoming, but there is no evidence to support this.[109] Hickok wore eyeglasses at various times to correct his ailing vision.

At Sidney in 1875, Wild Bill is alleged to have killed three buffalo hunters in Dyer's Saloon. William Frank (Doc) Carver, who was one of the finest rifle marksman in the world and later one-time partner of Buffalo Bill in the latter's famous Wild West Show, was there. Carver said that one of the men Bill killed was named "Big Jack," who was a friend of Jack McCall, the eventual assassin of Hickok. The whole town was talking, Carver said, about Hickok's killing of the three men, although Bill himself did not mention the incident.[110] To date, no contemporary evidence has been unearthed to substantiate Carver's story.

Hickok was back in Cheyenne in the early part of 1876. He met Mrs. Agnes Lake for the third time. On March 5, 1876, in the home of S. L. Moyer, Wild Bill and Mrs. Lake were married by the Reverend W. F. Warren.[111] Mr. and Mrs. Moyer were the witnesses.[112] Bill and his bride spent their honeymoon at Cincinnati,[113] the bride's hometown. At the time of her marriage to Hickok, Agnes Lake was fifty years of age, having been born Agnes Mersman in Alsatia in 1826.[114] She had a daughter, Emma Lake, by a previous marriage, thereby making Wild Bill a stepfather.

In the spring of 1876, Wild Bill left Cincinnati without his wife and headed for his last camp—the gold fields of Deadwood, Dakota Territory, in what is now the state of South Dakota. Mrs. Hickok was to follow as soon as Bill made a "strike." Bill never made his "strike" and she never saw him again. He was killed a few months later. She survived him until 1907.[115]

Wild Bill reached Cheyenne by June 1876. From there he and his friend Charles H. ("Colorado Charlie") Utter struck out for Fort Laramie, Wyoming. In July at the famed post Hickok and Utter joined a wagon train which was headed for the Dakotas. At the fort Hickok met for the first time Martha Jane Cannary, the now famous "Calamity Jane." Jane was under military guard as a post prostitute (or "camp follower") and a drunkard. Military authorities at Fort Laramie put her on the wagon train bound for the Dakotas. During the trip she lived as the mistress of Steve Utter, Colorado Charlie's brother. Her relationship with Wild Bill was rather casual.[116] She merely

Deadwood, South Dakota boomtown of the Black Hills gold fields, became Wild Bill's last haunt. He was killed here in 1876, the year this photograph was taken.

shared his whiskey bottle, but not his bed.

At Deadwood Hickok and Charlie Utter tried their hand at mining, but Bill had little success. He soon turned to his old standby —gambling. He made his headquarters in Carl Mann's and Jerry Lewis's Number Ten Saloon. Harry ("Sam") Young, whom Hickok had known at Hays City in 1869, was one of the bartenders at the Number Ten. Hickok had a premonition that Deadwood was to be his last camp. He expressed this belief to both Colorado Charlie and Tom Dosier, another friend. Finally, on August 2, 1876, at 4:10 P.M., the end came for Wild Bill. He was sitting in a poker game in the Number Ten Saloon with Carl Mann, Charlie Rich and Captain William R. Massie, a Missouri riverboat skipper from St. Louis. Hickok was violating one of his cardinal rules: he was sitting with his back to a door. Twice, without success, he had asked Rich to exchange positions with him.

Bill was having a particular run of bad luck. He borrowed a poker stake from Harry Young, who was on duty behind the bar. An ex-buffalo hunter named John ("Broken Nose Jack") McCall, with whom Hickok had occasionally played cards, walked unnoticed to within a few feet of Wild Bill. McCall suddenly drew a pistol and shouted, "Take that!" He fired. The bullet struck Hickok in the back of the head, killing him instantly. The bullet emerged from Bill's right cheek and struck Captain Massie in the left wrist. Hickok slowly slipped from his stool, dropping his cards (four of the cards were aces and eights—henceforth known as the famous "Dead Man's Hand"). Rich and Massie ran out of the front door of the saloon. McCall snapped two shots at bartender Harry Young and George

Dead Man's Hand—the hand Hickok held when shot

M. Shingle, one of the saloon patrons, but both times the pistol failed to fire. It was found to have been defective after the shot which killed Wild Bill. McCall made his escape quickly from the saloon. He later hid in Jacob Shroudy's butcher shop. Authorities (not Calamity Jane) later apprehended him there.

Why McCall had killed Hickok is anyone's guess. McCall later said that Wild Bill had killed his brother at Hays City, which obviously was a lie. It is known that Hickok and McCall had had trouble over a gambling debt.[117] Some claim that Deadwood's crooked gambling element was fearful that Wild Bill would be appointed city marshal and crack down on their tinhorn ways. Still others maintain that McCall was simply jealous of Hickok's fame and wanted to become a famous and important man by killing Wild Bill. It would seem that the reader has his choice of motives.

Jack McCall was about twenty-five years old when he killed Wild Bill Hickok. He was from Jefferson County, Kentucky, and had left home when he was about eighteen.[118] Most of his adult life was spent as a buffalo hunter on the Great Plains. In 1869 he was at Hays City where he saw Hickok for the first time. Sometime during the summer of 1876 McCall had come to Deadwood.

Hickok was buried the next day, August 3, on a hillside called Ingleside. Jack McCall was tried for his murder. Judge William L. Kuykendall presided at McCall's trial. George May acted as prosecuting attorney and McCall employed a Judge Miller as his defense counsel. Eleven jurors voted for acquittal and one (John Mann, brother of Carl Mann,[119]) for conviction. Judge Kuykendall, in an unprecedented move, declared Jack McCall a free man. McCall departed Deadwood soon after his trial. George May, on the promise of money which he never received from Mrs. Agnes Hickok, brought McCall to trial in a federal court.

Kuykendall had no authority to release McCall on the basis of a hung jury. The Dakota Territory was under federal jurisdiction and crimes committed there could be prosecuted by federal authorities. May had McCall arrested at Laramie and taken before a Judge Blair. McCall pleaded guilty to murdering Hickok.[120] He was to be tried in the federal court at Yankton, capital of the Dakota Territory, in present South Dakota. McCall was indicted on October 18.[121] This time he entered a plea of not guilty. He employed Oliver Shannon and ex-Brevet Brigadier General William H. H. Beadle as his defense attorneys.[122] On November 9 McCall and another man tried unsuccessfully to break jail.[123] McCall now admitted to federal authorities that Deadwood gambler John Varnes had paid him

Courtesy South Dakota State Historical Society, Pierre
"Colorado Charlie" Utter, on the left, erected a headboard over the grave of Wild Bill Hickok. Hickok died while playing poker and holding the famous "Dead Man's Hand." The other man is not identified.

money to kill Hickok. Hickok and Varnes reportedly had trouble at Denver over a card game.[124]

McCall came to trial finally at Yankton on December 4, 1876.[125] Chief Justice P. C. Shannon[126] of the Dakota Territory presided. Two days later the jury returned a verdict of guilty,[127] and McCall was sentenced to hang on January 3, 1877.[128] After unsuccessful appeals to the U.S. Supreme Court and President U. S. Grant, Jack McCall was hanged at Yankton on March 1, 1877.[129]

Hickok's remains were allowed to rest at Ingleside until August 3, 1879, when they were removed to Deadwood's Mount Moriah Cemetery (Calamity Jane is buried here, near the grave of Wild Bill). A huge headstone was erected over Bill's grave.[130]

It is interesting to note that when the remains of Hickok were disinterred, it was found that his face, head and upper portions of his body, as well as the many pleats of his dress shirt, although decomposed, remained visible on his form. The body seemed to have undergone some process of petrification, although it may have been a unique process of embalming by the disposition of the minerals in the soil which had percolated through the coffin into the body tissues. At any rate, it would seem that nature went to some lengths to preserve partially the remains of one of the West's greatest man-killers.

Most authorities consider Wild Bill to have been if not the deadliest man-killer in the West, then at least the most dedicated to his profession and the most famous. Charlie Gross, who probably knew Hickok better than anyone, studied Wild Bill at close hand during his days at Abilene. In a letter to his friend J. B. Edwards, an early-day Abilene resident, Gross recalled that Hickok used only flash powder and metal balls that he had molded, and that Wild Bill stated that he did not fully trust metallic

Hickok's paper target

cartridges.[131] When Gross questioned Hickok about molding his own lead, Bill replied, "When I draw and pull I must be sure." Hickok also used no holsters. He preferred to carry his pistols, butts forward, in his sash or waistband. Wild Bill drew his pistol with an inverted or twist of the wrist motion (the gun hand is turned under the gun butt). This was commonly called the "Cavalry Draw."

Wild Bill never missed an opportunity to practice target shooting. Gross recalled in later years that Hickok was a better shot right-handed than left.

"I never shot a man with my left hand except the time when some drunken soldiers had me down on the floor and were trampling me and then I used both hands," Gross recalled Hickok as saying.[132] (This was an obvious reference to Hickok's fight with the soldiers of the Seventh U.S. Cavalry at Hays City in 1870).

Charlie Gross was an eyewitness to some of Wild Bill's fancy target shooting. He remembered one occasion when Bill placed a piece of paper six inches in length on a tree, stood about twenty feet from the tree and fired six pistol shots with his right hand. In the center of the paper was a small dot. Two of Hickok's shots hit the dot and the other four shots struck the paper within an inch in a vertical line. (See drawing opposite page).

Hickok tried the same feat again, only left-handed. All six of his shots hit the paper in a vertical line, each shot above the other, but none struck the dot in the center of the paper.

Hickok never notched the handles of his revolvers to keep count of the number of his victims. No serious-minded gunfighter ever notched his guns.

Gross also recalled that Hickok never used the word "killed," but always said "shot" in reference to those he killed.

"Charlie, I hope you never have to shoot any man, but if you do shoot him, [shoot him] in the guts near the navel. You may not make a fatal shot, but he will get a shock that will paralyze his brain and arm so much that the fight is all over."[133]

Hickok's candid statement to his friend Gross not only summed up the Prince of Pistoleer's philosophy on man-killing, but also the Code of the American West: *survival at any cost.* Wild Bill broke this code only once. And it cost him his life.

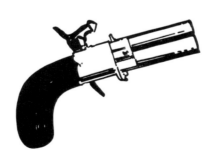

4.

DOC HOLLIDAY

(1852?-1887)

OHN HENRY HOLLIDAY was born to Henry B. Holliday (1819?-) and Alice Jane McKey (1829-1866)[1] at Griffin, Spalding County, Georgia. John Henry was baptized as an infant at the Presbyterian Church in Griffin on March 21, 1852,[2] so it is conceivable that he could have been born in late 1851. For a few years, at least, young John Holliday grew up in the aristrocratic southern style that his father's $17,000 estate[3] could afford. But the War Between the States destroyed the antebellum South and with it the Hollidays' way of life. Either during the war or shortly after, Henry Holliday moved his family to Valdosta, Lowndes County, Georgia. At any rate, Mrs. Holliday did not survive long after the war. From all accounts her death was a severe blow to young John. He and his father were never close after Mrs. Holliday's death. An open rift came between father and son when the senior Holliday married a second time to a woman about ten years John's senior.

It has always been written that Henry Holliday sent his son to the Baltimore College of Dental Surgery, now part of the University of Maryland, in the late 1860s. It has also been written that while studying dentistry in Baltimore John contracted tuberculosis (a disease to which he eventually succumbed) during an epidemic. Dr. Gardiner P. H. Foley, professor of dental history at the Baltimore college, the first and only college of dental surgery in the United States during Holliday's time, has made an exhaustive study of the records of the B.C.D.S. Dr. Foley has told the author:

John Henry "Doc" Holliday was the gunslinging dentist of the Old West. He was also a drunkard. Holliday became a good friend of the Earp brothers and followed them to Tombstone, Arizona.

"My reply has always been that there is no evidence to support the assertion that Doc Holliday attended a Baltimore dental school, let alone graduated.[4] In the periodical dental literature of the South, Georgia included, there is no mention of Doc Holliday, let alone identification of him as a dentist. I would assume that for the sake of his extra-professional reputation alone the Southern dental literature would have included some notice of him had he been deemed to merit such mention. Never in

the records of the Baltimore College of Dental Surgery is there a mention of Holliday. Neither address books nor catalogues list his name. As far as the dental literature of Maryland is concerned, he is completely ignored. Neither do I have any proof that Holliday claimed to be a graduate of a Baltimore dental school nor ever asserted an attendance at one."[5]

A check of the Baltimore city directories for the period of 1865 to 1874 also failed to show a John Henry Holliday as residing in the city.[6]

Old-timers, however, remember Holliday practicing dentistry in his hometown of Griffin at the corner of West Solomon and State streets. Rumor has him also practicing dentistry in Atlanta. And the city directory of Dallas, Texas, for the year 1873 lists Holliday and John A. Seegar as dentists.[7] The U.S. census report of 1870 for Valdosta, Lowndes County, Georgia, enumerated Holliday on June 8 as a "student" living at home. Some time between 1870 and 1873 young John Holliday learned the art and skill of dentistry as an apprentice under a practicing dentist, as was the custom in that era.

It has been written many times that tuberculosis and the indiscriminate killing of some Negro youths forced John Holliday to leave his native Georgia and go west where he eventually became famous as "Doc" Holliday. Doc is said to have contracted tuberculosis, circa 1870, and it is known that he died of the disease in 1887. It is humanly possible, however, for a person to have tuberculosis and live with the disease for seventeen years or longer without receiving any medical treatment.[8] Holliday succumbed eventually to miliary tuberculosis.

From the time of dissemination of miliary tuberculosis and the onset of innumerable tiny foci on the body, which is caused by the disease, most persons would not live longer than three or more months without modern treatment.[9] So it is conceivable that Holliday had tuberculosis (but not miliary tuberculosis) when he left Georgia, but he probably contracted the more dangerous disease years later at Leadville, Colorado. He did not contract the disease in a Baltimore epidemic. During the years when Holliday is alleged to have been a resident of Baltimore, the city did not have a tuberculosis epidemic.[10]

Doc Holliday's killing of the Negro youths is said to have occurred, circa 1870, at a swimming hole along the Withlacoochee River near Valdosta, Georgia. Doc is alleged to have killed at least one, possibly two Negro boys and wounded one or two others for bathing in his private swimming hole. The staff at the Georgia Historical Society has informed the author that after an exhaustive search into their records and those of Lowndes County, they were unable to find a contemporary record of the Holliday-Withlacoochee incident.[11]

John Myers Myers, a Holliday biographer, stated that in the files of the Arizona Pioneers' Historical Society is an affidavit signed by a surveyor named Moore, who said he was at Valdosta in 1881.[12] Moore stated in the affidavit that rumors in Valdosta were that Doc had killed a Negro in the Withlacoochee incident.[13] But a search by the staffs at the Arizona Pioneers' Historical Society and the Arizona State Library and Archives failed to locate the Moore affidavit.[14]

Whatever the reason or reasons Holliday left Georgia, it is known that by 1873 he was practicing dentistry at Dallas with Dr. John Seegar, formerly of Georgia.[15] Holliday had probably left Georgia in March or April, 1873.

His dental practice notwithstanding, it was in Dallas that Doc Holliday first gained fame as a gunfighting dentist. That Doc was disillusioned with the world around him, there can be little doubt. The world was not as idealistic as Doc would have liked, so he turned to drink after office hours. His drinking became excessive and his office hours less regular. Because his drinking kept him from his dental work,

Courtesy Robert E. Egan Collection, Dodge City, Kansas
Doc Holliday practiced dentistry haphazardly wherever he wandered in the frontier West. This advertisement appeared in the *Dodge City Times* of June 28, 1878. His office was in the famous Dodge House.

Courtesy Vincent R. Mercaldo Archives, Richmond Hill, N.Y.
"Big Nose Kate" Elder (or Fisher) was Doc Holliday's girl friend who followed him about the West. Wyatt Earp knew her in Wichita. Doc and Kate often quarreled. The pair broke up in Tombstone after Kate accused Doc of participating in a stagecoach holdup.

Doc turned to cards as a means of livelihood. Later, he rarely opened his office except to earn another gambling stake.

Holliday is said to have killed his first white man, a prominent rancher, at Dallas in a gambling dispute. Actually, Doc's only gun duel in Dallas had a less than fatal result. He and saloon owner Charles W. Austin exchanged shots with each other on New Year's Day, 1875, and were arrested for their disturbance.[16] Later that year Doc was

at Fort Griffin, Texas, a gathering point near the Western Trail for every kind of frontier riffraff in west Texas. Among them were hardcase Hurricane Bill Martin; Big Nose Kate Elder (who became Doc's mistress); John H. Selman, the man who assassinated Wes Hardin in 1895; and Lottie Deno, the West's most celebrated lady gambler, who operated a house of prostitution at Fort Griffin.[17]

On June 12, 1875 Doc and another gambler named Mike Lynch were arrested for gambling at Fort Griffin.[18] Both men "jumped bail"[19] and Doc went to Fort Concho, Texas. He left Concho under a cloud, going over to Fort Davis.[20] In 1876 he was at Jacksboro, Texas, a frequent hangout of soldiers from nearby Fort Richardson. Jacksboro was typical of a frontier town that was in the vicinity of an Army post. There were twenty-odd places in Jacksboro which served liquor, and fighting and friction between soldiers and citizens were commonplace. A troop of Fourth U.S. Cavalry once burned down a house of prostitution there. Doc is said to have killed a soldier of the Eleventh U.S. Infantry[21] at Jacksboro in 1876 during a card game. W. W. Bill Dennis, the county historian at Jacksboro, made an exhaustive study of the old records of Jacksboro and did not find any records pertaining to Doc Holliday.[22] Dennis told the author:

"There is a record for each dead body that was found at Jacksboro because the justices of the peace received five dollars for holding an inquest. That was big money then and there were lots of inquests held during what we call 'red-hot' times."[23]

Pat Jahns made a thorough study of the post records and monthly reports of Fort

Denver, the frontier Queen of the Rockies, was home to Doc Holliday at various times in his checkered career. After the Tombstone shoot-outs, Holliday fled to Colorado and was in Denver for a while.

Richardson and found no mention of any shooting incidents.[24]

By 1877 Holliday was back at Fort Griffin where he met his idol, Wyatt Earp. With Holliday when he met Wyatt was Doc's mistress, Katherine Elder, a burly prostitute who was better known on the frontier as "Big Nose Kate Fisher." Doc had probably met Kate at Fort Griffin in 1875, but Wyatt Earp had known her as an inmate in Bessie Earp's sporting house at Wichita as early as 1874.[25] According to the Wichita police judge reports, Kate was arrested and fined in June and August, 1874, for being a prostitute. On the latter occasion she used the alias of "Kate Earp."[26] The Kansas State census report of 1875 listed her as an inmate in Tom Sherman's combination dance hall and house of prostitution at Dodge City.

Doc allegedly knifed to death a man named Ed Bailey in a card game at Fort Griffin in January, 1878. Bill Dennis has also studied the old records of Shackleford County (in which county Fort Griffin was located), but found no record of Holliday killing anyone at Fort Griffin.[27] Legend, however, has Doc being arrested and jailed after killing Bailey, and Big Nose Kate setting fire to the town hotel and breaking Doc from jail while the townspeople were distracted by the fire.

The whereabouts of Holliday from the time he left Fort Griffin for the second time in 1877 to when he arrived at Dodge City in early June, 1878, is not known. One report has him and Kate operating a saloon along the Arkansas River near the Kansas-Colorado border.[28] After leaving Texas,

Collections in the Museum of New Mexico, Santa Fe
Las Vegas, in New Mexico Territory, was another locale for Doc Holliday, who operated a saloon, probably near this plaza. While here, he was involved in two shootings. The structure in the center was called the "hanging windmill," a ready-made scaffold with a "good drop" and available for instant use. It was torn down in 1880 after citizens complained that the hangings contaminated the water.

Doc probably went to Denver. Bat Masterson said he fled to Denver as early as 1876 after killing the soldier at Jacksboro.[29] Masterson said that Holliday knifed and severely cut a gambler named Bud Ryan at Denver in 1876 and that Ryan was still living as late as 1907.[30] The Denver newspapers carried no *contemporary* account of Doc's fight with Ryan,[31] although a biography of Holliday which appeared in the December 25, 1887, issue of the *Denver Republican* included an account of the knifing. There was a "Kid" Ryan at Denver in 1887 who was described as "a waiter bearing a hard reputation."[32] Ryan was involved in a saloon fight there in June, 1887, and severely

cut one Jack Brogan in the neck.[33] It is possible that Bud Ryan and Kid Ryan were one and the same.

Holliday was at Dodge City as early as June 8, 1878, when the *Dodge City Times* of that date printed the following advertisement:

DENTISTRY.
J. H. Holliday, Dentist, very respectfully offers his professional services to the citizens of Dodge City and surrounding country during the summer. Office at room No. 24, Dodge House. Where satisfaction is not given money will be refunded.

Doc obviously needed another gambling stake.

The actions of Doc Holliday while at

Dodge City are extremely sketchy at best. He was not involved in any trouble while there, or at least if he were, it did not make the local papers. Wyatt Earp stated at the preliminary hearing which followed the famous Tombstone killings of October 26, 1881, that he was "a friend of Doc Holliday because when I was City Marshal at Dodge City, Kansas [*sic*], he came to my rescue and saved my life when I was surrounded by desperadoes."[34] If Doc saved Wyatt's life at Dodge City (and Earp had no reason to lie about this), the incident never made the local newspapers.

How long Doc Holliday remained in Dodge City is not known. Possibly he remained there until sometime in 1879. Rumor has Doc one of the men with Bat Masterson and Ben Thompson aiding the Santa Fe Railroad in its right-of-way war with the Denver and Rio Grande Western Railroad near Pueblo, Colorado, during the spring of 1879. Probably after leaving Dodge, Holliday went to Leadville and Trinidad, Colorado. At Trinidad he is said to have wounded a gambler named "Kid" Colton. The district court records of Las Animas County (in which county Trinidad was located) were checked for a record of Holliday (or his often-used aliases of "Tom McKey" and "Tom McKee") and Colton without success.[35]

By July 1879, Holliday was at Las Vegas, New Mexico, operating a saloon with one Jordan Webb. Big Nose Kate was living with Doc. Wyatt Earp was there off and on in September, October, and November of that year. More so than any other town on the Western frontier, Las Vegas was overrun with a variety of hardcases and cutthroats. Two of the more notorious cutthroats there during Holliday's stay were David Rudabaugh, stage and train robber and companion of the famous Henry McCarty, alias "Billy ('The Kid') Bonney"; and Mysterious Dave Mather, con man, gambler, Las Vegas constable, killer, and a friend of a host of frontier celebrities such as Rudabaugh, Holliday, Earp, Masterson, Bassett, and Heinrich ("Dutch Henry") Borne, the most notorious horse thief in the West. In 1883 and 1884 Mather served a hitch as assistant marshal at Dodge City. John Joshua Webb, ex-peace officer at Dodge City, who once assisted in the arrest of Rudabaugh[36] and was now a close friend, was there. Webb was also an intimate friend of Bat Masterson. In 1880 Webb was made city marshal of Las Vegas. Also at Las Vegas in 1879 were Tom Pickett, another companion of Billy the Kid; Hyman G. Neill, alias "Hoodoo Brown," one-time acting coroner at Las Vegas; and J. J. Harlin, alias "Off-Wheeler," both notorious con men.

While at Las Vegas, Holliday is said to have been involved in two shootings, one of which resulted in a fatality. One of Doc's victims allegedly was Charles White, a gambler and part-time bartender. Holliday and White are said to have exchanged shots and that one of Doc's bullets grazed White's spine and momentarily stunned him. No contemporary record of the shooting, however, has been found.

Holliday shot and fatally wounded gambler Mike Gordon, an ex-Army scout, at Las Vegas on July 19, 1879. Gordon succumbed the next day. Gordon's mistress was employed at Holliday's and Webb's saloon and Gordon was unhappy about the situation. The girl refused to quit and Gordon set out

Collections in the Museum of New Mexico, Santa Fe
Lawmen, gunslingers, prostitutes, bankers, freighters, drummers, and merchants passed through the West's countless railroad terminals as they replaced the stagecoach stations. Doc Holliday, Wyatt Earp, and others of the "Dodge City Gang," used this one at Las Vegas, New Mexico. From here, Doc and Kate departed for Tombstone.

to shoot up Doc's place on July 19. Gordon fired a shot into the saloon. When he did not receive an immediate response, he fired a second time. Holliday stepped from the saloon and shot Gordon.[37]

By 1880 Doc and Kate had left Las Vegas for greener fields at Tombstone, Arizona. Wyatt Earp had already established himself when Doc and Kate arrived. Doc followed his trade as a professional gambler at Tombstone. He was a house dealer at the Oriental Saloon and, later, he made his gambling headquarters at the Alhambra Saloon. Doc later bought a percentage of the gambling interest at the Alhambra.

Besides his difficulties evolving from the attempted robbery of the Benson stage [see

chapter on Wyatt Earp], Holliday also had serious trouble with gambler M. E. ("Mike") Joyce, owner of the Oriental, and the notorious gunfighter Johnny Ringo. Holliday's first encounter with Joyce came between April 13 and May 30, 1881, when Doc shot Joyce in the hand at the Oriental Saloon. Holliday also shot one of Joyce's bartenders in the foot during the melee. Doc was indicted by the grand jury on May 30,[38] but nothing came of it. Holliday and Joyce had another dispute in mid-December 1881, when Joyce tried to shoot Doc. Sheriff Johnny Behan interfered and arrested Joyce for carrying firearms within the city limits.[39]

Perhaps what would have been the most

classical gun fight in Western history nearly occurred on the streets of Tombstone on January 17, 1882, between Doc Holliday and Johnny Ringo with Wyatt Earp as a witness. Ringo, who was a friend of the Clantons and McLaurys, accidentally came face-to-face with Holliday. Both gunmen instantly began calling each other vile names. Wyatt Earp, who was standing nearby, made an effort to keep these two legends of the pistol from drawing on each other. Deputy Sheriff Billy Breakenridge arrived in time and arrested both Holliday and Ringo for carrying firearms within the city limits.[40] The next day Holliday and Ringo were fined thirty dollars each for violating the city's firearms ordinance.[41]

Bat Masterson, who did not like Holliday, admitted to Doc's courage, but clarified his personality.

"Holliday had a mean disposition and an ungovernable temper, and under the influence of liquor was a most dangerous man. . . . He was hotheaded and impetuous and very much given to both drinking and quarreling. . . . I assisted him . . . not because I liked him any too well, but on account of my friendship for Wyatt Earp, who did. . . ."[42]

It was courage which prompted Doc Holliday to "take on" Johnny Ringo, considered by many Western buffs to have been, perhaps, the deadliest gunman in the entire Southwest. Doc's other redeeming trait was his word; once given, it was never broken. George Hinkle, who had no reason to have liked him, said Holliday's word was his bond.[43]

It was at Tombstone where the relationship between Doc Holliday, the Georgia gentleman, and Kate Elder, frontier prostitute, came to an abrupt end in early July, 1881. After Kate signed the affidavit, stating that he had been involved in the attempted holdup of the Benson stage, Doc told Kate to get out of his life. She knew Doc meant it when he had her arrested for threatening his life. Sometime thereafter Kate Elder left Tombstone. She survived Doc by a great many years and in later life tried to convince people that she was Mrs. John H. Holliday. Had Doc been alive at the time, he probably would have gone "gunning" for Kate for such a statement.

Holliday fled Arizona with Wyatt and Warren Earp in April, 1882, after killing Frank Stilwell and Indian Charlie Cruz. The Earps went to Gunnison, Colorado, and Doc to Pueblo, Colorado; later Holliday traveled to Trinidad, Leadville, and finally to Denver. Wyatt and Warren Earp were in semi-hiding, but Holliday remained in the limelight. Arizona authorities learned he was living in Denver in 1882, and in May of that year Pima County (Arizona) Sheriff Robert H. Paul—who had been shotgun messenger during the attempted holdup of the Benson stage—went to Denver with a warrant for the arrest of Holliday for Stilwell's murder. Paul was not the only person seeking Doc. A professional bounty hunter named Perry M. Mallon (or Mallen) also arrived in Denver about the same time, hoping to take Holliday into custody. Mallon was seeking a reported $1,500 reward for the return of Holliday to Cochise County, Arizona.[44]

Mallon brought Holliday into custody on May 15.[45] Mallon, however, had no legal authority to arrest Holliday, so he asked local police authorities to place Doc in jail. Colorado authorities notified Sheriff Paul

Courtesy Library, State Historical Society of Colorado
Leadville, Colorado, attracted the restless wanderers of the Old West, as did all the mining camps. Among them were Doc
Holliday and Luke Short. Holliday went to Colorado to escape the law after the O. K. Corral battle and the killing of
Frank Stilwell. But his gun blazed again in Leadville.

that Holliday was in custody and that he
would be held until his (Paul's) arrival in
Denver.[46] Meanwhile, Wyatt Earp learned
of Holliday's predicament. Earp contacted
Bat Masterson, who was in Denver, and
asked him to try to keep Doc from being
extradited to Arizona. Bat secured an audience with Colorado Governor F. W. Pitkin,

and after some discussion, Pitkin told Masterson he would not honor Holliday's extradition papers.[47]

Bat wanted insurance, however. He de-
vised a hoax. He made up a false charge
against Holliday on May 18, stating that
Holliday had fleeced a Denver man out of
$100.[48] Masterson had Holliday taken into

custody. On May 31 Holliday was taken before a Judge McBride in the District Court at Pueblo and waived examination. His bail was set and raised at three hundred dollars and a hearing was set for July 18.[49] Later his case was continued indefinitely. Masterson's ruse worked. Doc was protected indefinitely as long as he remained in Colorado.

Doc was in Leadville by 1884. At this time in his life Holliday projected a horrible appearance. His five foot ten frame was racked from tuberculosis. Never a stout man, his normal weight was 135 pounds. Death was hounding his footsteps and his cold blue eyes showed it. His blond hair was heavily streaked with gray and coupled with his tight, gaunt, pockmarked face, it gave him an appearance of a dead man.

If anyone was foolish enough to think that Doc's illness had mellowed his truculent disposition, he was mistaken. William ("Billy") Allen, who had been at Tombstone and talking with Johnny Behan only minutes before the famous street fight of 1881, was also at Leadville in 1884. He was working as a bartender in the Monarch Saloon where Doc gambled. In August 1884, Holliday borrowed five dollars from Allen. Allen kept taunting Holliday about the debt. When Allen went so far as to call him a welsher in public and behind his back, Doc decided to kill him. Holliday was in Hyman's Saloon on August 19 when Allen entered. Doc drew his pistol and fired. The bullet missed the bartender. Allen ran for the door and Holliday fired again. Doc's second bullet struck Allen in the arm, knocking him down. Holliday tried for a third shot at the prostrate Allen, but Henry Kelleman, a bartender at Hyman's, grabbed Doc's arm and kept him from firing again. Captain Bradbury of the Leadville police force entered the saloon and disarmed and arrested Holliday.[50]

On August 25 Doc was charged with as-

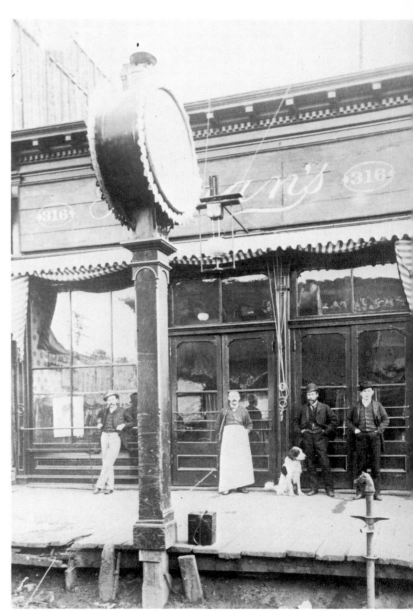

Courtesy Denver Public Library Western Collection
Though Doc Holliday was ill in Colorado, his temper hadn't mellowed. At Hyman's Saloon in Leadville, he fired on Billy Allen, a bartender who was berating Doc about a gambling debt. Allen was wounded and Holliday arrested.

Gravely ill from tuberculosis, Doc Holliday entered a sanitarium and health spa at Glenwood Springs, Colorado, in 1887.
He had suffered for many years from the disease. Here, in November of the same year, he died.

sault with an intent to kill and a Judge Old set his bail at $8,000.[51] Doc's trial did not come until March 27, 1885, when he went before a Judge Goldthwaite.[52] Doc was acquitted of the charge on March 28.[53] Some time after his trial Doc returned to Denver.

Rumor was that Allen and Doc had had a difference of opinion over Holliday's troubles at Tombstone, and that gambler Johnny Tyler, a friend of Tombstone gambler Mike Joyce, had Doc fired as a dealer at the Monarch Saloon, which was owned by Cy Allen, who may or may not have been a relative of Billy Allen. Tyler, who was at Leadville in 1884, was rumored to have had trouble at Tombstone with both Holliday and Wyatt Earp when he was a member of the gambling faction backing Joyce in the Oriental Saloon.

By the spring of 1887, Doc Holliday was gravely ill from tuberculosis. In May he went to the sanitarium at Glenwood Springs, Colorado. His tuberculosis was now mili-ary. Medical authorities could do nothing for him. He died there on November 8, 1887, and was buried the following day in the Linwood Cemetery. His passing was quiet and at the end he said, "This is funny. . . ." Indeed it was: Doc Holliday, against all odds, had died quietly in bed.

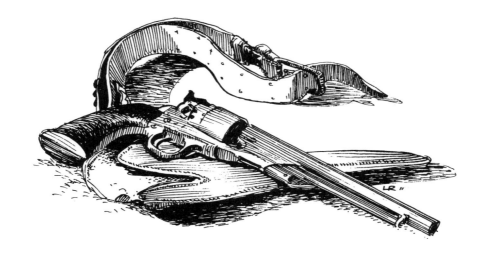

5.

BAT MASTERSON

(1853-1921)

BARTHOLOMEW (WILLIAM BARCLAY) MASTERSON was born to Thomas Masterson (1823-1921)[1] and Catherine McGurk (1836-1908)[2] at County Rouville, Quebec, Canada, on November 26, 1853.[3] Bat was not yet in his teens when Thomas Masterson moved his family in 1865 to a farm in Illinois, near St. Louis, after a brief sojourn in New York State. The Mastersons lived on their Illinois land until 1867 when they moved to a farm in Sedgwick County, Kansas, near present Wichita. Young Bat was then in his fourteenth year and he soon found the everyday life of a Midwest farm boy dull and unexciting. He endured the boredom of the farm for five more years and in 1872 talked his older brother, Edward John Masterson, and Theodore D. Raymond, a young friend and neighbor the Mastersons had known in Illinois, into leaving home with him.

Bat, Ed and young Raymond struck out in the summer of 1872. In a sense Bat never returned home, although he often went to visit his parents. The boys got only as far as Fort Dodge, Kansas. At this time the Santa Fe railroad was laying track toward present Dodge City, which would be founded as a townsite in July, 1872, as the western terminus of the Santa Fe. The Santa Fe had subcontracted the grading of a spur between Fort Dodge and the site of Dodge City to Raymond Ritter, a private contractor. Ritter hired the Mastersons and Raymond as graders. When the grading had been completed Ritter skipped out owing the boys their wages. Bat finally received the wages at gunpoint on April 15, 1873

Courtesy Kansas State Historical Society, Topeka
Bat Masterson was a dapper dresser, one of the most colorful of the Western gunfighters. He had style. He often
wore a derby, as did many Westerners, for contrary to legend, the bowler was far more popular that the broad-
brimmed ten-gallon hat.

when he and Henry H. Raymond, the older brother of Theodore Raymond, confronted Ritter as he returned to Dodge City via the Santa Fe.[4]

Disillusioned with their first venture in the West, Bat, Ed and Raymond went back to their homes. But Bat was not completely disappointed. By November 1872, he had returned to Dodge City, which was nothing more than the Santa Fe's terminus and a buffalo hunter's hangout on the historic Santa Fe Trail. Originally called "Buffalo City" by the hide hunters, the name was changed officially to Dodge City, deriving the name from Fort Dodge. During these

early years in Dodge City, brawling, vio-lence, and killings were considerably more common than during the city's more cele-brated cow-town era. Its Boot Hill began to rival that of Hays City. Railroad con-struction workers and buffalo hunters were among the first to be buried there.

Bat spent November and December, 1872, hunting buffalo on the plains of south-west Kansas and the Indian Territory. He made other hunts in April, July, and August, 1873.[5] Between hunts Bat was either at Dodge City or home visiting his parents. Occasionally he was at Wichita where he met Wyatt Earp in 1874. During most of 1873 Ed and Jim Masterson divided their time between buffalo hunts, working around Dodge City, and visiting home. Henry Ray-mond was the Masterson's constant com-panion. Bat seems to have divided most of his time during 1873 and the fore part of 1874 hunting buffalo, working at odd jobs around Dodge City, visiting his parents' farm, and "seeing the elephant" at Wichita. Sometime during these early years at Dodge, Bat lived with an ex-Ellsworth prostitute named Lizzie Palmer (nee Adams). Lizzie allegedly died from the effects of a wound received in a brawl with another woman fought over Bat Masterson and was buried on Dodge City's Boot Hill. Her remains were not recovered when the site of the original Boot Hill was razed in 1879.

By the year 1874 the great herds of buf-falo in southwest Kansas and the Indian Territory either had been killed or had mi-grated farther south, into the Texas Panhan-dle. It has been generally estimated that the buffalo—*bison* is the proper name of the species—numbered between thirty and sixty million when the Spanish explorer Francisco Vásquez de Coronado came to what is now the southwest part of the United States in 1540-1541. By 1870 the buffalo had been reduced to an estimated total of five million.[6] At one time buffalo hides brought $1.25, tongues went for twenty-five cents, and the hindquarters for a penny per pound.[7] The bones were sold for between eight and twelve dollars a ton.[8] It was easy to see why hunters such as Bat Masterson killed the buffalo in such wanton numbers.

With the last of the great southern herds concentrated in the Texas Panhandle, many of the buffalo hunters at Dodge City decided to move their base of operations. Bat Masterson was one of them. The hunters chose "Adobe Walls" as their headquarters. The Walls were the remains of a trading post built about 1843 by William Bent, a fur trader. It was situated between two forks of the Canadian River, at the scene of a fight between Colonel Kit Carson and his troops and the Kiowas and Comanches in 1864.

In the spring of 1874 Charles Myers and Fred Leonard, Dodge City traders, erected a sod trading post at the site of the ruins. Charles Rath, in partnership as a hide buyer with Bob Wright of Dodge City, also built a sod store at The Walls. Jim Hanrahan of Dodge City erected the inevitable saloon there. George (or William) Olds and his wife built a restaurant on the site, and Thomas O'Keefe established a blacksmith's shop. Myers and Leonard also raised a corral and log storehouse near their trading post.

A large group of buffalo hunters left Dodge City to occupy The Walls in early June 1874. Young Bat Masterson was among them. It was a dangerous enterprise

Courtesy Kansas State Historical Society, Topeka
Ed Masterson struck out in 1872 with his younger brother Bat to find adventure on the frontier. They got as far as Fort Dodge, then took jobs with the railroad. Later Ed became a law officer in Dodge City.

to say the least. During 1874 the Kiowas under their treacherous chief, Satanta, the Comanches under Quanah Parker, Gray Beard's band of Southern Cheyennes, and the Arapahoes were the major tribes of the Southern Plains in their last war against the white man. Historians have called it the "Red River War." Quanah Parker, son of the Comanche chief *Peta Nokoni* and Cynthia Parker, a white captive, was the most prominent leader of the war. Satanta had been a bloody menace to the Southern Plains for a decade. Prior to the prominence of Quanah Parker, he had been the most prominent leader of the Southern Plains tribes. In the first battle at Adobe Walls against Carson's troops, Satanta had sounded military bugle calls for the Kiowas.[9] The major power in uniting the Southern Plains tribes against the whites was the Comanche shaman Isatai, who harangued the tribal leaders into believing that his medicine would protect the tribes from the white men's bullets.

In late June Amos Chapman, an Army scout from Camp Supply, Indian Territory, arrived at Adobe Walls with a small detachment of enlisted men. The troopers with Chapman left the same day, but Chapman remained. He informed at least Jim Hanrahan that the Kiowas and Comanches were responsible for recent depredations against the whites in the Adobe Walls area. J. Wright Mooar, a buffalo hunter at The Walls, told a story many years later that Hanrahan, who had too much money invested in The Walls not to defend it, decided not to tell the other hunters about the presence of the Kiowas and Comanches in the area because he needed help in protecting his property. Mooar also stated that his brother, John W. Mooar, learned of the situation when he hid Chapman from the hunters in a wagon because Chapman was not fully trusted by the hunters at The Walls due to his close friendship with the Cheyennes. Chapman then informed John Mooar that the hostiles were in the immediate area. John drove to his brother's camp and warned him about the Indians. The brothers wasted no time in packing up and heading back to Dodge.[10]

Traders Charlie Myers and Charlie Rath also left Adobe Walls. Twenty-nine hunters and Mrs. Olds remained. At dawn the following day, one of the most celebrated In-

dian fights in Western history began, lasting for five consecutive days. Fortunately for the hunters, some of them were awake at the time of the hostile attack. The ridge-pole holding the roof of Hanrahan's saloon in place allegedly cracked loudly, awakening those sleeping in the saloon. The ridge-pole was examined, but nothing found wrong with it; a quirk of fate or a ruse on the part of Hanrahan, who—if the Mooar story is true—did not want his friends to be surprised by the Indians.

At the start of the fight two hunters, Ike and "Shorty" Shadler, were asleep in a wagon near the corral. They were killed in the first rush by the Indians. The remaining twenty-seven hunters and Mrs. Olds were scattered as follows:

In Hanrahan's Saloon—James Hanrahan, William Dixon, Bat Masterson, Michael Welsh, Oscar Shepherd, William H. Johnson, James W. McKinley, John McCabe, William Ogge (or Ogg), James (Bermuda) Carlyle, and Seth Hathaway.

In Leonard's & Myers' Store—Fred Leonard, William Tyler, William (Old Man) Keeler, Frank Smith, Samuel Smith, Hiram Watson, James (Mocassin Jim) Campbell, Henry Wirtz, Harry Armitage, Fred Myers, and Henry Lease.

In Rath's Store—George (or William) Olds, William Eba, Andy Johnson, James Langton, Thomas O'Keefe, and Mrs. Olds.[11]

For five consecutive days, June 27-July 1, the hunters were besieged by nearly two hundred Indians under Quanah Parker, Satanta, and Lone Wolf, the Kiowa. The shaman Isatai viewed the fight from a distant hill. Billy Tyler was killed the first

Dodge City became the hub for Bat Masterson's activities and adventures, both in the town and on the plains. For a time he served as a civilian scout out of Fort Dodge. He often tromped rutted Front Street (*above*) and the boardwalks which lined it, and patronized its saloons and deadfalls. The famous Long Branch Saloon is plainly visible to the right of the brick building on the far left.

day while trying to protect the livestock, and George Olds killed himself on the fifth day when his rifle accidentally discharged as he was descending a ladder. That same day, Henry Lease volunteered to go to Dodge City for help. Lease later brought help from Dodge, but after the fifth day the Indians ceased their attacks.

Tyler, Olds, and the two Shadler brothers were the only fatalities among the hunters.

After the battle ten dead Indians and a Negro were found on the field around The Walls. The Negro, who had blown a bugle during the fight, signaling his Indian allies when to charge and retreat, was killed by Harry Armitage as he was looting the Shadler wagon.[12] He was probably a deserter from the Ninth or Tenth U.S. Cavalry. Fred Myers killed two Indians and Fred Leonard at least one.[13] Bat Masterson is generally credited with killing one Indian, while Billy Dixon, using a .50 caliber Sharps rifle in what is allegedly the finest shot in Western history, felled an Indian from a reported distance of nearly a mile—1,538 yards. The horses of Quanah Parker and Isatai were dropped from under them during the first day and Quanah Parker was struck in the arm by a spent bullet. How many Indians actually lost their lives during the battle is not known. Indians usually carried their dead from the field and often lied about their losses, making it difficult to determine their precise casualties.

Bat Masterson returned to Dodge City in mid-July[14] and shortly thereafter embarked on a brief career as an Army scout. Bat enlisted at Fort Dodge as a civilian scout on August 5, 1874.[15] Bat was in time to take part in the punitive expedition of Brevet Major General Nelson A. Miles of the Fifth U.S. Infantry against the Southern Plains tribes. Masterson's salary was seventy-five dollars per month.[16] As an added stipulation, Bat was to earn a fifty dollar bonus for each dispatch he carried through Indian-infested country.[17] Although he carried at least one dispatch, he did not earn the bonus. He was assigned to the scouting detachment under First Lieutenant Frank D. Baldwin, who became only the second man in the U.S. Army to be awarded two Congressional Medals of Honor (Tom Custer was the other). Billy Dixon[18] and Amos Chapman[19] were among the detachment of scouts under Baldwin. Bat's immediate superior was Ben Clark, Miles' chief of scouts.

Major Charles E. Compton of the Sixth U.S. Cavalry left Fort Dodge on August 11, 1874[20] with a detachment of troops (including Baldwin and his scouts). General Miles and the main force left Fort Dodge two days later.[21] Field headquarters for the Miles expedition was to Camp Supply. Baldwin and an advanced scouting force of forty-nine men, including Masterson, reached Adobe Walls in late August and engaged the Indians in a light skirmish.[22] Baldwin's force left The Walls on August 20, traveling twenty miles down the north bank of the Canadian River where they crossed to the south bank.[23] Four of Baldwin's advanced scouts met a band of Indians at the mouth of Chicken Creek, and in a light encounter killed one of the hostiles.[24] Baldwin then sent Masterson and another scout, McGent, with dispatches to Miles.[25] Twelve miles west of Antelope Hills in the Indian Territory, Baldwin and his remaining scouts rejoined the main column on August 24.[26]

Six days later—August 30—Miles' troops had their biggest battle of the campaign. Lieutenant Baldwin's detachment of civilian and Delaware Indian scouts under their leader, Fall Leaf, were in advance of the main body of troops when it was attacked south of Mulberry (or Salt) Creek in northern Texas by a large body of Cheyennes. Miles' cavalry came to Baldwin's aid and chased the hostiles for a few miles. The Cheyennes were then joined by more of their numbers. With support from light field guns and Gatling guns, Miles' troops routed the Cheyennes from the field and pursued them for several miles.

Most writers have stated that Bat Masterson was with Baldwin on November 8, 1874 when he rescued two young white girls, Julia and Adelaide German (often erroneously spelled Germain), from the village of Gray Beard on Mulberry Creek. The German girls and their two sisters had been taken captive by the Indians near the Smoky Hill River in Kansas on September 11, 1874, after the hostiles had massacred the other members of their family. Masterson's service as a scout, however, had expired on October 12, 1874[27] with no record of re-enlistment as a scout.

On November 2, 1874, Bat was employed as a civilian teamster at Camp Supply[28] (at the junction of Wolf Creek and the north fork of the Canadian River in present Oklahoma). His salary was thirty-five dollars per month.[29] Bat's enlistment expired on December 26, but he re-enlisted as a teamster for thirty-five dollars on February 11, 1875 and served in this capacity until February 25.[30] The whereabouts and activities of Bat Masterson during most of 1875 are extremely sketchy. He probably worked around Sweetwater, Texas, which was established in 1875 on Sweetwater Creek as a trading post for Fort Richardson. (The name Sweetwater was changed to Mobeetie in 1879.) Between trips to Dodge City and his parents' farm, Bat probably spent the remainder of 1875 at Sweetwater.

Sometime during his stay at Sweetwater Bat met a dance-hall girl named Molly Brennan. Molly was rumored to have been at one time the sweetheart of Billy Thompson, brother of Ben Thompson. She was also said to have been the ex-wife of Joe Brennan, Ellsworth saloon owner. When Bat met Molly she was the love of twenty-nine-year-old Corporal Melvin A. King, a rough-and-tumble soldier of Company H, Fourth U.S. Cavalry, and veteran of the War Between the States. He was the same King whom Wyatt Earp allegedly tamed and curried at Wichita. Military records

show that King's real name was Anthony Cook[31] and that he was a veteran Indian fighter under Brevet Brigadier General Ranald S. Mackenzie. King's rank is generally listed as sergeant, but the Adjutant General's Office in 1876 and 1877 stated that he held the rank of corporal at the time of his death.[32]

King grew jealous when Molly Brennan became the sweetheart of Bat Masterson. On January 24, 1876, Masterson and King fought over her affections. When the gunsmoke had cleared Molly Brennan was dead, King lay dying, and Bat was severely wounded in the pelvic bone. King died on January 25[33] in the military cantonment at Sweetwater. For years it has been written that King fired at Bat, but that Molly threw her body in front of Masterson, receiving King's bullet and dying as a result. The bullet which struck Molly is said to have passed through her body and struck Bat in the pelvis. Then as Bat either fell or lay wounded, he fired at King, and it was fatal.[34] Legend, of course, has Ben Thompson rushing to the aid of the fallen Masterson to protect him from the would-be vengeance of some of King's Army friends.

The *Jacksboro* (Texas) *Frontier Echo* of February 11, 1876 carried a late account of the King-Brennan killings minus the alleged heroics of Thompson:

Telegraphic News: King, of H. Company, 4th Cavalry, and a woman, Molly Braman [sic], killed at San Antonio [sic] by a citizen.

If the reporter who filed the above dispatch did not err in stating that King and Molly Brennan had been murdered by the same person, it would seem that Bat Masterson was the one who killed his sweetheart

Western notables of all kinds, from wanted road agents to federal agents and inspectors, passed through this tiny depot at Dodge City, on a spur of the Atcheson, Topeka & Santa Fe from Fort Dodge. This was the first building passengers saw when disembarking from the steam cars, the last place when leaving the rowdy town.

(even though his name was not actually mentioned in the dispatch). Bat's wound was serious, but he eventually recovered. It has been said that military doctors treated the injury, but there is no record of this.[35]

The whereabouts of Bat Masterson during the remainder of 1876 are difficult to pinpoint. Probably he was often at Dodge City where old-timers remembered him walking about with a cane. The pelvic wound he had received in the King fight left him with a perpetual limp. Other reports place him at Cheyenne, Wyoming, Denver, and Sidney, Nebraska, at one time or another during 1876.

By the spring of 1877 Bat was living at Dodge City. By April of that year he and

Ben Springer had purchased a combination saloon and dance hall,[36] which was also a house of prostitution. Their saloon license was granted by the city council on May 1.[37] A little more than a month later, on June 6, Bat had a fight with City Marshal Larry Deger when the huge lawman was escorting little Robert Gilmore, alias "Bobby Gill," the town tramp, to jail. Bat felt that Deger was unnecessarily manhandling Gilmore and he interceded. Policeman Joseph W. Mason and about six Texas trail hands came to Deger's aid. Bat however kept fighting and Deger pistol-whipped him severely as the others held him. Bat was disarmed and taken to jail, and the following day Police Judge Daniel M. Frost fined him twenty-five dollars and costs.[38] About a month later Bat's friend, Mayor James (Dog) Kelley, returned ten dollars of the fine money to him.[39]

Before the summer had passed Bat had secured the position of undersheriff of Ford County under his friend and fellow gambler Charlie Bassett. Deger was concurrently a deputy sheriff of Bassett and in late July or early August, Bat dismissed Deger from his position.[40]

Mayor Kelley appointed Bat as a special policeman on September 17 at $2.50 per day.[41] He held this position until September 27.[42] During that time, he and his brother Ed (who was then assistant marshal under

Courtesy Kansas State Historical Society, Topeka
James H. ("Dog") Kelley (*left*) was a powerful figure in Dodge City, and four times its mayor. He was the political leader of the rough town's gambling and saloon faction. Shown with him is Charles S. Hungerford, a councilman and personal friend, and, at the lower center of the photograph, one of Kelley's favorite hounds.

Courtesy Kansas State Historical Society, Topeka
Lawrence E. Deger was the Dodge City marshal in 1876-77 when Bat Masterson began operating a saloon. He threw Masterson in jail for interfering with an arrest.

Deger) were involved in a shooting scrape on September 25 with a Texas cowhand named A. C. Jackson. Jackson mounted his cow pony and rode down Front Street. He stopped before the Alhambra Saloon and fired his revolver two or three times. Bat ordered him to stop but Jackson demurred and shot his revolver again. Bat fired at the drunken trail hand, but missed. Ed Masterson also triggered a wild shot at Jackson. Jackson spurred his mount and Bat and Ed fired second shots at Jackson, but again their bullets missed their mark. Bat mounted a horse and rode after Jackson,

Jim Masterson was also in Dodge and served as a deputy sheriff under his brother Bat, who was the choice of the voters over Larry Deger. As with the Earps, the Masterson brothers backed up each other.

but soon discovered that his pistol was empty and that he had no ammunition.[43]

By October Bat had decided to run for the office of sheriff of Ford County.[44] Charlie Bassett, the incumbent, was prohibited by the state constitution from seeking a third consecutive term. Bat had the political backing of Mayor Kelley, who headed Dodge City's sporting fraternity (of which Bat was a member), and incumbent Bassett, a professional gambler by choice and a peace officer by circumstances. Bat agreed to appoint Bassett as his undersheriff, if elected. Bat's opponent was his old adversary, Larry Deger. The election was held on November 6, 1877, and Bat defeated Deger

by only three votes, 166-163.[45] Mayor Kelley relieved Deger of his duties as marshal on December 4 and appointed Ed Masterson as city marshal.[46] Deger decided to retaliate against Bat Masterson and his political backers. He filed a contest of election suit, but in January 1878, he withdrew the suit because he wanted to avoid involving his friends in his trouble. [47]

Bat officially took office on January 14, 1878[48] and immediately appointed his assistants, although Bassett allowed him to assume the duties of sheriff as early as January 2.[49] Bat appointed Charlie as undersheriff. Bassett served concurrently as assistant marshal under Ed Masterson. Bat also appointed Simeon Woodruff as a deputy sheriff and John W. Straughn as jailor.[50] By August 1878, William Duffey had replaced Woodruff as deputy sheriff.[51] Later, at least by January 1879, Jim Masterson was serving as a deputy sheriff under his brother.[52] Although a Dodge City policeman and later city marshal, Jim concurrently held his commission as deputy sheriff. Bassett remained concurrently as undersheriff and city marshal (having succeeded the late Ed Masterson as city marshal in April 1878) until November 4, 1879, when he resigned both positions.[53] Jim Masterson succeeded Bassett as marshal.[54] Charlie, however, was back serving as Bat's deputy by at least early January 1880.[55] Another man, A. S. Tracy, was Bat's deputy at one time in 1878.[56] Bat also had two deputy sheriffs (on separate occasions) for the town of Speareville, located about fifteen miles northeast of Dodge City. The first man to hold the position was Murray Wear, and he was succeeded by L. M. Depuy on January 18, 1879.[57]

The notorious Long Branch Saloon was a hangout for the hard-drinking man. As shown in this rare interior photograph, it was a far cry from the lavish palaces depicted a century later on television Westerns. It was long, narrow, and utilitarian. At one time or another, most all the famous gunfighters drank at this bar, among them Wyatt Earp, Bat Masterson, Doc Holliday, Luke Short, and Ben Thompson.

Bat was in office less than a month when on January 27, five men were foiled in their attempt to rob the Santa Fe at the railroad station in Kinsley, a town about thirty-seven miles northeast of Dodge City. Bat organized a posse and started on the trail of the outlaws. Another posse was organized comprised of citizens of Kinsley, but Bat refused to cooperate with this posse. On February 1 Masterson, J. J. Webb, "Prairie Dog Dave" Morrow, and Kinch Riley captured two of the robbers, Dave Rudabaugh and Ed West, near the mouth of Crooked Creek about sixty miles south of Dodge City.

(Ironically, Rudabaugh and Webb later became close friends.)

For the remainder of February, Bat followed every lead concerning the whereabouts of the other Kinsley bandits. On March 15 two of the outlaws were arrested in Dodge City by Bat and Ed Masterson, Charlie Bassett, and Policeman Nat L. Haywood. The second pair of robbers was identified as J. D. Green and Tom Gott, alias "Dugan." They had been in Dodge City trying to learn about the activities of Masterson and his posse. Meanwhile, Dave Rudabaugh was released after agreeing to turn state's evidence against his fellow robbers.[58] The fifth robber, Mike Rourke, evaded Masterson's capture.

An interesting side story to the Kinsley affair was that in early February, Bat Masterson had the unpleasant task of arresting his friend, Bill Tilghman, for complicity in the attempted robbery.[59] (Tilghman later became city marshal at Dodge City and subsequently a deputy U.S. marshal in the Oklahoma Territory.) Tilghman, however, was dismissed from the jurisdiction of the court on the motion of J. E. McArthur, Edwards County attorney[60] (in which county Kinsley was located). In April of that year Bat again had to arrest his friend Tilghman on a charge of horse theft.[61] Again Tilghman was discharged by the court.[62]

The coming of Dodge City's cattle season in the spring of 1878 brought tragedy to Bat Masterson in a left-handed way. On the night of April 9, City Marshal Ed Masterson and Policeman Nat Haywood, who was acting assistant marshal in the temporary absence of Charlie Bassett, tried to quell a disturbance in the Lady Gay Saloon and Dance Hall. Alfred M. Walker, a trail boss, and five of his trail hands had driven a herd of cattle to Hays City and were celebrating the trail's end at the Lady Gay. One of the cowhands, twenty-seven-year-old John Wagner, was the chief hell-raiser; Ed Masterson disarmed him and gave his pistol to Walker with orders not to give it back until Wagner was sober. Walker, however, returned the pistol to Wagner. A few minutes later Walker, Wagner, and four of Walker's other cowhands—Thomas Highlander, John Hungate, John Reece and Thomas Roads— accosted Masterson and Haywood in front of the Lady Gay. Masterson saw that Wagner was again armed and attempted to disarm him. Wagner refused; he and Ed began scuffling. Haywood stepped forward to aid Masterson. Walker and another cowhand drew their pistols and Wagner snapped a shot in Haywood's face, but fortunately the cylinder only clicked.[63]

Wagner then fired his pistol. The bullet struck Ed Masterson in the stomach, the closeness of the shot setting his shirt afire. Ed drew his pistol and triggered four shots in quick succession. One bullet struck Wagner in the left side of the bowels.[64] Walker was hit three times, once in the left lung[65] and twice in the right arm which was shattered.[66] Some of the shots accidentally grazed the faces of two innocent bystanders.[67] Wagner ran into A. J. Peacock's saloon and collapsed to the floor.[68] Walker also rushed into Peacock's and out through the rear entrance, collapsing some distance from the back door.[69] He was carried to a room over Wright, Beverly & Co.'s store.[70] Wagner also was taken there. Although seriously wounded, Walker eventually recovered.[71] Wagner however succumbed on April 10.[72] Ed Masterson staggered into G. M. Hoover's saloon and collapsed on the floor.[73] George Hinkle, the bartender, was the first to inform Bat that Ed had been shot.[74] Ed was carried to Bat's room[75] on Bridge Street (now Second Avenue) where he died within the hour. Bat was beside himself with grief at the death of his favorite brother. He arrested Highlander, Hungate, Reece and Roads for their part in the death of his brother, but they were released for lack of evidence.[76]

It is a generally accepted theory among Western buffs that Bat Masterson was the

Chalk Beeson was co-owner of the Long Branch. He knew all the Dodge City notables and witnessed the buildup of a lot of action across his bar. Like the major watering holes in all the Western towns, the Long Branch was a combination social hall, business "office," and liars' club where many a tall yarn was spun.

one who shot Wagner and Walker, and not his brother Ed. Both the *Ford County Globe* and the *Dodge City Times* (which at that time was particularly pro-Bat and rarely missed an opportunity to publish his name), did not mention Bat's name in connection with the shooting of Wagner and Walker. However, on at least two occasions Tom Masterson, Jr., stated that it was Bat who shot the two cowhands.[77] The younger Masterson said that Policeman Haywood had fled and Ed had Wagner pinned against a building when Bat arrived at the scene. Bat then shot Wagner, but Ed could not see Bat in the bad light; he released Wagner and reached for his pistol, thinking another cowhand had fired the shot. When Ed let go of Wagner, Walker shot him in the abdomen, and in turn was shot by Bat Masterson.[78] We know, however, that Wagner confessed to killing Ed Masterson.[79] Tom Masterson, of course, was not an eyewitness to the shooting.

One eyewitness, George W. Reighard, a

Dodge City freighter, nearly a half century later said that it was Bat Masterson who shot Wagner and Walker,[80] but his account of the shooting contains many inaccuracies. Ham Bell, who watched the shooting from a window in Peacock's saloon, said many years later that he would not make any statement, one way or the other, as to who shot Wagner and Walker.[81] Bat Masterson also never made a public statement on the incident.

The death of his brother took something out of Bat. Life itself was never quite the same for him. While Bat was recovering from his grief, Dodge City was experiencing its most violent year as a cow town. In May of that year Thomas Gallagher, a cowhand, was killed by lightning near Buckner Creek, eighteen miles northwest of Dodge City. That same month Alice Chambers, the ex-mistress of Phil Coe, died in a saloon brawl and reputedly became the only woman buried on Dodge City's famous Boot Hill. On July 13, Deputy U.S. Marshal Harry T. McCarty of Ford County was fatally shot while drinking at the Long Branch Saloon. In August, George Hoyt was killed and in September, several homesteaders and cow-hands in Ford County were murdered by the Cheyennes under Dull Knife and Little Wolf.

More bloodshed came on the early morning of October 4, 1878, when variety actress Fannie Keenan was mistakenly killed by cowhand Jim ("Spike") Kenedy, son of Texas cattleman, Mifflin Kenedy. Fannie Keenan was also known as Dora Hand in Dodge City. She had played several variety houses in the South and was well known in both Memphis and Saint Louis. Prior to coming to Dodge in 1878, she had played a two-year engagement in Saint Louis.[82]

The tragic circumstances which led to Fannie Keenan's death began on August 17, 1878, when Jim Kenedy was drunk and disorderly in Mayor Dog Kelley's Alhambra Saloon. Kelley had City Marshal Charlie Bassett arrest Kenedy for being disorderly[83] at the Alhambra and Comique Theater. Kenedy, like many other Texas trail hands who came to Dodge City, considered peace officers as Bassett, Wyatt Earp and the Mastersons nothing more than "fighting pimps" who enforced the law as Dog Kelley wanted it enforced. Kenedy decided to assassinate Kelley.

On the early morning of October 4, Kenedy rode up to the front of Kelley's shack below the Dead Line and fired two shots into the air and two more through the front door. What Kenedy did not know was that Kelley was not in his shack. He had been ill two or three weeks and on September 30 was hospitalized in the infirmary at Fort Dodge.[84] Fannie Keenan and another variety actress, Fannie Garrettson, were asleep in the two-room shack. The first bullet which penetrated the front door struck the floor and went through the carpet, then glanced upward through the plaster partition dividing the two rooms, and finally lodged in the back room. The second bullet hit the front door at a slightly higher elevation than the first. This projectile struck the bedclothing of the first bed, which was occupied by Miss Garrettson, passed through two quilts and the partition. It struck the bedclothing of the second bed which was occupied by Fannie Keenan, passed through the coverings, and entered her right side,

Courtesy Library, State Historical Society of Colorado
Trinidad, in southern Colorado, was the scene of a dramatic exchange in 1879 when Bat Masterson learned that local authorities were holding Dutch Henry Borne, a notorious horse thief. Masterson traveled to Trinidad and, after much red tape, was able to bring the prisoner to Kansas for trial.

just beneath the arm, killing her almost instantly.[85]

Just why Fannie Keenan and Fannie Garrettson were sleeping in Dog Kelley's house has never been explained. Legend has Miss Keenan as Kelley's mistress. Others say that the girls were only renting the mayor's place during his hospitalization. At any rate, Fannie Keenan was laid to rest with honors in Dodge City's new Prairie Grove Cemetery.

Assistant Marshal Wyatt Earp and Policeman Jim Masterson were among the first to reach the murder scene. They soon became suspicious of Kenedy and another man who were in a nearby saloon. The two officers decided to question the pair, but Kenedy fled before they could do so. His companion was taken into custody, but it was later proved that he had nothing to do with Fannie Keenan's murder.

Later that day Bat Masterson organized a posse consisting of himself, Charlie Bassett, Wyatt Earp, Bill Duffey, and Bill Tilghman, who was specially deputized to serve as a posse member. (The others were peace officers of one type or another.) Bat and his posse caught up with Kenedy late on the afternoon of October 5 near Meade City, about thirty-five miles southwest of Dodge City. Kenedy tried to outride the posse and was fired upon. His horse was shot from under him by three bullets and

Bat Masterson returned his famed prisoner, Dutch Henry Borne, to Kansas from this railroad station at Trinidad, Colorado. However, his efforts were in vain, for Borne was acquitted of his crime in Ford County. Bat was attracted by what he saw in Colorado and later went there to live.

he was severely wounded in the left shoulder.[86] Kenedy was returned to Dodge City, but was later acquitted of Fannie Keenan's murder.

The murder of Fannie Keenan culminated Dodge City's most violent year on the frontier. But Bat Masterson's troubles as sheriff of Ford County continued. In late December, Bat received word that the West's most notorious horse thief, Henrich ("Dutch Henry") Borne, was at Trinidad, Colorado. Bat telegraphed authorities in Trinidad to arrest Borne and hold him. He arrived there on New Year's Day 1879, only to find that Trinidad authorities wanted five hundred dollars to release Borne to Kansas authorities, claiming they could receive that amount for him in Nevada.[87] After much legal red tape, Bat took his cele-

brated prisoner to Dodge City on January 7. Despite Bat's trouble in bringing him to Kansas, Dutch Henry was acquitted of his Ford County crimes because of lack of evidence.[88] By January 18 Bat had been appointed a deputy U.S. marshal[89] to serve under U.S. Marshal Benjamin F. Simpson. Bat held his commission until May 1880, when he was replaced by Ham Bell.[90]

As sheriff and deputy U.S. marshal, Bat Masterson was kept busy, but he nevertheless found time to invest in several South Side saloons, dance halls and houses of prostitution. While he was frequently out of Dodge City on legal business, Bat usually left his surly-tempered, quick-triggered brother Jim in charge of his gambling interests. It is little wonder that the Mastersons, Wyatt Earp and Charlie Bassett were called "fighting pimps" by the Texas trail hands. While on duty as sheriff in Dodge City, Bat looked as if he were anything but a cow-town peace officer. He dressed in fashionable tailor-made Eastern clothes. He wore a white derby hat and carried a cane. He carried a stocky 175 pounds on a five foot ten inch frame. He had gray eyes and brown hair. His mustache (which he shaved in later life) was thick, but he kept it closely clipped and did not allow it to droop as was the custom of the era. Strangers arriving for the first time in Dodge City were frequently mistaking him for an Eastern dude.

In February 1879, Bat traveled to Fort Leavenworth with Charlie Bassett, Jim Masterson, an A. J. French and one "Kokomo" Sullivan to identify several Cheyenne warriors who were being held by the Army for several depredations committed in September, 1878. The real purpose of Bat's mission was to escort the identified warriors to Dodge City where they would be tried for their crimes. The identification was made and military authorities transferred seven of the Cheyennes (belonging to Dull Knife's band) to the custody of Kansas Adjutant General P. S. Noble, who had a warrant for their arrest. General Noble then turned custody of the prisoners over to Bat and his party.[91] The seven Cheyennes had a preliminary hearing at Dodge City and were granted a change of venue to Lawrence.[92] Masterson and Bassett transported the prisoners to Lawrence, but they were later acquitted for lack of evidence.[93] This arrest cost the county $4,000,[94] and this fact was later used against Bat in his reelection campaign.

Meanwhile, Bat was having trouble with his superior, George B. Cox, chairman of the board of Ford County commissioners. The *Ford County Globe* in its issue of March 18, 1879 reported that the Masterson-Cox relationship had not been amicable and that Cox had resigned his position. The *Globe* alleged that the cause of Cox's resignation was because of a lack of harmony between

Courtesy Library, State Historical Society of Colorado
Railroad officials of the Santa Fe sought Bat Masterson's help during the Royal Gorge "war" with the Denver and Rio Grande. Masterson quickly recruited a force in Dodge to help the Santa Fe. He made Canon City (*above*) his headquarters and left gunfighter Ben Thompson in charge.

the board of county commissioners and Masterson and his deputies. Masterson had given himself *carte blanche* as sheriff, to the dissatisfaction of Cox.

Shortly after Commissioner Cox's resignation Bat became involved in the now-famous war between the Santa Fe and the Denver, Rio Grande and Western Railroad. The Santa Fe contested the Rio Grande's right-of-way through the Grand Canyon of the Arkansas River—the Royal Gorge—near Pueblo, Colorado. On March 20, 1879, Santa Fe officials at Canon City, Colorado, wired Masterson asking him to recruit a company of men to aid their line in its fight.[95] Bat rounded up thirty men and left Dodge City two days later.[96] He had no legal authority to help the Santa Fe and was acting in the capacity of a private citizen.

Legend has Doc Holliday among Masterson's hired gunfighters. There are no records, however, of the Santa Fe which show the names of the men with Bat nor how much they were paid, although there are reports that they were paid variously from $1.50 to $3.00 a day and higher. Ben Thompson reportedly was with Bat's group.[97]

Bat returned to Dodge City on April 5,[98] leaving Thompson in charge of the men he left behind. Bat, however, went back to Canon City on June 9, 1879[99] to take command of a roundhouse which blocked the Rio Grande's right of way through the Royal Gorge. The *Dodge City Times* of June 14 reported Bat's defense of the roundhouse:

"... He [Masterson] had been placed there, but surrendered his authority upon writs being served by U.S. officers...."

After surrendering the roundhouse, Bat returned to Dodge City with fifty men on June 12.[100] The war between the Santa Fe and Rio Grande was eventually settled out of court.

By September, 1879, opposition to Masterson's reelection as sheriff was forming. The out-county farmers were reportedly tired of Masterson.[101] George Hinkle proved to be Bat's opposition. Bat was nominated on the Independent ticket and the *Dodge City Times* backed Bat for reelection while the opposition was supported by the *Ford County Globe*. The *Globe* accused Masterson of causing Ford County an unnecessary expense of four thousand dollars in the arrest of the seven Cheyenne Indians the previous February.[102] The *Times* earlier explained Bat's expenses by saying that he had to police thirteen unorganized counties attached to Ford for judicial purposes and that it cost something to oversee such a large territory.[103]

The election was held November 4 and Hinkle defeated Masterson by a vote margin of 404 to 268.[104] Robert Fry, editor of the *Speareville News,* had worked for Masterson's defeat, and even after the election he continued to write articles that were detrimental to Bat's character. Fry published a letter from one Charles Roden, who had worked against Masterson in the election, in which Roden said that Bat struck him several times in the office of Dodge City attorney T. S. Jones, and that outside the office, Jim Masterson searched his pockets for a pistol. Roden stated that afterwards he discovered that his wallet was missing.[105] Attorney Jones later informed Fry that Roden acted as if he were going to draw a pistol and that Masterson, who was unarmed (Jones was obviously in error when he stated that Masterson, a gunfighter and peace officer, was unarmed), struck him several times.[106] Bat finally tired of Fry's libel and decided to do a little libeling of his own. He wrote the *Dodge City Times* and stated in part, ". . . The word sonofabitch I strictly confined to the Speareville editor, for I don't know of any other in Ford County."[107] It must have given Bat a great deal of satisfaction when as a deputy U.S. marshal he arrested his old political adversary, Daniel M. Frost, co-editor of the *Ford County Globe,* on November 30, 1879. Frost was charged with purchasing stolen U.S. government property.[108]

Bat officially left office on January 12, 1880[109] and the following month struck out for Leadville, Colorado. During the next several months Masterson divided his time between Dodge City, Leadville, and Gunnison County, Colorado. Bat was at Dodge City living with Annie Ladue, a nineteen-year-old concubine,[110] when in July 1880 he received a wire from Ben Thompson in Texas asking him to rescue Ben's brother Billy from a possible lynching at Ogallala, a Nebraska cow town[111] on the Western Trail. Billy Thompson and another Texas man, Jim Tucker,[112] had shot each other in a gun duel at Ogallala in June and Billy had been seriously wounded.[113] Ben feared that the citizens of Ogallala would lynch Billy. Bat, who throughout his life showed a staunch loyalty to his friends, went to Ogallala and brought Billy Thompson to Dodge City in a wagon.[114] Legend has Bat sneaking Billy out of Ogallala under the watchful eyes of the law and hiding at the home of Buffalo Bill Cody at North Platte, Nebraska, until

Thompson was well enough to travel. (Cody's home at North Platte and later his famous Scout's Rest Ranch there were famous for Western hospitality. The Codys' played host to many Western personalities while they lived at North Platte.) Later in the year, Bat became a resident of Kansas City. In early December, 1880, he returned to Dodge City,[115] but on February 8, 1881, he left Dodge for Tombstone[116] where he joined his friend Wyatt Earp at the Oriental Saloon.

Bat was at Tombstone in April, 1881, when he received a telegram from his brother Jim, now an ex-marshal, to come to Dodge City and aid him in a difficulty with A. J. Peacock and Alpha (Al) Updegraff. Jim Masterson and Peacock were partners in the Lady Gay Saloon and Dance Hall, and one of the girls employed there was allegedly robbed by a friend of Jim Masterson. Updegraff, who was a bartender at the Lady Gay, told the girl to file charges against Masterson's friend. Jim tried to get Updegraff to talk the girl out of preferring charges, but the bartender refused. Masterson then attempted to fire Updegraff, but Peacock, who was a friend of Updegraff, objected. Trouble between Masterson and Updegraff became worse, each man took a shot at the other, and Updegraff had Masterson arrested. Peacock and Updegraff were soon "posted" that Bat Masterson was coming to Dodge City to aid Jim.

Bat arrived at Dodge City on April 16. He immediately saw Peacock and Updegraff as he stepped from the train. He called to them, and the two men darted for cover. All three immediately commenced firing. Several friends of the three men joined in the shooting. Jim Masterson, Charlie Ronan, and Tom O'Brien backed Bat in the shoot-out. The firing ceased when Bat and Peacock ran out of ammunition, and Updegraff had one bullet left.[117] Updegraff and a James Anderson were the only men hit during the brief fight. Updegraff received a bullet in the right lung,[118] from which he later recovered. Anderson was struck in the back from a ricocheting bullet.[119]

Mayor Alonzo B. ("Ab") Webster and Sheriff Fred Singer placed Bat under arrest. He was taken to the police court and fined ten dollars, including costs, for his part in the fight.[120] Later in the day, Bat and Jim Masterson left Dodge City after Jim Masterson sold his interest in the Lady Gay. It was thought that Updegraff's wound would prove fatal, but he eventually recovered. If it was Bat's bullet which struck Updegraff, then he was the last man—red or white—that Bat Masterson shot. Beyond 1881, Masterson was able to live on his reputation as a gunfighter.

From 1881 to 1887 Bat Masterson made frequent visits to Dodge City, taking quite an active interest in politics there. He was with Luke Short during Short's troubles there in 1883. On November 1, 1884, Bat published his one-edition-only newspaper the *Vox Populi* at Dodge City.[121] And in March, 1886, as a special deputy sheriff of Ford County, he closed (temporarily) all the saloons in Dodge City and filed arrest warrants against the saloon owners.[122] (Kansas had been legally "dry" since 1880.)

Despite his visits to Dodge and his periodic trips to various Western towns and cities, Bat Masterson became a permanent resident of Denver for twenty-one years, 1881-1902, except for brief residencies at Lamar and Creede, Colorado. By 1889

Masterson had settled down as a professional gambler in Denver, which was then the sporting capital of the nation. In 1890 Bat was managing Ed Chaise's Palace Saloon and Gambling House.[123] The Palace Saloon also had a variety theater and on November 21, 1891, Bat married Miss Emma Walters, one of the actresses at the theater. This was Bat's first and only marriage, although in 1886 he had eloped with Mrs. Nellie Spencer (nee McMahon), the wife of Louis Spencer, a well-known Denver variety actor.[124] Masterson and Spencer had fought over the woman on the night of September 8, 1886, and Bat struck the actor with his pistol.[125] The papers reported that Bat and Nellie had eloped to Dodge City,[126] but no record of their marriage (if, indeed, they were married) has been found. The marriage of Bat and Emma lasted until Bat's death in 1921. Mrs. Masterson died in 1932.[127] There were no children born to the union.

Early in 1892 Masterson secured employment with the Denver gambling firm of Watrous, Banninger and Company. During 1892 and 1893 Bat was in the mining town of Creede managing this company's gambling operations.[128] (Robert Ford, the killer of Jesse James, was also at Creede in 1892 operating a saloon before he was killed there on June 8, 1892). The *Leoti* (Kansas) *Standard* of March 3, 1892, reported that Bat was city marshal at Creede. The obituary of Masterson which appeared in the *Rocky Mountain News* of Denver on October 26, 1921, stated that he had been a deputy sheriff at Creede. Lute Johnson, a correspondent of the *Denver Republican*, met Masterson at Creede about this time and reported that he had been for several years a

Creede, in southern Colorado near the upper Rio Grande River, was as rough and tumble as it appears here, a tent city as tough as the torn mountains surrounding it. A famous Western ballad declared that "There Is No Night in Creede." Bat Masterson was engaged in gambling operations here, then became a lawman.

Creede was a typical mining camp of the Rocky Mountains with its hastily constructed buildings clinging to the steep hillsides. The railroad ran there, bringing in the miners and taking out the ore. It also brought in a full share of toughs, who soon learned to fear Bat Masterson.

deuputy sheriff of Arapahoe County, when the city of Denver was located in Arapahoe County.[129] A list of Colorado marshals and sheriffs for the period of 1859 to 1964 does not list Bat Masterson.[130] The sheriff's office records for Denver, when it was in Arapahoe County, does not list Masterson.[131] Quite possibly Bat was city marshal at Creede before that town had a regular police force. In many frontier towns when the city had no regular police force, several citizens merely hired a man for the job, usually one with a fast-gun reputation. Bat was probably signed up in this capacity.

There seems to be some additional evidence that Masterson was city marshal at Creede from one of correspondent Johnson's undated dispatches: "... *All the toughs and thugs fear him as they do no other dozen men in camp. Let an incipient riot start and all that is necessary to quell it is the whisper, 'There comes Masterson'. ...*"[132] Judging from Johnson's report, Masterson did a competent job as city marshal at Creede. Creede was one of the last boom towns before the passing of the frontier; at the time Bat was there, it was overrun with gunmen, cardsharps, con men, and prostitutes. The local Boot Hill was called "Shotgun Graveyard."[133] The frontier was then in its twilight years, and both Creede and its marshal were throwbacks to an older era and more violent way of life. Bat must have felt right at home.

By 1894 Bat was again residing full time in Denver, by then the capital of the West. In 1897 he traveled to Carson City, Nevada, where he lost a large amount of money backing heavyweight champion "Gentleman Jim" Corbett in his fight with Bob Fitzsimmons. Fitzsimmons knocked out Cor-

bett in the fourteenth round with his famous "solar-plexus punch." In 1899 Bat became associated with a motley group of Denver sporting men, including Otto Floto, the celebrated sports editor of the *Denver Post*, who lent the use of his name to a circus owned by Harry H. Tammen and Frederick G. Bonfils, the circus-crazed publishers of the *Denver Post*. Tammen and Bonfils were later business associates of Buffalo Bill Cody. Masterson, Floto, and Company formed the Colorado Athletic Association, a fight promotion organization. Bat's position with the association was that of official referee.[134] Floto, however, decided to take full control. Masterson and a few of the backers in the original association broke away by July, 1899, and formed the rival Olympic Athletic Club.[135] Bat was elected president.[136] Bat and Floto had a falling out because of Masterson's new club. On one occasion Bat and the sports editor had words and Bat struck Floto with his cane.[137] The rivalry between the two clubs resulted in a financial drain on both Masterson and Floto. Unfortunately for Bat, Floto had powerful and influential friends, which meant an unlimited source of revenue. Bat also was paying heavy bribes to the Denver police force to allow him to promote prize fights within the city limits. (During the early days of the Masterson-Floto rivalry, prize fighting was illegal in Colorado.)

By 1902 Bat Masterson was a disillusioned, almost-broke, middle-aged man. The frontier and a way of life that Bat and others like him had known all their lives was gone forever. Even the days of the free-lance professional gambler were over. Gamblers had now formed cliques and began concealing their gambling activities under the cloak of respectability. A disillusioned Bat Masterson turned to drink. Denver authorities became tired of a drunken ex-frontier relic and asked him to move on. It hurt his pride beyond comprehension, but he left the city. Although somewhat late in life, leaving Denver in 1902 was the turning point for Masterson.

Bat traveled east to (of all places) New York City, arriving there in June 1902. En route from Chicago Bat had met two men, Joseph C. Sullivan and Leopold Frank. Masterson, Sullivan and Frank had played cards with George H. Snow, an elder in the Mormon Church, on the train to New York. Elder Snow lost $16,000 to the three men. On arriving in New York, Snow informed the police department that he had been fleeced by Masterson and his companions. A Detective Captain Gaugan of the New York City police department arrested Bat, charging him with grand larceny and carrying a concealed weapon. Sullivan and Frank were also arrested. Marked cards were found in their possession.[138] John Considine, Sr., the theatrical manager (his clients at one time or another included Charlie Chaplin, Marie Dressler and Will Rogers) came to Bat's aid by paying his $1,000 bail.[139] The charge against Bat was eventually dropped when Snow admitted that he wasn't certain that Masterson had cheated him.[140] Later in the month the New York police again arrested Bat on a charge of carrying a concealed weapon.[141]

Considine had met Masterson out West and had always considered Bat one of his best friends. Fortunately, Bat had made other friends in the West who would prove useful to him in New York. One of these was William E. Lewis, editor of the *New York Morning Telegram.* Lewis talked Bat into joining the paper as a sports writer. Alfred H. Lewis, brother of William, became fond of Bat and later wrote a highly fictionized novel based on Masterson's exploits at the Adobe Walls fight. Some of the more prominent people who became friends of Bat in New York were Damon Runyon; Charles Stoneham, owner of the New York Baseball Giants; Louella Parsons, later famous as a Hollywood columnist; Victor McLaglen, part-time prize fighter and later famous as an actor; and heavyweight champions Jack Johnson, Jess Willard, and Jack Dempsey.

In New York Bat had the fortunate pleasure of meeting President Theodore Roosevelt, who had a special fondness for men who had lived on the frontier during the wild days. While Roosevelt was President, Bat was a frequent guest at the White House. Some of Bat's friends had served in Roosevelt's "Rough Riders" regiment during the Spanish-American War. Roosevelt offered Masterson an appointment as U.S. marshal for the Oklahoma Territory in 1905. Masterson declined on the grounds that he would be a mark for every young boy who wanted to make a fast-gun reputation for himself. Bat's fighting days were behind him and he knew it. Besides, he was beginning to relish the cosmopolitan atmosphere of New York. Roosevelt, nevertheless, wanted Bat as a peace officer and at the personal request of the President, Bat was appointed a deputy U.S. marshal[142] for the Southern District of New York on March 28, 1905.[143] Bat technically served under U. S. Marshal William Henkel at a salary of

$2,000 a year, which was one of the highest salaries ever paid (at that time) to a deputy U.S. Marshal.[144]

Masterson was assigned to the U.S. Attorney's Office for the Southern District.[145] He seems to have done very little in his capacity as a deputy marshal. Bat's main duty was being in charge of the grand jury room.[146] Most of his time was taken up with journalism, and in 1907 he wrote or dictated a series of articles for *Human Life Magazine* on five gunfighters he had known in the old days. Alfred H. Lewis may have ghost-written the articles for Bat, but the articles, nonetheless, brought Bat much recognition as a journalist.

On June 16, 1909, Henry A. Wise, the U. S. Attorney for the Southern District of New York, notified the U.S. Attorney General that Masterson's services were no longer needed.[147] President William Howard Taft was informed of Wise's decision on June 23, 1909.[148] On June 29, Taft authorized the U. S. Attorney General to discharge Bat.[149] Alfred Lewis belatedly wrote President Taft on July 10 asking him to retain Bat as a deputy U.S. marshal.[150] Marshal Henkel was informed by the Attorney General on July 12 that Masterson was to be dismissed unless he was needed in that capacity.[151] Two days later Henkel informed the Attorney General that Masterson was not needed,[152] and on July 15, the Attorney General authorized Henkel to advise Masterson that his office would be abolished and discontinued from and after August 1, 1909.[153]

Bat decided to continue his journalistic career full time and became sports editor of the *Morning Telegraph*. As the sports editor of a major New York newspaper, Bat grew into quite a prominent journalist, one of the leading prizefight critics in American journalism. He had come a long way since the dusty streets of Dodge City.

Bat's twilight years were not as tranquil as one might suspect. He was involved in several disputes which were usually settled verbally rather than with violence as had been Bat's custom. On one occasion in May, 1907, at the Belmont race track in New York, Bat resorted to the old ways when he clubbed Walter St. Denis, sports editor of the *New York Globe*, in a dispute.[154] In 1911 he became involved with Frank D. Ufer, a millionaire sportsman, over the ability of a heavyweight fighter named Carl Morris, whom Ufer managed. Ufer declared in print that Masterson had shot drunken Mexicans and Indians in the back and that he (Bat) was a badman. Masterson retaliated by filing a defamation of character suit against Ufer. On February 1, 1913, the suit came to trial[155] and Bat eventually was awarded $3,500 in damages.[156] Two of Bat's character witnesses were Major General Frank D. Baldwin, his old commander from his Indian War days, and Lieutenant General Nelson A. Miles, retired commanding general of the United States Army.[157]

Later, Bat had trouble with Dick Plunkett, whom he had known at Creede. Plunkett made a remark that Masterson was an unsavory character and Bat took offense. He accosted Plunkett and a companion in the bar of the Waldorf-Astoria, but the house detective and two policemen intervened and led Bat away before he could tangle with Plunkett.[158]

Occasionally, Masterson wrote about things other than sports. In December,

1906, he wrote that Chester Gillette, a convicted murderer, had received a travesty of justice at the hands of the court at Herkimer, New York. An arrest warrant was issued for Bat, his publisher, Henry N. Carey, and his editor, William E. Lewis, by Judge Irving R. Devendorf at Herkimer on December 11, 1906, charging them with criminal contempt of court.[159] Masterson and Carey were arraigned before Judge Devendorf at Herkimer on December 17.[160] Bail was set and raised at $2,000 each.[161] Masterson and Carey went to trial at Herkimer on December 17 before Judge Devendorf and later were fined fifty dollars each.[162] Bat and his publisher were ably defended by their attorney, Clarence J. Shearn.[163] Lewis was not tried with Masterson and Carey because of illness.[164]

By 1921 Bat Masterson had become so entrenched in the twentieth century cosmopolitan life of a New York journalist that one could excuse him if the old times on the frontier seemed like a vague memory. It was almost as if he had never been west of the Hudson River. People invariably plagued him about reliving the old days over a round of drinks. He refused to talk much about them. He shaved his mustache, the last vestige of the old era across the Missouri. (In 1921 the mustache had become a symbol of the past to modern American men.)

The end came for Bat at his sports desk on October 25, 1921. Cause of death was a heart attack. He was buried in New York's Woodlawn Cemetery. Somehow Bat's death was out of time and place. A somewhat less prosaic death would have been more fitting, perhaps, for the famed gunfighter who had been so much a part of the frontier.

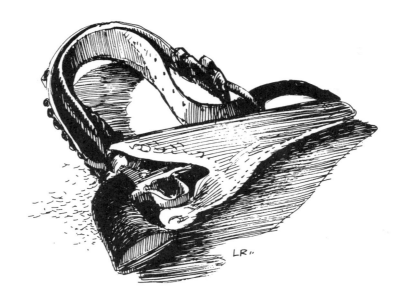

6.

LUKE SHORT

(1854-1893)

UKE L. SHORT was born to J. W. Short[1] (1812-1890)[2] and Hettie Brumley[3] (1827-1908)[4] somewhere in Mississippi in the year 1854.[5] J. W. Short moved his family to Texas by way of Arkansas in 1856.[6] In Texas Luke grew to manhood on his father's farm. When old enough, he left home and hired out as a cowhand. During the 1870s when the Texas cattle trade was at its peak and the drives to the Kansas railheads were a common occurrence, Luke was trailing herds north.

In the Kansas cow towns, Short became disinterested in pursuing the hard work of a cowhand. He was fascinated at the ease with which the professional gamblers made their money at the expense of drunken drovers. He decided to strike out farther north on his own. Sometime in 1876 Short arrived

at Sidney, Nebraska, the last outpost of civilization before reaching the gold-laden, Sioux-held Black Hills of the Dakotas.

In Sidney Luke became a partner of some whiskey peddlers. The names of these men are lost to history, but together with Short, they established what ostensibly was a trading post and in reality was a place where Indians could purchase liquor. Short's "trading post" was about 125 miles north of Sidney near the Nebraska-Dakota Territory line. Luke's chief customers were young Sioux braves who strayed from the Red Cloud Reservation.

Selling whiskey to Indians was, of course, a federal crime. The possibility of being apprehended by the authorities was not the only problem confronting Luke and his partners. Drunken and disgruntled Sioux

Courtesy Kansas State Historical Society, Topeka
Luke Short appears more dandy than dangerous gunfighter in this photograph. He became a wealthy gambler who liked expensive clothes. His right-hand pocket was specially made, a built-in holster, deeper and lined with leather for his gun.

braves were a more immediate threat to the partners. Luke is said to have later admitted that he personally killed six drunken braves and buried each one in a secluded place.[7] Bat Masterson, who was a personal friend of Short, said that Luke was eventually arrested by a detachment of soldiers and taken to Sidney.

At Sidney, Luke was escorted aboard a train bound for Omaha, but sometime thereafter he escaped from his soldier guards.[8] The records of the War Department at the National Archives include no references to the arrest of Short by military authorities in 1877 or 1878.[9] (Luke is said to have been operating his trading post in 1877.) The Social and Economic Records Division of the National Archives has a record of letters received by the Bureau of Indian Affairs relating to the Red Cloud Reservation for the period 1876 to 1878. These records show five men were arrested for selling whiskey to Indians on March 20, 1876. Two of these men were named Day and Fisher; the other three were unnamed. Two other men, Yomans and Lisco, were arrested near Sidney on March 22, 1877, for the same offense. There is no mention of Short in these records.[10]

By 1878 Short had decided to engage in a less precarious occupation. What he did prior to October of that year is not known. For three days, October 6-8, he was employed as a dispatch courier at Sidney[11] during the Cheyenne uprisings of Dull Knife and Little Wolf. Luke was hired at a salary of ten dollars per day[12] to carry dispatches from Ogallala, Nebraska, to Major Thomas T. Thornburgh, Fourth U.S. Infantry, who was in the field. Short was paid thirty dollars for his three-day service.[13] From October 9-20 he served as a civilian scout for Thornburgh (who was killed in the Ute Indian War of 1879), enlisting at Sidney at a rate of $100 per month.[14] When his twelve-day hitch had expired he was paid forty dollars by the government.[15]

Luke reached the mining town of Leadville, Colorado, sometime in the latter part of 1878 or early 1879. Leadville was overrun with miners eager to be departed from their hard-earned diggings. And Leadville had more than its share of tinhorn gamblers

Early in his career, Luke Short made money by selling whiskey illegally to the Indians at a "trading post" north of Sidney, Nebraska. He arrived at Sidney in 1876. The sketch by Lieutenant J. E. Foster shows the barracks in the upper left, near a sizable village, the last outpost going to the Black Hills. Short returned here a few years later to scout for the Army.

Sioux braves from the Red Cloud Reservation were among Luke Short's best customers at his trading post. This is how a reservation encampment appeared to Lieutenant W. H. Carter who made the sketch about the time Short was peddling whiskey there. Somewhere in the center is where Short allegedly buried six of his disgruntled customers.

ready to do just that. Rumor has Luke Short shooting his first white man at Leadville over the placing of a gambling debt. Some sources say the victim's name was Brown and that he tried to bully little Luke into allowing him to have his (Short's) bet which Luke had already placed. Luke objected and the man reached for his pistol. According to the story, Short was quicker. He shot the man in the cheek, seriously wounding him. Since Leadville had no newspaper at this time and such shootings were a common occurrence in such mining camps, this episode in Short's life might have been true.

From Leadville Luke drifted down to Dodge City. There he made friends with fellow gamblers Bat Masterson and Wyatt Earp. Masterson and Earp secured Short employment as a house dealer at Chalk Beeson's and Will Harris's Long Branch Saloon. From 1879 to early 1881, Short seems to have remained in relative obscurity at Dodge City. (For a professional gambler on the frontier to have remained in obscurity for such a length of time was not an easy task.) By early 1881 Luke was a house dealer in the Oriental Saloon at Tombstone. Wyatt Earp had an interest in the Oriental. Other house gamblers there at the time were Bat Masterson and Doc Holliday. The Oriental Saloon, therefore, had the dubious distinction of having had, at one time, the presence of Earp, Holliday, Masterson, and Short, all considered among the West's front-ranked gunfighters. Tombstone residents often referred to this gambling clique as the "Dodge City Gang."

Short's stay at Tombstone was brief, but eventful. On February 25, 1881, he killed his first white man, a well-known sporting man by the name of Charles Storms.[16] Bat Masterson in his biographical treatise on "Famous Gunfighters of the Western Frontier," said that "Charlie Storms was one of the best known gamblers in the entire West and had, on several occasions, successfully defended himself in pistol fights with Western gunfighters."[17] Short and Storms had a difference of opinion over a card game in the Oriental Saloon. (Rumor is that the two men had had trouble at Leadville.) Masterson, who was a friend of both men, intervened and kept Short and Storms from drawing on each other. Storms, however, returned later in the day and confronted Short. Both men drew their pistols. Short crowded in close, firing three times. One bullet struck Storms in the heart and another broke his neck.

On May 2, 1881, Luke was given a hearing in the death of Storms by the District Court at Tucson (to which Cochise County was attached for judicial purposes) and released.[18] He returned to Dodge City later in the year. Luke again secured a position as house gambler at the Long Branch Saloon, then as always, the most popular bistro in Dodge. He remained in this position until February 6, 1883, when he bought out co-owner Chalk Beeson's interest in the Long Branch.[19]

In the early spring of 1883 Dodge City's city administration underwent a political change which resulted in what has been called by Western historians the famous "Dodge City War." The central figure in the war (actually it was a war of words rather than bullets) was Luke Short. By 1883 Wyatt Earp, Charlie Bassett and the Masterson brothers had long since departed Dodge, although Bat Masterson continued

Luke Short was working for Wyatt Earp as a dealer in the Oriental Saloon in Tombstone when he killed gambler Charlie Storms over a card game. Short was given a hearing at Tucson *(above)* and then released.

to make periodic visits to the city. Dog Kelley and his saloon ticket were out of favor and, more important, out of political office. On April 3, 1883, a reformed ticket headed by ex-Marshal Larry Deger was elected to head the city administration.[20] On April 23 Mayor Deger and his city council passed two ordinances, one prohibiting the keeping of a house of prostitution[21] and the other making the keeping of a bordello the same as having no visible means of support and, therefore, punishable under the city vagrancy act.[22]

The Deger faction considered the Long Branch Saloon a house of prostitution because Luke and his partner, Will Harris,

who was also vice-president of the Bank of Dodge City,[23] employed the services of three female "entertainers" in their watering hole. The city administration also considered the Long Branch as one of the vilest establishments in Dodge City because Luke hit rowdy customers on the head with chairs and at one time employed Jack McCarty, a con man and convicted robber, as house gambler.[24]

On April 28 the three female "entertainers" were arrested.[25] Short did not mind the apprehension of his female employees as much as he did the fact that other establishments in Dodge City, whose owners were a part of the Deger faction, were allowed to retain their "entertainers."[26] Two nights later Short and Special Police Officer Louis (or Lewis) C. Hartman, who was also city clerk, passed each other on Front Street. Hartman had assisted in the arrest of Short's female employees.[27] Short drew his pistol and fired two shots at Hartman. In his anxiety to flee, Hartman stumbled and fell. Short thought he had killed him and as he walked away, Hartman drew his pistol and fired a wild shot at Luke.[28]

Luke was arrested and posted bond of $2,000.[29] He also filed a counter charge against Hartman.[30] Luke appeared for a hearing on May 2 and was ordered to leave town. He was given an armed escort aboard an eastbound locomotive later in the day.[31] Five other gamblers were rounded up by a vigilante committee and given similar treatment that same day, including Johnson (Johnny) Gallagher,[32] a personal friend of both Luke Short and Wyatt Earp. Two of the gamblers, Tom Lane and L. A. Hyatt, returned to Dodge the following week, but were not allowed to remain.[33]

Luke went to Kansas City where he immediately began plans to go back to Dodge. He sought the advice of attorneys on his legal rights at Dodge City. He kept abreast of things in Dodge by writing his partner, Will Harris, and State Congressman George Hoover. He also began enlisting help from fellow gamblers Bat Masterson, Wyatt Earp, Charlie Bassett and Johnny Gallagher about aiding him in his return. With the assistance of W. F. (Billy) Petillon, his friend and clerk of the District Court of Ford County, Luke petitioned Governor George W. Glick of Kansas on May 10 for state action in his behalf.

Newspapers in eastern Kansas began picking up stories of "the war" and playing them up. As a result, each side started making charges and countercharges, many of which were impossible to verify. On May 13 Bat Masterson, who was ever-ready to assist a friend in time of trouble, arrived at Kansas City from Denver to offer his services to Short.[34] Bat also went to Silverton, Colorado, and recruited Wyatt Earp.[35] Charlie Bassett, who was then a house gambler at the Marble Hall Saloon in Kansas City, offered his services.[36] Luke was slowly recruiting his army of gunfighters and preparing his "invasion" of Dodge.

Sheriff George T. Hinkle of Ford County, on behalf of the Deger faction, telegraphed Governor Glick explaining why Short had been forced to leave Dodge City.[37] Bob Wright, county commissioner, and another Dodge citizen, Richard J. Hardesty, wired Governor Glick explaining that Dodge City was presently a "peaceful and quiet" town.[38] Meanwhile, the governor alerted two companies of the Kansas National Guard to stand by for possible action.[39]

Governor Glick on May 12 informed Sheriff Hinkle by telegram that it was the latter's duty to preserve order at Dodge City and to protect lives and property there.[40] Hinkle telegraphed Glick the same day that he would do his best to keep law and order, but that he could not be responsible for the actions of any individual.[41] Meanwhile, a reporter of the *Topeka Daily Capital* interviewed Luke Short and Billy Petillon on May 11 at Topeka. In the interview Short and Petillon charged that Mayor Deger was a political dupe of ex-mayor A. B. ("Ab") Webster, who allegedly was the real power behind the political throne in Ford County. Short and Petillon asserted that Webster,

Wyatt Earp was living at Silverton, Colorado, in 1883 when Luke Short sent for him to help in the "Dodge City War." Short, who was co-owner of the Long Branch Saloon, had been ordered to get out of town after a shooting. He planned to return.

also the owner of a saloon, wanted to close the Long Branch, the most popular and profitable watering hole in Dodge City.[42]

After reading Governor Glick's telegram to Sheriff Hinkle on May 12, several of the town's leading citizens, including Hinkle, Hoover and Wright, telegraphed the governor on May 13 that he had been misinformed and that he should send the State Adjutant General to Dodge City to investigate matters.[43] Meanwhile, Dodge City received word that Luke Short and his army of gunfighters were on their way to Dodge via the next train. Hinkle organized a posse to greet the westbound train on May 15, but when the train stopped, it did not contain Short nor any of his gunfighting cohorts.

Meanwhile three Dodge citizens—Wright, Congressman Hoover and Chalk Beeson—went to Kansas City to confer with Short[44] in the hope of averting possible bloodshed.

Governer Glick sent the State Adjutant General, ex-Brevet Brigadier General Thomas Moonlight, to Dodge to study the situation. He arrived on May 16.[45] General Moonlight conferred with several of the town's citizens who were extremely apprehensive about Short's impending return. The next day he telegraphed Glick that Luke Short would be allowed to return to Dodge City to settle his business affairs.[46] Moonlight sent a second telegram almost immediately to the governor stating that Short could be protected against public as-

Luke Short, with friends Bat Masterson and Charlie Bassett to help back him up, boarded the steam cars to invade Dodge City from this ornate railroad station at Kansas City. En route they picked up Wyatt Earp. Expecting trouble in the invasion of the gunfighters, citizens asked for the state militia.

sault if he came, but not from private assault.[47] In a third wire to the governor later in the day, Moonlight informed Glick that Sheriff Hinkle could not protect Short against private attack at Dodge City.[48] Moonlight could do no more, so he left Dodge on May 18.

Luke Short left Kansas City and traveled to Caldwell, a cow town near the Kansas-Indian Territory line. He arrived at Caldwell in late May.[49] Sheriff Hinkle, fearing that Short's invasion was imminent, wired Governor Glick a petition signed by several citizens on May 31, requesting that he send General Moonlight to organize a company of state militia.[50] Several of the same citizens later signed a request to Governor Glick asking him not to grant power to or-

At the end of the "Dodge City War"—which proved to be no war at all—Luke Short and his invasion force posed for this memorable picture, taken in Dodge City. Standing, *left to right:* W. H. Harris, Luke Short, Bat Masterson, and W. F. Petillon; *seated:* Charles E. Bassett, Wyatt Earp, M. F. McLane, and Neil Brown. The picture has been captioned by historians, "Luke Short and His Dodge City Peace Commission."

ganize such a militia because of the excitement it was causing. Moonlight wired Hinkle on June 4 that the governor thought it best to defer the organization of militiamen for the present because of this inconsistency on the part of several citizens of Dodge City.[51]

Short met Petillon at Caldwell and on June 3 they went to Kinsley, Kansas, where they found Wyatt Earp,[52] who had arrived from Silverton, Colorado. On June 5 the bloodless invasion came when Luke Short, Wyatt Earp, Bat Masterson, Charlie Bassett, M. F. (Frank) McLane, *et al.*, arrived

in Dodge City.[53] The inevitable had come.

Major Harry E. Gryden of the Kansas State Militia, a Dodge City resident, telegraphed General Moonlight on the night of June 5 that everything had been settled between the opposing factions.[54] Gryden's optimism wasn't shared by other Dodge citizens. Several citizens, including Sheriff Hinkle, Mayor Deger, and Commissioner Wright, wired the governnor on the morning of June 6 that Dodge City was overrun with desperate characters and that law and order could not be preserved. The telegram also requested that two companies of state militia be sent immediately.[55] Glick wired back that he was sending Moonlight to Dodge City.[56] Moonlight wired Major Gryden to keep peace at all costs.[57] Later, the overly optimistic Hinkle wired the governor that everything had been settled and that Luke Short's gunfighters had left town.[58] Hinkle, however, sent another wire to Glick on June 6 stating that a fight was imminent and that Short had not sent his gunfighters out of town.[59] Mayor Deger decreed that all gambling houses were to be closed until an agreement could be reached.[60]

Moonlight arrived on the night of June 6 and effected an amicable peace settlement between the Short and Deger factions. Bat Masterson and Wyatt Earp left Dodge on June 10,[61] their services being no longer needed by Luke Short. Before leaving town, however, they posed with Short, Billy Petillon, Charlie Bassett, Will Harris, Neil Brown and Frank McLane in a famous photograph[62] which has been labeled by historians as "Luke Short and his Dodge City Peace Commission."

In what was probably an aftermath of the Dodge City War, Luke had Police Judge Robert E. Burns arrested in late August 1883, charging him with misconduct in office and the collection of illegal fees.[63] Finally on November 19, 1883, Short and his partner Will Harris sold the Long Branch Saloon to Roy Drake and Frank Warren.[64] Short and Bat Masterson, who had returned to Dodge City, then left for Fort Worth.[65] Luke however was back in late December 1883 and early January 1884, celebrating the holiday season.[66] He paid another visit to Dodge City in early May 1884.[67] In early August 1884, Luke decided to sue Dodge

Western History Collections, University of Oklahoma Library
Jim Courtright was a two-gun tough who ran his own private detective agency at Fort Worth, Texas. As in numerous other instances in the Old West, Luke Short killed Courtright in a quarrel over money.

City for $15,000 for running him out of town during the Dodge City War.[68] Luke and the city eventually settled their differences out of court.[69]

During the last decade of his life Luke Short made his gambling residence at Fort Worth. In this time he lived with a woman known only by the name of "Hettie." As a Fort Worth gambler, Luke grew wealthy. Gambling became illegal in Fort Worth and Luke was forced to run his games behind closed doors. Many of his customers were from the elite society of the city. Luke was not out of place hobnobbing with Fort Worth's upper crust. He was a neat, fastidious dresser which gave him a rather dignified appearance. He was clean-shaven except for a thick, drooping mustache. He had thinning brown hair and blue eyes. He stood five feet six inches in height and weighed about 125 pounds. (He became tremendously heavier after he contracted dropsy in later life.) His head was rather large and did not seem to match his small body. His clothes were tailor-made and his right trouser pocket was tailored extra long, the inside lined with leather. Here he carried his pistol. (Usually, the frontier gambler carried his pistol in a shoulder holster under his coat).

By February 1887, Luke had a one third interest in Jake Johnson's White Elephant Saloon at Fort Worth.[70] Short and Johnson were soon approached by Timothy Isaiah ("Longhaired Jim") Courtright, a two-gun hardcase whose home was at Fort Worth and who had a well-known reputation as a gunfighter in both Texas and New Mexico. Courtright, ex-city marshal at Fort Worth, was the head of his own private detective agency. He also had a protection racket whereby he would police the various resorts in Fort Worth for a small piece of the action in each saloon. Jake Johnson was a friend of Courtright and he seems to have been willing to give Courtright protection money for his services if Short would agree. Since Luke was his own policeman, he refused to pay for "protection."

Courtright tried bullying Short into paying. Talk in Fort Worth was that Courtright would force Luke into a shooting if he didn't pay. Luke prepared himself for a possible showdown. The fight came on February 8, 1887.[71] Courtright sent word via Johnson that he wanted to see Short. Luke was entertaining his old friend Bat Masterson, who had come to Fort Worth for a visit, when the word arrived. (What Courtright may or may not have known was that Short had sold his one-third interest in the White Elephant to Johnson on February 7.[72])

Short met Courtright near a shooting gallery (of all places). Luke could see that Courtright had been drinking. The two men exchanged small talk and then Short reached inside his coat pocket. Courtright yelled at him not to go for his pistol. Luke told him that he never carried his pistol there. Courtright drew the pistol holstered on his right hip (he had another pistol holstered on his left hip). Luke quickly drew his gun from his right trouser pocket. Because Short had to reach under his coat and Courtright had only to pull his pistol from the holster on his hip, he beat Luke to the draw. However, as he drew his pistol upward, the hammer snagged on Courtright's watch chain, giving Short ample time to pull his own weapon.

Luke crowded in close (as was his custom) and fired six times in rapid succession. (The old legend that gunfighters only carried five cartridges in their revolvers and rested the hammer of each pistol on an empty chamber seems to have been just that—legend.) The first bullet broke Courtright's revolver cylinder. Two other shots went wild and three others struck Courtright in the heart, right shoulder and right thumb, breaking it.[73] Courtright was dead minutes after he hit the ground.

Short was arrested, but released on $2,000 bond on February 9 by a Judge Smith.[74]

The Federal Building in Fort Worth was the scene of Luke Short's trial for killing Jim Courtright. He was released on a plea of self-defense. Later he was involved in another shooting in Fort Worth. He died in September, 1893, in Kansas.

He employed attorneys Alex Steadman, Robert McCart and a third named Capps to defend him.[75] Short was eventually released on self-defense.

After killing Courtright, Luke lived in relative obscurity at Fort Worth until December 23, 1890 when he and Fort Worth saloon owner Charles Wright shot each other over a gambling dispute. Wright ambushed Short from behind, shooting him in the left leg and knocking off a part of Luke's left thumb with a shotgun blast. Despite his wounds Luke managed to wound Wright in the wrist, fracturing it, before the latter fled for his life.[76]

Luke Short's gunfighting days became numbered because of dropsy. In late August 1893, he went to Geuda Springs, Kansas, a mineral spa, for his health.[77] Hettie and Luke's brother, Young Short, accompanied him. Luke was too ill for anything to help him. He died at Geuda Springs on September 8, 1893, of dropsy.[78] His remains were returned to Fort Worth and buried in the Oakwood Cemetery. It was a relatively quiet passing for one of the deadliest gunfighters in the West.

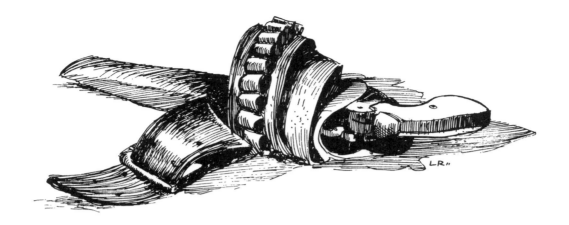

7.

BEN THOMPSON

(1843-1884)

ENJAMIN F. THOMPSON was born to
William (. . .-. . .) and Mary A.
Thompson[1] (. . .-1883?) at Knot-
tingley, England on November 11, 1843.
During the early years Ben received the cul-
tured education of the typical British youngster of his day. But the culture, the fine
breeding, and the education somehow went
astray and a hard-drinking, Texas-reared
man-killer emerged. Bat Masterson, who
knew him well, commented on Thompson's
ability of exterminating his fellow man:

*"It is very doubtful if in his time there
was another man living who equalled him
with the pistol in a life and death struggle."*[2]

It was the ultimate summing up of
Thompson the gunfighter, but Masterson's
comment only scratched the surface in summing up Thompson the man.

By 1858 the Thompson family had immi-
grated to Austin, Texas, where young Ben
continued his education in a private school.
Thompson's father is said to have been an
officer in the British Navy, but available records from Great Britain failed to show him
in the Royal Navy as an officer between
1796 and 1861.[3] At an early age Ben's father died and as the eldest son, he had to assume the responsibilities of earning a living
and supporting his widowed mother and the
other children. He secured a job as a printer's apprentice for the *Austin Southern In-
telligencer*, a daily newspaper.[4] But fate
was destined to intervene and keep Ben
from a career in journalism.

Even as a teen-ager in Austin, Thompson
was involved in the kind of trouble which
was to mark his later life: the shedding of

Ed Bartholomew Collection, Toyahvale, Texas
English-born Ben Thompson was one of the West's most feared gunmen. Bat Masterson said his skill could be matched by few, if any. This is how Thompson appeared at age twenty-nine. He first shed blood while a teen-ager.

human blood. On perhaps at least two occasions in the 1850s, he was involved in serious shooting scrapes. One of the shooting incidents resulted in his temporary imprisonment. In one affair he allegedly shot and wounded a youngster in a hunting dispute.[5] And in October 1858, he shot and wounded a Negro youth named Joseph Smith (some sources say Joe Brown) in a quarrel.[6] Ben was arrested for the Smith shooting, but was released by Judge E. F. Calhoun in a preliminary hearing because no witness appeared against him.[7] He was re-arrested and given a preliminary hearing before a Justice Graves. He was then bound over for trial in the Travis County District Court.[8] In early December he appeared be-

fore Judge A. W. Terrill,[9] being sentenced to sixty days in jail and fined one hundred dollars.[10] On March 12, 1859, Texas Governor Hardin R. Runnels remitted a portion of Ben's fine and ordered him released from jail before his term had been served.[11]

After his release, Ben settled down to the quiet life of a printer's devil. He was struck by the wanderlust, however, and about 1860 he went to New Orleans, where it is said he secured a job as a bookbinder for Samuel W. Slater, formerly of Austin.[12] In New Orleans Thompson is believed to have killed his first man. The story has yet to be substantiated, but it bears repeating. One evening Ben was a passenger aboard an omnibus when a drunken Frenchman named Emil de Tour molested a young lady passenger. Thompson came to the girl's rescue and de Tour slapped Ben's face. Thompson drew a knife and slashed the Frenchman in the shoulder, inflicting a superficial wound. A few days later de Tour's friends found Ben in his printshop and offered Thompson the Frenchman's challenge of a duel. After some disagreement as to the choice of weapons, knives were finally decided upon. Thompson and de Tour allegedly met in a darkened room somewhere in New Orleans and Ben fatally stabbed de Tour. Floyd Benjamin Streeter, the distinguished Western historian, fruitlessly combed the old municipal records of New Orleans in the hope of finding any mention of the duel.[13] A search of the city directories for the period 1858 to 1861 also failed to list anyone named "Emil de Tour."[14]

At any rate, Ben returned to Austin. In 1860 Texas was on the eve of secession and although he was an Englishman by birth, Thompson was a Texan by choice; he de-

Still in his teens and already with a record, Thompson wandered to New Orleans where he took a job with a book bindery. One evening aboard a double-decked streetcar, Thompson allegedly knifed a drunk for molesting a young woman. Later, in a duel, he allegedly killed the man. The streetcar where the first incident occurred was similar to the one shown in this 1864 photograph.

cided to cast his lot with his adopted state and the Confederacy when Texas left the Union in 1861. During the war Ben married Miss Catherine Moore of Travis County. She bore him a son, Ben, Jr., and a daughter. But the War Between the States was to have a far greater effect on Thompson than either marriage or fatherhood.

Thompson joined Company D of the Sec-ond Regiment Texas Cavalry (also known as the Second Regiment Texas Mounted Rifles at Camp Carrizitas, Texas, on June 16, 1861 for a period of one year.[15] In July 1862, when the regiment was reorganized, Thompson's company was designated as Company I. One of the highlights of Ben's Army service was his friendship with the noted Samuel Stone Hall, who became fa-

This was a familiar scene to Ben Thompson, along Congress Avenue in Austin, Texas. Although English by birth, Thompson became a dyed-in-the-wool Texan and rode for Texas and the Confederacy during the War Between the States.

mous as one of the most prolific and popular dime novelists in the country. It has been said that two of the characters in Hall's dime novels were patterned after Ben Thompson and his younger brother Billy.[16]

Sometime during Thompson's first year of military service, he is alleged to have wounded seriously First Sergeant William D. Vance and wounded fatally First Lieutenant George W. Hagler, both of Company H, Second Regiment Texas Cavalry, in a dispute over the distribution of rations at Fort Clark, Texas. Thompson is said to have deserted his regiment after the fight. This affair is substantiated at least by the *Austin Daily Capital* in its issue of March 13, 1884, which published a Thompson obituary.

This newspaper referred to Hagler as "Lt. Hughes." A search of the old military records failed to show that Hagler was killed[17] or that Vance was wounded.[18] Thompson's military service records, however, show that he was absent without leave on July 28, 1863 and is not shown to have been on duty again until November 28, 1863.[19]

Ben reenlisted in the Second Texas Cavalry for two years on June 20, 1862 at Edinburg, Texas.[20] By this time he held the rank of sergeant.[21] He was, however, reduced to the rank of private after being absent without leave.[22] On November 28, 1863 he was placed on detached service from his regiment to drive some mules to Houston.[23] On April 16, 1864 Thompson was placed on recruiting service for his regiment.[24] In August of that year he was detached to duty with the Quartermaster Department.[25] And on October 10, 1864, he was again detached to drive a herd of cattle to Bolivar Point, Texas.[26] Thompson was paroled as a private from Company I, Second Regiment Texas Cavalry, by the office of the U.S. Provost Marshal at Galveston, Texas, on August 28, 1865.[27] Thompson's regiment, which was part of General Edmund Kirby Smith's Army of the Trans-Mississippi, had surrendered on May 26, 1865. Kirby Smith was the last Confederate general to surrender. Major General P. H. Sheridan, in command at New Orleans, feared that the Texas troops of Kirby Smith's army would not permanently lay down their weapons. Sheridan dispatched Brevet Major Generals George Custer and Wesley Merritt, later regimental commander of the Fifth U.S. Cavalry, to Texas to insure a cessation of the hostilities. It would seem, however, that Thompson was a prisoner of the Union Army sometime between May 26-August 28, 1865.

It is often written that during the latter part of the war, Thompson killed at least three, possibly four, men, and wounded a fifth in private quarrels. He is alleged to have killed First Lieutenant Martino (Martin) Gonzales, Company H, Thirty-third Regiment Texas Cavalry, and at least one of Gonzales' men, Miguel Zertuche, in a gambling dispute at Nuevo Laredo, Mexico. Another of Gonzales' men, Sergeant Juan Rodriguez of the Third Battalion Texas Cavalry, allegedly was fatally wounded either by Thompson or accidentally by one of Gonzales' men in the dispute. Gonzales and some of his men were Mexican-Texans serving in the Confederate Army and were sta-

tioned at Laredo, Texas, across the Rio Grande from Neuvo Laredo. A search of the old military records reveals that there is no record of Miguel Zertuche serving in the Confederate Army.[28] The records also reveal that Gonzales was paroled from the Confederate Army in October 1865,[29] and the service records of Rodriquez are incomplete, but they show that he was serving with the Confederate Army as late as July 1863[30] with no apparent record of further military service. The *Austin Daily Capital* of March 13, 1884, in its obituary of Thompson, stated that he killed Gonzales (whom the newspaper erroneously described as an officer in the Mexican Army) after the war while serving for Emperor Maximilian of Mexico. If Thompson killed Gonzales, it was after the latter had been paroled from the Confederate Army.

While on recruiting assignment in Austin, Thompson is said to have become involved in a friend's quarrel, killing John Coombs, and on the same occasion wounding a companion (name unknown) of Coombs. The aforementioned *Austin Daily Capital* substantiated Ben's killing of Coombs. Since the Coombs affair was a local incident, *The Daily Capital* would have been in a position to know the facts. It also has been written many times that Thompson was tried and acquitted for killing Coombs. The District Court at Austin, however, has no record of Thompson in connection with the Coombs affair,[31] nor has the War Department a record relating to a trial of Thompson for the killing of Coombs.[32] (During the Reconstruction Era the state of Texas was attached to the Fifth Military District for judicial purposes.)

The War Between the States left many Southern soldiers disillusioned and many of them turned to other means of violence. After the war, Thompson left his wife for the time being to fight for another "lost" cause in Mexico. In 1864 the French government of Emperor Charles Louis N. Bonaparte—Napolean III, nephew of Emperor Napoleon Bonaparte—had ousted Benito P. Juárez, the constitutionally-elected president of the Republic of Mexico, and appointed the Archduke F. Maximilian Hapsburg of Austria as puppet emperor. Maximilian was the younger brother of Emperor Franz Josef Hapsburg I of Austria.[33] Napoleon III was attempting to gain a territorial foothold in North America. This was a clear violation of the Monroe Doctrine.

Juárez formed a government in exile and began a revolution to regain his presidential seat. The official position of the United States was open sympathy toward the Juárez government. During the War Between the States, the United States could do little else. Once the war had ended, however, this country had a large veteran army ready to intervene, if necessary, in Juárez' behalf. The United States sought to exert diplomatic pressure, at least initially, against the French government to withdraw from Mexico, which Napoleon III did, leaving Maximilian in a precarious situation.

Most of the Mexican people were against Maximilian. And Napoleon III removed his troops, lest their presence provoke United States intervention on behalf of the Juárez government. Maximilian was forced to hire American mercenaries, mostly Yankee-hating, disgruntled ex-Confederate soldiers, to fight for his throne. Juárez himself was not adverse to employing outsiders in his army.

His agents approached General George Custer about the possibility of accepting the rank of major general and the position of adjutant general in Juárez' army. Custer requested a year's leave of absence from the U.S. Army, but his request was denied. He seems to have toyed at least with the idea of commanding Juárez' ragtag cavalry.

Among Maximilian's motley group of ex-Confederate mercenaries was Ben Thompson. (One of Maximilian's more distinguished ex-Confederate mercenaries was former Brigadier General Joseph O. Shelby, who had refused to surrender to Union authorities.) Thompson's service with Maximilian was *unofficial*, however. A search of Mexican records at both the Office of the Secretary of National Defense and the National Archives of the Republic of Mexico failed to turn up any document pertaining to Ben Thompson or his service for Maximilian.[34] Since Thompson was a foreign mercenary, he would not have been a member of the regular Army of the Republic of Mexico.[35] There seems to be little doubt, however, that Thompson fought as a mercenary for Maximilian. At least one contemporary newspaper substantiated his service.[36] Thompson reportedly held the rank of captain and fought for Maximilian until the latter's capitulation[37] in May, 1867. Ben served with the command of General Tomas Mejia, one of the few Mexican generals whose loyalty was with Maximilian. Mejia was later executed with the emperor and another loyalist general by the Juárez government.

While garrisoned with Mejia's troops at Matamoros, Mexico, Thompson and a fellow officer are said to have been drunk and disorderly, and were arrested by a squad of

Billy Thompson, Ben's younger brother, built his own reputation as a gunfighter. However, Ben's notoriety overshadowed him. This 1872 photograph of Billy was taken at Ellsworth, Kansas, where the brothers teamed together.

Mexican policemen. According to the story, one of the policemen (name unknown) jabbed Ben with a pistol. Thompson and this policeman met sometime later at a dance house and quarreled. The Mexican lunged at Ben with a knife and Thompson reportedly shot him several times, killing him.

Meanwhile, Maximilian's hope of retaining his throne were declining. He moved the throne to Queretaro to stave off inevitable defeat. The American mercenaries who had fought for him began deserting in his hour of need. Mejia called for volunteers to defend Queretaro. Ben Thompson, never one to desert a cause regardless of how futile fighting for it may have been, was among those Americans who answered Mejia's plea. Juárez' forces seized Queretaro, however, without a fight through the treachery of one of Maximilian's lieutenants. With the fall of Queretaro to Juárez' forces, Thompson fled to Vera Cruz and later returned to Austin.

Ben settled down with Catherine in Austin and pursued gambling as a profession. Meanwhile, Ben's brother William (Billy) Thompson, Jr., about four years younger, was making a reputation for himself, one that would have rivaled that of other famous gunfighters had not Ben's fame so completely overshadowed him. Billy became a fugitive when he fatally shot Private William Burk, the chief clerk in the office of the U.S. Adjutant General of Texas, in an Austin bordello on March 31, 1868.[38] Burk succumbed to his wound the following day[39] and Billy escaped to the Indian Territory with Ben's aid.

Ben lived quietly in Austin until September 2, 1868, when he shot his wife's brother, James Moore, in the side during a family dispute.[40] He then stormed into the office of Justice of the Peace W. D. Scott and threatened to kill him or anyone else who attempted to arrest him.[41] But Ben was arrested and tried by a Reconstruction military commission at Austin for an assault with an intent to kill and for theatening to kill.[42] On October 20, 1868 he was found guilty on both charges and sentenced to four years in Rusk Prison, the Texas State Penitentiary at Huntsville.[43] Thompson entered the Huntsville penitentiary on November 1 and was assigned number 1285.[44]

Ben remained at Huntsville until 1870 when he received a full pardon from President Ulysses S. Grant.[45]

For the remainder of 1870 Ben stayed in Austin gambling. As a professional gambler, Ben found that a pistol was as much a part of his profession as a deck of cards. Legend has him the inventor of the shoulder holster—an ideal way then as now to conceal a weapon. In the spring of 1871 Thompson and Phil Coe, an old gambling crony whom he had met during the war, opened the Bull's Head Saloon at Abilene. Abilene was the leading cattle-shipping point in Kansas in 1871, and the Texas trail hands spent much money in the cow town. The Bull's Head was one of the most profitable saloons in Abilene. Thompson and Coe drew their clientele from the flush trail hands. Anything went at the Bull's Head and the sky was the limit.

Billy Thompson was also at Abilene in 1871. During the cattle-shipping season he was a house dealer at the Bull's Head. During the off-season in the winter of 1871-72 he went to Ellsworth, where he took up residency with a prostitute named Emma Williams.

While Ben was at Kansas City in October, 1871, visiting Mrs. Thompson and their young son who had come there at Ben's request, Phil Coe was killed by City Marshal Wild Bill Hickok. Ben lost everything in the Bull's Head with Coe's death, for Thompson's partnership with Coe was verbal. With no written papers to support their arrangement, the entire business passed into the hands of Abilene businessman Thomas Sheran. Sheran had purchased Coe's interest in the saloon on August 2 of that year.

While in Kansas City, Ben and his wife and son were involved in a carriage accident. Mrs. Thompson was injured so severely that one of her arms had to be amputated. At Kansas City Ben learned of Coe's death. Knowing that he had no written contract, he and his family returned to Austin where Ben awaited the cattle-shipping season of 1872.

Ben joined his brother Billy at Ellsworth during the cattle-shipping season of 1872, after a brief sojourn in Wichita earlier in the year. The Thompson brothers operated as free-lance gamblers at Ellsworth in 1872 and 1873, residing at the Grand Central Hotel. Ellsworth was the number two railhead in Kansas behind Wichita in 1872 and 1873. Abilene ceased to be the boss cow town after 1871. Ellsworth, which was on the Kansas Pacific Railroad, shipped 40,161 head of cattle in 1872[46] and 30,540 head in 1873.[47]

Ben was an impressive sight in the gambling haunts of Ellsworth. He stood five feet eight inches in height and weighed about 180 pounds. He had wavy black hair, blue eyes, a thick black mustache (which became thicker in later life), and a small lower lip goatee which he shaved later in his life. (Eventually he became bald to the crown of his head, except for a small patch of hair near the front.)

Billy Thompson lived for a time with Emma Williams, until she took up with Wild Bill Hickok who resided briefly in Ellsworth in 1872. Hickok's ex-deputy at Abilene, Brocky Jack Norton, was Ellsworth's city marshal in 1872 and 1873. Lizzie Palmer, the celebrated cow-town prostitute, also was there in 1872, as was the controversial cattleman, Isom P. ("Print") Olive. Molly Brennan, who became famous as the

Ed Bartholomew Collection, Toyahvale, Texas
Ellsworth was a typical Kansas cow town when the Thompson brothers were there, with saloons, eateries, and various deadfalls strung along Main Street. The famous Drover's Cottage is plainly seen at the right. This is how Ellsworth looked in 1873 when Ben Thompson "treed" the town.

lover of Billy Thompson, Corporal Melvin A. King and Bat Masterson, was in town in 1872 and 1873 where her husband Joe Brennan operated a saloon. (The women seemed to have gotten around almost as much as the men.) Brennan's saloon was the Thompson brothers' favorite gambling haunt.

During the summer of 1873, a bitter feud resulted between the Thompsons and the Ellsworth police force, which culminated in tragedy for an innocent party. The Ellsworth police force at one time that summer consisted of City Marshal Norton and Policemen John ("Happy Jack") Morco, a swaggering braggart and self-proclaimed gunfighter; John S. ("High Low Jack") Branham, late of the Wichita police force; John ("Long Jack") DeLong; and Edward O. Hogue, who was also a deputy sheriff of Ellsworth County. Hogue had been chief of police (in lieu of the city marshalship)

and city marshal at Ellsworth on two separate occasions. He had been replaced as city marshal by Norton. Later during the summer of 1873, he was reappointed city marshal. Hogue was later a deputy sheriff at Dodge City.

The trouble between the Thompson and the Ellsworth police force began on June 10, 1873[48] when Hogue arrested Billy Thompson for being drunk and unlawfully carrying and discharging a pistol within the city limits.[49] On June 11 Billy was fined five dollars plus ten dollars in court costs by Police Judge Vincent B. Osborne.[50] Ben Thompson also had discharged his pistol on June 10 and the next day, he appeared voluntarily in the police court and was fined ten dollars plus costs by Judge Osborne.[51] (This is the only known police record of Ben Thompson in the Kansas cow towns.[52]

Then on June 30, Happy Jack Morco arrested Billy Thompson for unlawfully carrying a pistol on his person within the city limits, for being drunk and disorderly, and for assaulting Morco.[53] On July 1 Thompson was fined ten dollars plus fifteen dollars costs by Judge Osborne for being drunk and carrying a concealed weapon.[54]

The bloodshed occurred on August 15, 1873. Ben Thompson, John Sterling, Neil Cain and Cad Pierce, all Texans and professional gamblers, were playing cards in Joe Brennan's saloon. Thompson had a financial arrangement with Sterling. After the card game ended, Ben met Sterling in Nick Lentz's saloon and asked him to settle up. Sterling was drunk and refused. Angry words were exchanged and Sterling slapped Thompson's face. Ben was not armed. He reached for Sterling but Morco, who was a friend of John, drew his pistol and kept Thompson from accosting the gambler. Ben warned Morco to keep Sterling away from him.

Later, Morco and Sterling returned to the front of Brennan's saloon. One of them shouted, "Get your guns you Texas sonofabitches and come out and fight!" Ben Thompson was inside. He ran out the back door, went to Jake New's saloon and got his Winchester rifle and a pistol. He left New's and met Billy, who was drunk and had Ben's English-made double-barreled shotgun. Billy had heard that Ben was in trouble. Ben, however, advised Billy that he was too drunk to be of any help and that he should go to the hotel and stay out of action. Billy had both barrels of the shotgun cocked and he accidentally discharged one load. The blast struck the sidewalk in front of New's saloon where Texas cattle barons Seth Mabry and Eugene B. Millett were standing. Ben tried to remove the remain-

Western History Collections, University of Oklahoma Library
Sheriff Chauncey B. Whitney, of Ellsworth, tried to quiet things down when the Thompson brothers went on a rampage. He was shot by the drunken Billy. Ben called Whitney "our best friend."

ing cartridge from the shotgun, but it was made of brass and had swollen in the chamber, being impossible to extract without firing.

Meanwhile, someone informed Ben that Morco and Sterling were out to "get him." Ben took Billy's shotgun and handed it to a third party. Ben then walked to the railroad tracks in the middle of the street and called out, "If you damn sonofabitches want a fight, here we are!" Billy reclaimed his shotgun and joined Ben in the middle of the street. The Thompsons were ready for blood.

Sheriff Chauncey B. Whitney of Ells-

Courtesy Ellsworth County Historical Society
Billy Thompson made a quick getaway after shooting Sheriff Whitney, who was unarmed. A friend got his horse from a livery stable behind the Grand Central Hotel. Billy rode to the front to exchange guns with Ben, then took off. Seen at the far right, next door to the hotel, is the printing office of the *Ellsworth Reporter*, from where the editor witnessed Ben Thompson's duel with the police.

worth County, who had been in the famous Beecher's Island Indian fight of 1868,[55] and was former city marshal at Ellsworth, and ex-policeman Long Jack DeLong approached the Thompsons and attempted to placate them into avoiding trouble. The four men agreed to talk things over in Brennan's with a round of drinks. As all but Ben had entered the saloon, someone yelled, "Look out . . . !" Ben turned and saw Sterling and Morco, who had a pistol in each hand, in a fast run toward him. When Sterling and Morco saw Thompson turn and face them, they stopped. Happy Jack was about thirty feet from Ben. Sterling was some distance to the rear. Sterling broke and ran into Jerome Bebee's store. Morco

started to do the same. As he darted into the doorway of Bebee's, Ben fired his rifle. The bullet missed Happy Jack's head by inches and lodged in the door casing. The shot brought Sheriff Whitney and Billy Thompson out of Brennan's. Whitney was a few feet in front of Billy, who was staggering. Billy pointed the shotgun at his brother and Whitney. Both Ben and Whitney told Billy to be careful with the gun because he was drunk. Whitney tried twice to get out of the direction Billy was pointing the gun. Billy staggered and his shotgun[56] went off. The blast struck Whitney in the shoulder, arm, chest and lungs.[57]

"For God's sake, Billy, you have shot our best friend!" cried Ben.

GOVERNOR'S PROCLAMATION.

WHEREAS, C. B. Whitney, Sheriff of Ellsworth County, Kansas, was murdered in the said county of Ellsworth, on the 15th day of August, 1873, by one William Thompson, said Thompson being described as about six feet in height, 26 years of age, dark complexion, brown hair, gray eyes and erect form; and Whereas, the said William Thompson is now at large and a fugitive from justice;

NOW THEREFORE, know ye, that I, Thomas A. Osborn, Governor of the State of Kansas, in pursuance of law, do hereby offer a reward of FIVE HUNDRED DOLLARS for the arrest and conviction of the said William Thompson, for the crime above named.

L. S.

IN TESTIMONY WHEREOF, I have hereunto subscribed my name, and caused to be affixed the Great Seal of the State. Done at Topeka, this 22d day of August, 1873.

THOMAS A. OSBORN.

By the Governor:

W. H. SMALLWOOD, Secretary of State.

Courtesy Kansas State Historical Society, Topeka
A price of $500 was placed on the head of Billy Thompson for killing the sheriff of Ellsworth County. The Kansas governor, a former U.S. marshal, signed the proclamation. Now wanted in both Texas and Kansas, Billy fled to Colorado.

"I don't give a damn! I would have shot him, if he had been Jesus Christ!" Billy replied.

Whitney had been unarmed when he was shot by Thompson. There was little Ben could do but aid his brother in getting out of Ellsworth as quickly as possible. Ben literally held off the entire population of the city while Billy made his escape. Neil Cain, a friend of the Thompsons, secured Billy's mount from Sam John's livery stable in the rear of the Grand Central Hotel at North Main and Lincoln. Cain held the horse while Billy mounted.[58] Billy rode to the front of the hotel and exchanged the shotgun for Ben's rifle.[59] Billy rode out of Ellsworth via a brief stopover in "Nauchville" (the red-light district of Ellsworth) to visit Molly Brennan.[60]

Meanwhile, Ben kept Ellsworth at bay. Mayor James Miller summarily dismissed the entire Ellsworth police force (then consisting of Marshal Norton and Policemen Morco and Hogue) because they refused to arrest Ben Thompson. Mayor Miller approached Thompson and asked him to give up his arms. Ben consented (this was after Billy had made his escape) on the agreement that Morco surrender his.[61] Mayor Miller accepted Thompson's terms and Ben turned over his weapons to Deputy Sheriff Hogue.[62]

Whitney passed away on August 18. It became "unhealthy" for Texas gamblers to remain in Ellsworth after his death, so Ben Thompson left. Billy Thompson went to Buena Vista, Colorado. Kansas Governor Thomas A. Osborn, an ex-U.S. marshal, offered a $500 reward for his arrest and conviction. Billy was now a fugitive from both Texas (for the Burk killing) and Kansas. He remained in Buena Vista for some time. Buena Vista was a lawless little community near Leadville. The town was overrun with the outlaw element and they popularly elected Billy mayor of Buena Vista.[63]

Three years later Billy Thompson was arrested by the Texas Rangers. Captain John Sparks of the Rangers apprehended Billy on October 26, 1876,[64] near Austin. Texas authorities allowed Kansas to have priority in the Whitney killing and Billy was extradited to stand trial. Ben secured the services of attorneys A. H. Case and Phil Pendleton, ex-prosecuting attorney of Ellsworth County, to defend Billy.[65] In March, 1877, Billy's trial was postponed until September 5, 1877.[66] Ben secured the services of a third attorney, J. D. Mohler, to assist Case and Pendleton.[67] Billy was acquitted on September 14.[68] His acquittal cost Ben a small fortune in attorneys' fees.

The cattle-shipping season of 1874 found Ben Thompson dealing monte and faro in W. W. (Whitey) Rupp's Keno House at Wichita. While in Wichita in 1874 he resided first at the Douglas Avenue House and later boarded in a private home.[69] During the cattle season of 1875, he was a house dealer in the Long Branch Saloon at Dodge City. The cattle season of 1876 again found Ben Thompson with his gambling head-quarters in Dodge City. Ben spent several cattle seasons in Dodge. During his many sojourns in the "Cowboy Capital" Ben became a friend of Bob Wright, Dodge's first citizen and a co-founder of the cow town. On at least one occasion Ben boasted to Wright about his six-gun prowess and man-killing ability. He told Wright that he never carried more than one gun and never missed the man at whom he shot, and always shot his victim in the head. He also boasted to Wright that when he shot his victim, he would always look around the crowd and see if the victim had any friends or if there were any damaging witnesses against him. He would then shoot them to destroy the evidence.[70] Obviously Thompson went overboard in his boasting to Wright.

During the cow town's off season Ben would almost invariably make his gambling headquarters in Austin. One of his frequent haunts was the Capital Variety Theater, which was owned by Mark Wilson. Thompson and Wilson had little liking for each other. On December 25, 1876, the hostility between the two culminated in bloodshed.

On Christmas Eve Wilson had ejected several rowdies and drunks from the theater. One of those was James Burdett, a friend of Ben Thompson. Burdett had befriended Billy Thompson in one of the latter's frequent brushes with the law. Thompson was never one to let a friend down. Word got back to Wilson that Thompson was coming to the theater on Christmas night to "settle up" for Burdett. Wilson prepared for Thompson's "invasion" by hiring the services of two additional house policemen.[71]

On Christmas night Thompson and Burdett were at the theater. Burdett was in a front seat and Thompson, not finding a seat, was sitting atop a table in one of the aisles. During the performance one of the patrons (probably Burdett) set off some firecrackers. Wilson stepped to the front of the audience and demanded to know who had created the disturbance. Suspecting Burdett, Wilson ordered his arrest. Burdett had some lamp black in his hand; he threw it in Wilson's face. A policeman named Allen stepped forward and started to escort Burdett from the theater. Thompson intervened and tried to quell Burdett's arrest. Wilson became angry and told Thompson to mind his own business. Ben replied that it was his business. Wilson then accused Thompson of having been the instigator of the disturbance. Thompson denied the charge, and Wilson called him a liar. Ben reached over Allen's shoulder and slapped Wilson's face, cutting him with his ring. Allen grabbed Thompson, forcing him backwards.

Wilson went down the aisle for a shotgun. Someone shouted a warning. Thompson turned as Wilson pulled the trigger. Allen, or someone else, tilted the shotgun upward just as Wilson fired. The blast went over Thompson's head and struck a wall. Ben drew his pistol and fired four times at Wilson, hitting him in the head, neck, chest and fingers.[72] Wilson was dead before he hit the floor. In the meantime, Charles Matthews, Wilson's bartender, fired at Thompson with a rifle. The bullet cut through Ben's coat and creased his hip. Ben turned and shot at Matthews. The bullet struck the bartender in the mouth. At first it was believed that Matthews was mortally wounded, but he must have recovered for no record has been found of Thompson being tried for his kill-

Courtesy Library, State Historical Society of Colorado
The Grand Canyon of the Arkansas River—the Royal Gorge —was a coveted right-of-way sought by rival railroads. Ben Thompson joined Bat Masterson in recruiting an "army" to defend the gorge for the Santa Fe railroad. Thompson was said to have sold out to the Denver and Rio Grande.

ing[73] nor has a newspaper account of his death been found.[74]

Before the New Year Ben was given a preliminary hearing by Judge Fritz Tegener and committed to jail without bail.[75] Thompson employed the services of William M. (Buck) Walton, an attorney and long-time friend who later became Thompson's original biographer. Ben also hired two additional attorneys, Green and Hill, to aid Walton.[76]

Thompson was released eventually on a writ of *habeas corpus*.[77] Authorities brought him before the Court of appeals at Galveston; bail was set and raised at $5,000.[78] In April 1877, the Travis County Grand Jury indicted both Thompson and Burdett for murder.[79] Burdett, however, was later found guilty of an assault and given a small fine.[80] Thompson's case went to trial on May 31 in Austin and on the same day the jury returned a verdict of not guilty.[81] Ben was acquitted in time to make the cattle season at Dodge City.

The cattle-shipping season of 1878 again found Ben Thompson at his usual Dodge City haunts. In March 1879, the Santa Fe in its Royal Gorge right-of-way feud with the Denver, Rio Grande and Western Railroad wired Sheriff W. B. (Bat) Masterson at Dodge City asking him to recruit a company of gunfighters. According to the *San Antonio Express* of March 13, 1884, which published an obituary of Thompson, Ben was the leader of the Santa Fe's gunfighters. (Actually, Masterson was the leader and Thompson was his chief lieutenant.) The *Express* also reported that in June of that year, Thompson surrendered the Santa Fe's roundhouse near Canon City, Colorado (which blocked the Rio Grande's right-of-

Courtesy Nebraska State Historical Society, Lincoln
Near this spot at Ogallala, Nebraska, Bat Masterson tried to save Billy Thompson from a lynch mob. He was sent by Ben, who was in Texas. Masterson tried smuggling Billy out on a locomotive, but the depot was heavily guarded. He finally used a wagon to get Billy out of town.

Courtesy Austin-Travis County Collection, Austin (Texas) Public Library
The Iron Front Saloon (at left) in Austin, Texas, became the business headquarters for Ben Thompson. He had heavy investments in the gaming tables which were over the saloon. He then became a law officer and his reputation sharply reduced local crime.

way through the Royal Gorge), without firing a shot for a bribe of $2,300 and several diamonds. Other sources in Texas at the time claimed the bribe was $5,000.[82] There is no record, however, of any payment to Ben Thompson by the Denver, Rio Grande and Western Railroad.[83] The *Dodge City Times* of June 14, 1879 stated that Masterson surrendered the roundhouse upon writs served by United States officers.

During much of 1879 Ben gambled in the various Colorado towns of Pueblo, Denver, Trinidad and Leadville. On October 2, 1879, he was back in Austin announcing his candidacy for the city marshalship.[84] The election was held on November 3, 1879[85] and Thompson ran on the Democratic ticket

in a field of three, losing to the Republican incumbent, Ed Creary, by a vote margin of 1,174 to 744.[86]

By 1880 Thompson decided to make his permanent gambling headquarters in Austin. He invested heavily in the gaming tables at the Iron Front Saloon and did quite well. Meanwhile on June 26, 1880, Billy Thompson was wounded in a gunfight with Jim Tucker at Ogallala, Nebraska. Ben dispatched his friend Bat Masterson to Billy's aid.

Later that year Ben Thompson ran again for the single office of city marshal and chief of police in a field of five candidates. He was elected to office on December 14, 1880,[87] defeating his closest competitor,

When Ben Thompson became a public official, the *Austin Daily Statesman* kept close tab on his activities, not always to his liking. The newspaper criticized his conduct and twice Thompson visited the offices, trying with threats to change the editor's mind. The editor had an easy time keeping track of him for the Iron Front Saloon was handy, beneath the *Statesman* composing room.

John Kelly, by a vote margin of 849 to 621.[88] He took office officially on December 27.[89] Ben was given the rank of captain of police and he received a salary of $150 per month.[90] With the Texas man-killer as captain of Austin's police force, would-be lawbreakers thought twice about running afoul of the law. His first month in office, the crime rate dropped and arrests were down from the previous month.[91] Between the time Ben took office and October 17, 1881, he and his policemen made a total of 1,200 arrests.[92] Thompson had several deputies to assist him, with Police Sergeant John Chenneville as his chief lieutenant.[93]

His police duties and gambling activities, however, were not enough to occupy Thompson's mind and he took to drinking excessively. He became an insomniac and imbibed a full quart of Hennessy brandy every night.[94] Instead of waiting for someone else to break the law, Thompson would do it himself by getting drunk and shooting at the street lamps. On at least three occasions during his last years (when he did not wear the badge of city marshal), *The Daily Democratic Statesman* of Austin criticized Thompson's drunken conduct. And on two of those occasions, Thompson visited the editorial office of the *Democratic Statesman* and attempted to intimidate the editors. Nonetheless, Ben was reelected city marshal on November 7, 1881, defeating J. R. Kirk by a vote margin of 1,173 to 933.[95]

In July 1882, Thompson took his son and daughter to San Antonio to visit friends. The Thompson children had long wanted to see the city and Ben finally secured a leave of absence as Austin's marshal to make the

Western History Collections, University of Oklahoma Library
Jack Harris, owner of a San Antonio variety theater, was one of Thompson's bitterest enemies. A feud with Harris and his partners over a gambling debt ran on for several years.

trip. Ben however had three deadly enemies at San Antonio: Jack Harris, owner of a variety theater and his two gambling associates, Joseph C. Foster and William H. Simms, cousin of Pink Simms. Simms was from Austin; he and Thompson had once been friends and gambling associates. Since about 1880, Thompson had had a bitter feud with the three San Antonio gamblers.

The friction began over a card game between Thompson and Foster. Ben had lost money to Foster; he accused the latter of cheating and refused to pay the debt. Foster reached for his pistol, but Thompson outdrew him. For some reason known only to Thompson, Ben did not shoot. Foster wisely let the matter drop. Harris then publicly warned that Thompson had better not enter the variety theater again or make an appearance on the streets of San Antonio, or he would kill him on sight. But Thompson returned to San Antonio sometime later, meeting Harris and Simms in a local saloon. Thompson and Harris had words about Harris's threats and his refusal to allow Thompson in his place again. Ben warned that he would kick his way into the theater if anyone tried to keep him out. Thompson also told Harris that he had little use for him and that if he wanted to settle things, he was willing. Harris did not accept Thompson's challenge.

Thompson and his children arrived in San Antonio on the evening of July 10, 1882. Harris was "posted" that Ben Thompson was in town. Billy Simms was particularly nervous about Thompson's presence. Simms and Foster hated Thompson, but neither had the nerve to face him in a head-on clash. Jack Harris, however, was a man of another breed. Ben went to Harris's variety theater on the afternoon of July 11, but none of the trio made an appearance. Ben returned that evening. He became belligerent and insulted the characters of Foster and Harris to Barney Mitchell, one of Harris's bartenders in the theater's saloon. Thompson called Foster a thief and accused Harris of living off the earnings of the women he employed at the theater. He told Mitchell to tell Foster and Harris what he had said. Mitchell refused, saying that he (Thompson) should tell them himself. As he was talking, Thompson backed slowly toward the entrance with his hand on his pistol. He collided accidentally with a musician who

The variety house of Jack Harris was at the rear of this gaudy building, at the corner of Commerce and Soledad streets in San Antonio. There were gambling rooms on the second floor. It was here that Ben Thompson gunned down Harris and where, later, Thompson walked into a trap.

had just entered. Ben turned and faced the man, thinking it was Harris, Foster, or Simms.

Meanwhile, one of Harris's more loyal employees, went to his home and warned him about Thompson's presence at the variety house and about his threatening mood. Simms also slipped out of the theater to warn Harris. Simms met Harris on his way to the theater and gave him a pistol.

In the meantime, Thompson left the theater and met a policeman named Jacob Ripps on the street outside, engaging him in conversation about Harris's place. Thompson warned Ripps that if he tried to keep him out of the theater he (Thompson) would just as soon shoot him. Ben then joined a jeweler friend named Leon Rouvant in the

theater's bar for a round of drinks. As Harris was coming toward the show house, he was stopped by Ramon Biencourt, a private citizen, and warned about Thompson. A few minutes later John Dyer, another of Harris's bartenders, met his employer at the theater's west door and told him about Thompson.

Harris went into the ticket office, and secured his shotgun. He held the gunstock in his right hand and rested the barrels across his crippled left forearm. Harris's actions were hidden from Thompson's view by a Venetian blind screen which stretched across the entire width of the room, between the front doors and the theater bar. Thompson walked from the saloon and met Simms on the street. They shook hands and engaged in conversation. Ben warned Simms that there was going to be trouble inside. Thompson then walked down the street and Simms entered the variety hall. A few minutes later Ben returned to the front of the theater. Harris was now behind the blinds. A few patrons hurried from the hall; one of them shouted that Harris had a gun. Thompson noticed someone behind the blinds and stepped forward to get a better look. He made out the form as Harris and called to him. Harris shouted a challenge to Thompson. Ben drew and shot into the screening. The bullet cut through the blinds, ricocheted along the wainscotting of a wall, and struck Harris in the right lung, inflicting a mortal wound. Thompson stepped to one side and fired a second shot at Harris, but the bullet went wild. Thompson took another wild shot and then stepped backward toward the street.

Harris fell backward against a wall when hit by Thompson's first bullet. He managed to raise himself and stagger upstairs where he collapsed in an aisle. Simms was standing atop another staircase with a cocked pistol when Harris was shot, but he made no move to confront Thompson. Harris was carried to his home where he died later that night. Ben surrendered himself to police authorities the following day.[96]

Ben was given a preliminary hearing before Justice of the Peace Anton Adam, who committed Ben to jail without bail.[97] Ben employed a battery of attorneys for his defense: Walton, Hill, Sheeks, Sneed, Wooten, George F. Pendexter, John A. Green, Sr., John A. Green, Jr., N. O. Green and J. Minor[98] (or Miner). Thompson's attorneys asked for a writ of *habeas corpus* before District Court Judge George H. Noonan on

July 28 without success.[99] *Habeas corpus* was sued for before Judge Samuel Wilson in the Court of Appeals, but Wilson refused to grant it on lack of jurisdiction.[100] Thompson's attorneys then sued for the writ before Judge Noonan, but it was again denied.[101]

Thompson was indicted for murder on September 6[102] by the Bexar County Grand Jury. His trial was set for September 12, but was postponed until January 1883.[103] Thompson's trial began before Judge Noonan at San Antonio on January 16, 1883.[104] On January 20 he was acquitted of Harris's killing.[105]

Meanwhile, the Harris killing had cost Ben his job as city marshal at Austin. Ben resigned on August 7, 1882,[106] effective September 1 of that year,[107] but the city council refused to accept it. Instead, they granted him a sixty-day leave of absence.[108] However, the city council accepted Thompson's second resignation on October 23, 1882.[109]

The death of Harris did not end the bitter feud between Thompson and the variety theater faction. Foster, who now controlled the showhouse with Simms, announced publicly that Thompson would not be allowed to enter the place again. Thompson made threats against Simms for his part in warning Harris of his (Thompson's) presence at the theater on the day of Harris's death. Fearing Thompson, Simms left Texas and went to Chicago.[110] He returned later to San Antonio to settle his financial affairs with Foster.[111] Both Foster and Simms realized that their lives were in danger as long as Ben Thompson lived.

Ben Thompson's running feud with Foster and Simms culminated in further tragedy in March 1884. On March 11 of that year John King Fisher, a gunfighter of some

Gunfighter John King Fisher, who was widely known, ran onto Thompson and suggested they visit the Harris theater. The pair was bushwhacked inside the variety hall.

note, an ex-cattle thief and deputy sheriff of Uvalde County, Texas, met Ben Thompson in Austin. Thompson and Fisher were previously acquainted and the two gunmen made the rounds of the Austin saloons. During the course of their saloon-hopping Fisher, who was a friend of Joe Foster, suggested that he and Thompson visit the Harris variety theater in San Antonio. Thompson demurred. (Ben had refused an earlier invitation from Foster to visit the theater because he suspected a trap.) The friendship between Fisher and Foster dated back to about 1881. Foster was in the San Antonio jail about that time and Fisher supplied him with daily meals at no cost to Foster. Some have claimed that Fisher was merely trying to lure Ben into a trap. Others say that Fisher was only attempting to get mutual friends together to become bygones. At any rate, Thompson agreed reluctantly to accompany Fisher as far as San Antonio on the latter's trip home.

The two gunmen boarded the train in an inebriated state. To observers, Thompson appeared more intoxicated than Fisher. Ben was in a belligerent mood. He and Fisher took a bottle of whiskey from a foreign passenger on the train. When a Negro porter was delinquent in one of Thompson's requests, Ben struck the man on the head with the whiskey bottle, drawing blood. Fisher told Thompson to leave the Negro alone or he (Fisher) would deal with Thompson. The Negro's blood had splattered against Thompson's Lincoln-styled beaver hat; the upper part became stained with blood, so Thompson took a knife and cut out the crown.

Somewhere along the route Simms and Foster were informed via telegraph that Thompson and Fisher were on their way to San Antonio. Simms and Foster notified one of their house policemen, Jacob S. Coy, about the impending arrival. The San Antonio police force was alerted to Thompson's coming. Rumor was that the San Antonio police had been instructed to shoot Thompson at the slightest provocation.

Thompson and Fisher arrived on the night of March 11. They visited the Turner Hall Opera House to see Ada Gray starring in *East Lynne*. When the two gunmen left the opera house, Fisher suggested that they visit Harris's theater. Ben objected at first, then consented to go.

Billy Simms was extremely nervous about Thompson's inevitable arrival at the variety

Ben Thompson and John King Fisher traveled these tracks from Austin to San Antonio on their last fateful journey. At first Thompson didn't want to go, but Fisher talked him into it. Their enemies were tipped off that the gunslingers were coming.

hall. He went for a walk to help settle his nerves. When he returned, he met Thompson and Fisher. The latter had his pistol conspicuously displayed on his person. Simms greeted both men in a friendly manner. The three were then joined by Jake Coy. The four men had a round of drinks and then Thompson, Fisher, and Simms went upstairs to the balcony. They were joined later by Coy after he had notified the local police about Thompson's presence at the theater and had stationed another house policeman upstairs.

Thompson sat in a seat to Fisher's left. Simms sat in a seat nearer the end of the hall. Coy sat near Thompson. Ben sent a waiter boy to Simms, asking him to come to where he was sitting. Simms joined Thompson in a seat on the latter's left. A round of drinks was ordered by Thompson. Fisher declined a drink and ordered a cigar. Thompson told the waiter to bring two cigars. When the drinks had been brought,

Thompson joked that there was poison in his drink. He then refused to pay for the order. The waiter refused to leave. Thompson asked the youngster if he was waiting for money and the waiter replied that he could wait as long as Thompson. Fisher told Thompson to pay for the order. When the drinks had been consumed, Thompson began talking about Jack Harris and how he had been killed. Fisher objected to the topic of conversation. He stood up and said he thought that he and Thompson were out for some fun. Ben told him to be patient.

Thompson, Fisher, Simms, and Coy started toward the stairs when Ben thought he saw Joe Foster. He asked Simms if it was Foster and Billy answered in the affirmative. Thompson asked Simms to send for Foster. Simms dispatched a waiter with Thompson's message. Foster came over to where Thompson and the others were standing. He removed his eyeglasses and adjusted them. Ben reached out to shake his hand, inquiring if he wanted a drink. Foster hesitated, saying he only wished to be left alone and that he wanted no trouble with Thompson, that the world was big enough for the both of them. Thompson became angry. Heated words followed and voices were raised. Thompson made a remark about what had happened to Jack Harris. Simms, Foster and Coy backed slowly away from Thompson and Fisher. It was about 11:00 P.M.

Suddenly, a fusillade erupted. More than two dozen shots were fired. When the smoke had cleared, Thompson and Fisher were dead; Foster had been struck twice, once in the knee which severed an artery and shattered the bone, and once in the thigh;[112] and Coy had received a crippling wound in the calf of the right leg.[113] Thompson was struck by nine bullets; any one of eight would have proved fatal.[114] Fisher had been hit by thirteen bullets.[115] Coy's wound left him permanently crippled. Foster's leg was eventually amputated; he died of complications of the wound on March 22.

Drs. Worthington and Wooten (who was one of the most scientifically minded medical men in Texas[116]) performed an autopsy on the body of Ben Thompson. The autopsy showed that five of the nine bullets which hit Thompson had entered the head; a sixth bullet struck his left jaw; a seventh hit his left arm and penetrated his heart; another bullet entered the left hip and exited his body on the right side under the ribs; and still another creased his back across the shoulders.[117] The *official conclusions* of the autopsy were that Thompson was *standing erect and still when struck simultaneously at least by five different persons using both*

Western History Collections, University of Oklahoma Library
Billy Simms, who was co-owner of the variety hall, feared Thompson, but he met the two men and they had a round of drinks. Simms realized that he would never have peace of mind until Thompson was dead.

rifles and pistols who were standing a little above and to the left of him.[118]

It was obvious. Thompson and Fisher had been murdered by concealed assassins hired by Simms and Foster. The coroner's jury, for some reason, chose to ignore the autopsy report and to accept the biased testimony of Simms and Coy that Thompson had entered the variety theater in a belligerent mood and had slapped Foster and attempted to kill him, but was stopped by Coy who wrestled with Thompson for his pistol. Captain Shardein of the San Antonio police force testified that Thompson's pistol was found with five empty chambers. That

Thompson had fired his pistol or was wrestling with Coy or anyone else was a medical impossibility, according to the autopsy report. (Obviously someone had fired Thompson's pistol five times to make it appear as if he had triggered the weapon before he was killed). Simms and Coy could hardly be called impartial witnesses.

At least three impartial eyewitnesses—Thomas McGee, a Texas rancher,[119] and Alex T. Raymond and John R. Sublett, two traveling salesmen[120]—stated postitively that neither Thompson nor Fisher drew a weapon. Raymond and Sublett also said that either Simms or Coy had taken Thompson's revolver and shot him twice in the head and once in the body and that the other one had shot Fisher in a similar manner.[121] These *coup de grace* shots were unnecessary, for both Thompson and Fisher died instantly. Raymond and Sublett also said that Foster had accidentally shot himself in the leg while drawing his pistol.[122] The jury, however, ruled that Thompson and Fisher had met their deaths justifiably at the hands of Simms, Coy, and Foster.[123] This was an obvious falsehood; Simms, Coy, and Foster had been armed only with pistols and had been standing on a level with Thompson and Fisher.

After the killings, Simms assisted Foster down the stairs. Simms had a pistol in his hand. He had drawn the gun shortly before Thompson and Fisher were killed. (Fisher had yelled at him not to draw the weapon.) As Simms was helping Foster, Billy Thompson who had been drinking a few doors away and heard about the shooting, rushed into the theater and started up the stairs. He was met by both Simms and Captain Shardein. The police captain searched Billy for weapons, but found none. Billy was then escorted from the theater to avoid further trouble.[124] Some of the women employed at the showhouse crowded around the two dead men, wanting to view Ben's body.

King Fisher's part in the whole affair has always been something of a mystery. It is doubtful that Foster would have used his friend willingly as a dupe in bringing Ben to the theater and then having him assassinated along with Thompson. Fisher was probably killed because of his close proximity to Thompson when the latter was fired upon. It's possible, however, that Foster might not have been too sure of Fisher's loyalty once Thompson had been killed, and therefore, was not averse to letting Fisher fend for himself. Fisher probably had been acting as an arbitrator and was killed as a matter of circumstance.

The assassins were never officially identified, much less arrested. However, it was later rumored that three of the assassins had been a bartender named McLaughlin, a gambler known only as "Canada Bill," and an actor at the variety hall named Harry Tremain.

The body of Ben Thompson was sent to Austin and interred in the Oakwood Cemetery. In a way, Thompson's death was the high-water mark of the American frontier. His breed of men had become a relic of the past, even in 1884. Those men who had the foresight to adapt to the changing frontier survived; those who didn't, perished.

Ben Thompson was a product of the era which he helped to make. Therefore, he is to be judged within the context of that era. At best, he was a violent man in a violent time. One is as extinct as the other.

NOTES

1. CLAY ALLISON

1. F. Stanley, *Clay Allison,* p. 18.
2. Military service records of R. A. C. Allison, Light Tennessee Artillery, Confederate States Army, Old Military Records Division, National Archives, Washington, D.C.
3. Ibid.
4. Ibid.
5. Ibid.
6. Stanley, p. 102.
7. Military service records of R. C. Allison, Nineteenth Regiment Tennessee Cavalry, Confederate States Army, Old Military Records Division, National Archives, Washington, D.C.
8. Ibid.
9. Letter, Clay Allison to the Editor to the *Ford County* (Kansas) *Globe* (Dodge City), February 26, 1880, published in the *Globe* of March 2, 1880.
10. Military service records of R. C. Allison, Nineteenth Regiment Tennessee, Confederate States Army, Old Military Records Division, National Archives, Washington, D.C.
11. Ibid.
12. Ibid.
13. Stanley, p. 59.
14. Ibid., pp. 58-59.
15. Ibid., p. 59.
16. Ibid.
17. Ibid., p. 194; letter, Ernest R. Archambeau to Dale T. Schoenberger, no date on letter.
18. *The Daily New Mexican* (Santa Fe), July 19, 1887.
19. Stanley, p. 201.
20. Ibid.
21. Stanley, *The Grant That Maxwell Bought,* p. 147.
22. Letters, F. Stanley to Dale T. Schoenberger, July 26, 1965; Tom Hill, County and District Court Clerk, Hemphill County, Tex., to Dale T. Schoenberger, no date on letter.
23. Information given to Dale T. Schoenberger by the Pecos, Texas, Chamber of Commerce.
24. Ibid.
25. Stanley, *Clay Allison,* p. 88.
26. Ibid.
27. Ibid., p. 94.
28. Ibid.
29. Ed Bartholomew, *The Biographical Album of Western Gunfighters,* p. 44.
30. *The Weekly New Mexican* (Santa Fe), October 18, 1870.
31. Bartholomew, p. 44; Stanley, *Clay Allison,* p. 95.
32. O. S. Clark, *Clay Allison of the Washita,* p. 19.
33. Stanley, *The Grant That Maxwell Bought,* p. 68.
34. *The Daily New Mexican,* January 13, 1874.
35. Harry E. Kelsey, Jr., "Clay Allison: Western Gunman," *Brand Book of the Denver Westerners,* 1957, p. 388.
36. Stanley, *Desperadoes of New Mexico,* p. 177.
37. Old-timers say that Chunk Colbert wanted to kill Clay Allison because Clay had bested his uncle. Others say that Colbert wanted to enhance his reputation by killing Allison.

38. Stanley, in his *Clay Allison,* pp. 98-99, says that Chunk Colbert was killed in a one-room cafe next door to the Clifton House.
39. *The Daily New Mexican,* January 13, 1874.
40. Ibid.
41. Kelsey, p. 388. Kelsey, interview with Clarence Stockton, nephew of Tom Stockton, March 25, 1954.
42. Letter, Mrs. Dorotha M. Bradley, Assistant Archivist, New Mexico State Records Center and Archives, Santa Fe, to Dale T. Schoenberger, July 12, 1966.
43. *Raton* (New Mexico) *Range,* July 22, 1887.
44. Ibid.
45. I can find no record of this incident.
46. *Las Animas* (Colorado) *Leader,* September 24, 1875.
47. *Colorado Chieftain* (Pueblo), November 3, 1875.
48. Stanley, *Clay Allison,* p. 132.
49. *Raton Range,* July 22, 1887.
50. *The Daily New Mexican,* June 1, 1875.
51. *Colorado Chieftain,* November 12, 1875.
52. *Raton Range,* July 22, 1887.
53. Jim Berry Pearson, *The Maxwell Land Grant,* p. 71.
54. Stanley, *Clay Allison,* p. 80.
55. Letter, Mrs. Dorotha M. Bradley, Assistant Archivist, New Mexico State Records Center and Archives, Santa Fe, to Dale T. Schoenberger, July 12, 1966.
56. *Raton Range,* July 22, 1887. This printing press was found in the Cimarron River in the early 1950's. Judge Henry L. Waldo later issued a warrant for Clay Allison's arrest because of this incident.
57. Agnes Morley Cleaveland, *No Life for a Lady,* p. 8. Mrs. A. M. Cleaveland was the daughter of W. R. Morley.
58. Letter, Elmer O. Parker, Old Military Records Division, National Archives, Washington, D.C., to Dale T. Schoenberger, November 14, 1967.
59. *The Daily New Mexican,* March 30, 1876. This newspaper stated that Clay Allison was arrested at Cimarron.
60. *Raton Range,* July 22, 1887.
61. The killing of soldiers by a civilian came under civilian jurisdiction.
62. *The Daily New Mexican,* October 10, 1876. Davy Crockett was killed by peace officers in October, 1876.
63. Stanley, *The Grant That Maxwell Bought,* p. 68; Stanley, *Fort Union* (New Mexico), p. 225.
64. Letter, Mrs. Virginia Rust, Assistant in Manuscripts, Henry E. Huntington Library and Art Gallery, San Marino, California, to Dale T. Schoenberger, June 29, 1966. The William G. Ritch papers are in the possession of this library. It is interesting to note that Frank Springer was one of the owners of the *Cimarron News and Press* at the time Clay Allison destroyed the paper's printing equipment.
65. Ibid. In 1875-1878 Colfax County court trials and hearings were held at Taos by territorial decree.
66. Ibid.
67. *Colorado Chieftain,* December 31, 1876.
68. Ibid., December 27, 1876.
69. Luke Cahill, "Recollections of a Plainsman," p. 48, manuscript, State Historical Society of Colorado, Denver.
70. *Las Animas Leader,* December 22, 1876.
71. A. K. Richeson, interview with William Thatcher, January 17, 1934, p. 9, manuscript, State Historical Society of Colorado, Denver.
72. Cahill, p. 48.
73. *Colorado Chieftain,* December 31, 1876.
74. Ibid., January 3, 1877.
75. Cahill, p. 48.
76. *Las Animas Leader,* December 22, 1876.
77. *Colorado Chieftain,* December 31, 1876; January 3, 1877.
78. Kelsey, p. 398.
79. *Las Animas Leader,* December 22, 1876.
80. Kelsey, p. 399.
81. *Colorado Chieftain,* January 3, 1877; *Las Animas, Leader,* January 5, 1877.
82. *Las Animas Leader,* January 5, 1877.
83. *Colorado Chieftain,* February 6, 1877.
84. *Las Animas Leader,* January 12, 1877.
85. *Colorado Chieftain,* January 9, 1877.
86. Ibid.
87. *Las Animas Leader,* February 16, 1877.
88. Kelsey, p. 400.
89. *Las Animas Leader,* February 9, 1877.
90. Miscellaneous Record Book "B," Colfax County, New Mexico, Courthouse, Raton, N.M.
91. *Las Animas Leader,* January 5, 1877.
92. Ibid., March 30, 1877.
93. Stanley J. Sierson, Jr., Chief of Detectives, East Saint Louis, Illinois, Police Department, in a letter to the author, dated August 24, 1965, said that the city's police records for 1878 are no longer available.
94. I can find where no Saint Louis newspaper referred to Clay Allison as "a murderer of fifteen men."
95. Clay Allison was mistaken when he said that he had served under Ben McCulloch during the last two years of the war. McCulloch was killed in 1862. Allison probably meant Colonel Robert McCulloch of the Confederate Army.
96. "Mexico" referred to the New Mexico Territory. "Old Mexico" was used in reference to the country.
97. Letter, Milt Hinkle to Dale T. Schoenberger, March 17, 1964. Milt Hinkle is the son of George T. Hinkle, the bartender in George M. Hoover's saloon at Dodge City and twice sheriff of Ford County. Milt Hinkle during his younger days was a famous Wild West performer and rodeo cowboy.
98. *Dodge City,* (Kansas) *Times,* July 26, 1878.
99. Letter, Pink Simms to Floyd Benjamin Streeter, October 27, 1935, Walter S. Campbell collection, Dodge City File, General Research Correspondence, Division of Manuscripts, University of Oklahoma Library, Norman; Stanley Vestal, *Dodge City: Queen of Cowtowns* (Bantam edition), p. 122.
100. Charles A. Siringo, *A Lone Star Cowboy,* pp. 101-2; Siringo, *Riata and Spurs,* p. 59. Siringo claimed that he and another cowhand, John Ferris, were ordered to join the twenty-odd cowhands backing Clay Allison.
101. Letter, Thomas Masterson, Jr., to Floyd Benjamin Streeter, September 17, 1935, Walter S. Campbell Collection, Dodge City File, General Research Correspondence, Division of Manuscripts, University of Oklahoma Library, Norman; Vestal, p. 123.
102. Vestal, p. 236.
103. Copies of the Dodge City, Kansas, police court dockets for the period of July to December, 1878, Walter S. Campbell Collection, Dodge City File, General Research Correspondence, Division of Manuscripts, University of Oklahoma Library, Norman.
104. Letter, Milt Hinkle to Dale T. Schoenberger, March 17, 1964.
105. Ibid., March 6, 1964.
106. Stanley, *Clay Allison,* p. 173.
107. *Ford County Globe,* March 2, 1880.
108. *Las Vegas* (New Mexico) *Daily Optic,* March 31,

1881; *Cimarron* (New Mexico) *News and Press*, April 7, 1881; *Raton Range*, July 22, 1887.

109. Marriage Book "A," pp. 37-38, Colfax County, New Mexico, Courthouse, Raton, N.M. The marriage license of John W. Allison and Betty McCullough was not recorded until 1884.

110. Stanley, *Clay Allison*, p. 212.

111. Ibid., p. 228.

112. Ibid., p. 111.

113. *Raton* (New Mexico) *Comet*, January 21, 1887.

114. *Cheyenne* (Wyoming) *Democratic Leader*, June 13, 1886.

115. *Las Vegas Daily Optic*, July 7, 1886.

116. Letter, Mrs. Katherine Halverson, Chief, Historical Division, Wyoming State Archives and Historical Department, Cheyenne, to Dale T. Schoenberger, September 24, 1965.

117. *Las Vegas Daily Optic*, July 7, 1886.

118. The Daily New Mexican, July 19, 1887.

119. Ibid.

120. Information given to Dale T. Schoenberger by the Pecos, Texas, Chamber of Commerce.

121. *The Daily New Mexican*, July 19, 1887.

122. Stanley, *Clay Allison*, p. 111.

123. Miguel Antonio Otero, *My Life on the Frontier* (1864-1882) 1:127; Stanley, *Clay Allison*, p. 220; letter, F. Stanley to Dale T. Schoenberger, July 25, 1965.

124. Otero, p. 127; Stanley, *Clay Allison*, p. 228.

125. Information sent to Dale T. Schoenberger by the Public Health Department, City of Fort Worth, Texas.

126. *Globe Live Stock Journal* (Dodge City), July 26, 1887.

2. WYATT EARP

1. Stuart N. Lake, *Wyatt Earp: Frontier Marshal*, pp. 4, 372.

2. Ibid., p. 4.

3. Letter, from the office of Ted R. Carpenter, County Recorder, San Bernardino, California, to Dale T. Schoenberger, December 1, 1967.

4. Frank Waters, *The Earp Brothers of Tombstone*, p. 29; Bartholomew, *Wyatt Earp: The Untold Story*, p. 24.

5. Bartholomew, *Wyatt Earp: The Untold Story*, pp. 24-25.

6. Waters, 29; Bartholomew, *Wyatt Earp: The Untold Story*, p. 25. The United States census report of 1870 for Lamar, Barton County, Missouri, Lamar Township, taken on September 3, enumerated Wyatt Earp, who gave his occupation as "farmer," and Irilla Earp, who gave her age as twenty-one, and was listed as the wife of Wyatt Earp.

7. Waters, p. 29.

8. Ibid.

9. *South-West Missourian* (Lamar), June 16, 1870.

10. Bartholomew, *Wyatt Earp: The Untold Story*, pp. 33-42.

11. Ibid.

12. United States District Court Judge Isaac C. Parker, the infamous "Hanging Judge," gained his reputation on the bench at Fort Smith.

13. Wayne Gard, *The Chisholm Trail*, pp. 190, 203, 212, 219, 232.

14. Ibid., p. 190.

15. Letter, Floyd Benjamin Streeter to Frank Waters, January 4, 1938; Waters, pp. 37-38.

16. Floyd Benjamin Streeter, *Prairie Trails and Cow Towns*, p. 108.

17. Ibid., p. 167.

18. *Wichita* (Kansas) *City Eagle*, October 29, 1874.

19. The municipal records of Wichita do not substantiate the claim that Wyatt Earp served as a member of the Wichita city police force *at any time in 1874*.

20. "Proceedings of the Governing Body," Records of the City of Wichita, Kansas, Journal "B," p. 42; *Wichita City Eagle*, April 8, 1875.

21. "Proceedings of the Governing Body," Records of the City of Wichita, Kansas, Journal "B," pp. 44, 53; *Wichita* (Kansas) *Weekly Beacon*, April 28, 1875. It is of interest to note that Bessie Earp and her "girls" were fined on several occasions by the police court, but after Wyatt Earp became a member of the city police force, Bessie and her girls were never fined.—letter, Ben L. Witherspoon, Deputy City Clerk, Wichita, to Dale T. Schoenberger, July 24, 1962.

22. "Proceedings of the Governing Body," Records of the City of Wichita, Kansas, Journal "B," pp. 66-67, 71.

23. Ibid, pp. 55, 62, 66, 71, 75, 77, 78, 81, 85, 90, 96, 100.

24. Letter, Donald C. Gisick, Deputy City Clerk, Wichita, Kansas, to Dale T. Schoenberger, March 15, 1967. The total of 366 was for the period of April 12, 1875 to April 30, 1876.

25. Letters, Waldo E. Koop to Dale T. Schoenberger, June 26, 1962; Ben L. Witherspoon, Deputy City Clerk, Wichita, Kansas, to Dale T. Schoenberger, July 16, 1962.

26. Letters, Waldo E. Koop to Dale T. Schoenberger, June 26, 1962; Ben L. Witherspoon, Deputy City Clerk, Wichita, Kansas, to Dale T. Schoenberger, July 16, 1962; July 24, 1962; Bartholomew, *Wyatt Earp: The Untold Story*, pp. 112, 114, 126-27, 150.

27. Bartholomew, *Wyatt Earp: The Untold Story*, pp. 126-27.

28. Lake, pp. 115-17, 123, 132; letter, Waldo E. Koop to Dale T. Schoenberger, July 1, 1962.

29. Harry Sinclair Drago, *Wild, Woolly and Wicked*, pp. 215-19; Drago, interview with Sam Jones, June 20, 1959.

30. Bartholomew, *Wyatt Earp: The Untold Story*, pp. 160-65. A copy of this letter is in the collection of Ed Bartholomew, Fort Davis, Texas. In 1925 Wyatt Earp had a script written about his life on the fron-

tier. He had hoped that his friend William S. Hart, the cowboy film star, would play the part on the screen.—letter, Wyatt S. Earp to William S. Hart, July 3, 1925. One of the reasons for the script was that Wyatt was displeased with the many "lies" that were being written about him. Ibid.

31. *Wichita City Eagle,* May 6, 1875; *Wichita Weekly Beacon,* May 12, 1875.
32. *Wichita Weekly Beacon,* May 26, 1875; *Wichita City Eagle,* May 27, 1875.
33. *Wichita Weekly Beacon,* December 15, 1875.
34. Ibid., January 12, 1876.
35. Gambling and prostitution were not legally prohibited in Wichita until 1876 and 1875, respectively. Gamblers and prostitutes, however, paid regular "fines" which were a source of income to the city. If they defaulted in the payments, they were arrested and fined in the police court. Wyatt Earp gambled in the back room of a saloon, as did other gamblers, to avoid paying the regular fine.
36. *Wichita Weekly Beacon,* April 5, 1876. Morgan Earp, Wyatt's brother, was also at Wichita at this time. He was fined a total of three dollars for an unnamed offense on October 1, 1875.—"Miscellaneous Papers," Records of the City of Wichita, Kansas.
37. Ibid.
38. Bartholomew, *Wyatt Earp: The Untold Story,* p. 157.
39. *Wichita Weekly Beacon,* April 5, 1876.
40. "Proceedings of the Governing Body," Wichita, Journal "B," p. 112.
41. *Wichita Weekly Beacon,* April 5, 1876.
42. "Proceedings of the Governing Body," Wichita, Journal "B," p. 103.
43. Ibid., pp. 66-67, 71.
44. Ibid., p. 107.
45. Ibid., p. 112.
46. "Miscellaneous Papers," Records of the City of Wichita, Kansas.
47. "Proceedings of the Governing Body," Wichita, Journal "B," p. 115.
48. *Tombstone* (Arizona) *Nugget,* November 17, 1881.
49. Bartholomew, *Wyatt Earp: The Untold Story,* p. 114.
50. *Wichita Weekly Beacon,* May 24, 1876.
51. Letter, Milt Hinkle to Dale T. Schoenberger, no date on letter. Bill Tilghman's horse, "Chant," won the Kentucky Derby in 1894.
52. *Dodge City* (Kansas) *Times,* October 14, 1876.
53. "*Strausbach* vs. *E. Cramer,*" District Court, Civil Records, Ford County, Kansas, Dodge City; Vestal, p. 235; Bartholomew, *Wyatt Earp: The Untold Story,* pp. 174-75.
54. Gard, p. 232.
55. Ibid., p. 218.
56. Ibid., p. 231. Government records rounded off the total 321,928 to 322,000.—Tenth United States census report, *Statistics of Agriculture,* p. 975, Census Division, National Archives, Washington, D.C.; Walter Prescott Webb, *The Great Plains* (Grosset's Universal Library edition), p. 223; Vestal, p. 83.
57. Gard, p. 236.
58. Ibid., p. 239.
59. Ibid., p. 253.
60. Ibid.
61. Ibid., pp. 218, 232, 236, 239, 253, 255, 256, 257.
62. Dodge City, Kansas, Ordinance Book, 1:4, Kansas State Historical Society, Topeka.
63. Letter, Milt Hinkle to the author, no date on letter.
64. Letter, Dr. Samuel J. Crumbine to Walter S. Camp-

bell (Stanley Vestal), January 24, 1950, Walter S. Campbell Collection, Dodge City File, General Research Correspondence, Division of Manuscripts, University of Oklahoma Library, Norman. Only three cowhands were killed in fights at Dodge City between 1875-1886.
65. *Dodge City Times,* March 31, 1877. Wyatt Earp was not listed as a Dodge City police officer in the *Times* after March 31, 1877, until he was appointed assistant marshal there in May, 1878.
66. Walter Noble Burns, *Tombstone: An Iliad of the Southwest,* p. 56.
67. W. B. (Bat) Masterson, "Famous Gunfighters of the Western Frontier," *Human Life Magazine,* 1907.
68. Bartholomew, *Wyatt Earp: The Untold Story,* p. 175.
69. Letter, Lonnie Lee, the grandson of J-Bob Lee, to Dale T. Schoenberger, December 10, 1964. Jim Slade, a hardware clerk at Dodge City in 1876, told Lonnie Lee, who met Slade at Lewiston, Idaho, during the 1920s, that he could still remember Wyatt Earp walking around Dodge City with a bandaged head after his fight with Red Sweeney. Lee said he met the girl whom Earp and Sweeney fought over at Globe or Miama, Arizona, during the 1920s.
70. Ibid.
71. Letter, Lonnie Lee to "Mail Roundup," *Real West Magazine,* VIII, Number 39 (January, 1965):80.
72. Nyle H. Miller and Joseph W. Snell, *Why the West Was Wild,* p. 153.
73. John Barbour, Associated Press wire story, March 19, 1967.
74. Letter, George R. Henrichs, Executive Director, Dodge City, Kansas, Boot Hill Museum, to Dale T. Schoenberger, July 12, 1963.
75. Masterson, "Famous Gunfighters of the Western Frontier," *Human Life Magazine,* 1907.
76. *Wichita Morning Eagle,* July 24, 1938.
77. Lake, p. 205.
78. Letter, Milt Hinkle to the author, January 18, 1964.
79. Ibid., no date on letter.
80. Ibid., January 18, 1964.
81. Letter, Pink Simms to Frank Waters, no date on letter; Waters, p. 40.
82. Letter, T. F. Hobble to Dale T. Schoenberger, March 27, 1967. T. F. Hobble is the son of Frank A. Hobble. Hamilton B. (Ham) Bell, a resident of Dodge City from 1874 to 1947, was non-committal on Wyatt Earp.—Letter, Robert E. Eagan to the author, April 4, 1967. Eagan interviewed Bell's secretary for the author.
83. *Dodge City Times,* July 21, 1877.
84. Masterson, "Famous Gunfighters of the Western Frontier," *Human Life Magazine,* 1907.
85. *Dodge City Times,* May 11, 1878.
86. *Ford County Globe,* May 14, 1878.
87. *Dodge City Times,* June 8, July 6, August 10, September 7, October 5, and December 7, 1878.
88. Ibid., August 10, 1878.
89. Lake, p. 205.
90. *Ford County Globe,* August 27, 1878.
91. Eddie Foy and Alvin F. Harlow, *Clowning Through Life,* p. 112.
92. *Dodge City Times,* July 26, 1878.
93. *Ford County Globe,* July 30, 1878.
94. *Dodge City Times,* July 26, 1878. It is believed that this other cowhand was Joe Day, Charles French, or a man named Harrison.
95. *Ford County Globe,* July 30, 1878.

96. *Dodge City Times,* August 24, 1878; *Ford County Globe,* August 27, 1878.

97. *Ford County Globe,* August 20, 1878.

98. Copies of the Dodge City police court dockets for the period of July to December 1878, Walter S. Campbell Collection, Dodge City File, General Research Correspondence, Division of Manuscripts, University of Oklahoma Library, Norman. Jim Kenedy (spelled correctly with one *n*) was the half-breed son of Captain Mifflin Kenedy, the former partner of Cattleman Richard King of the famous King Ranch of Texas.

99. Ibid.

100. *Dodge City Times,* October 5 and October 12, 1878; *Ford County Globe,* October 8, 1878.

101. *Dodge City Times,* December 7, 1878.

102. Ibid., April 12, 1879; *Ford County Globe,* April 15, 1879. The salary reduction of Wyatt Earp obviously was because of the end of Dodge City's cattle season. Earp's salary cut was more than restored with the beginning of the cattle season of 1879.

103. William A. Settle, Jr., *Jesse James Was His Name,* pp. 101-2.

104. Copies of the Dodge City police court dockets, January to December, 1879, Walter S. Campbell Collection, University of Oklahoma Library.

105. *Dodge City Times,* May 24, 1879.

106. *Ford County Globe,* June 10, 1879.

107. Copies of the Dodge City police court dockets, January to December, 1879, Walter S. Campbell Collection, University of Oklahoma Library.

108. Miller and Snell, p. 157.

109. *Ford County Globe,* September 16 and October 28, 1879.

110. Letter, Milt Hinkle to "Frontier Post," *Frontier Times Magazine,* Spring, 1961; Bartholomew, *Wyatt Earp: The Untold Story,* p. 315.

111. *Ford County Globe,* September 9, 1879.

112. Vestal, pp. 126, 236.

113. Copies of the Dodge City police court dockets, July, 1878, to September, 1879, Walter S. Campbell Collection, University of Oklahoma Library. Stanley Vestal states that Wyatt Earp made a total of 35 arrests during this period, and that 64 arrests were recorded for 1878. Vestal, p. 126. Vestal's surviving handwritten copies of these dockets record only 44 arrests for 1878; another eleven entries are listed on page 236 (Bantam edition) of his book, *Dodge City: Queen of Cowtowns,* making a total of 55 *known* arrests for 1878. Since Vestal was under the false impression that Earp was city marshal, he erroneously credited Wyatt as the arresting officer when the arrest was recorded as being made "by the marshal." Vestal also reported that only 29 arrests were made for 1879, but his own copies of the dockets reveal that a total of 41 arrests were made that year.

114. Ibid. A total of 78 arrests were recorded for this period. In addition to the totals of Wyatt Earp and Jim Masterson, City Marshal Charlie Bassett made 12 arrests and Officer John Brown, who was dismissed from the police force in August, 1878, made five arrests.

115. Vestal, p. 126.

116. Bartholomew, *Wyatt Earp: The Untold Story,* p. 307.

117. Ibid., p. 309.

118. *Ford County Globe,* September 30, 1879.

119. *Tombstone Nugget,* November 17, 1881.

120. Letter, Margaret J. Sparks, Reference Librarian, Arizona Pioneers' Historical Society, Tucson, to Dale T. Schoenberger, July 27, 1966.

121. Waters, pp. 182-83.

122. *Ford County Globe,* March 30, 1880.

123. *Tombstone* (Arizona) *Epitaph,* October 20, 1880.

124. Ibid.

125. Ibid.

126. Ibid., October 28, 1880.

127. "Minutes of the Common Council," Records of the City of Tombstone, Arizona Territory.

128. Ibid.

129. Ibid. Mayor J. P. Clum also was editor and publisher of the *Tombstone Epitaph.* The *Epitaph's* editorial policy was slated toward the Earps and their interests.

130. Waters, p. 102. Johnny Behan was later superintendent of the Arizona Territorial Prison at Yuma.

131. Waters, p. 102.

132. *Tombstone Nugget,* November 17, 1881. The post records of Camp Rucker for 1880 reveal much livestock theft from the post, and that Lieut. J. H. Hurst led his expedition in search of thieves in July, 1880. —Telegram, Captain Alexander B. McGowan to the commanding officers of Camp Huachuca and Fort Lowell, Arizona, July 25, 1880; letter, Lieut. Joseph H. Hurst to Captain Alexander B. McGowan, July 29, 1880, Post Records of Camp Rucker, Arizona Territory, 1880, Old Military Records Division, National Archives, Washington, D.C. A search of the reports submitted by Lieut. Hurst reveals that he did not engage the services of the Earp brothers in any official quartermaster capacity.—letter, Elmer O. Parker, Assistant Director, Old Military Records Division, National Archives, Washington, D. C., to Dale T. Schoenberger, August 13, 1970. In his letter, Hurst stated that his pursuit of the thieves was unsuccessful.

133. George Whitwell Parsons, *The Private Journal of George Whitwell Parsons,* Arizona Pioneers' Historical Society, Tucson.

134. *Tombstone Nugget,* March 19, 1881. Undersheriff H. M. Woods was also editor of the *Nugget.* The paper's editorial policy was slanted against the Earps and their interests.

135. Waters, p. 134.

136. Ibid.

137. *Tombstone Nugget,* July 6, 1881.

138. Waters, p. 140. Wells, Fargo and Company's undercover detective in the Tombstone area, Frederick J. Dodge, in a letter to Stuart N. Lake, dated September 15, 1930, stated that he knew Doc Holliday was involved in the outlaw gang around Tombstone, and intimated that Holliday had killed Budd Philpot. Dodge, a friend of the Earps, admitted in the same letter that Wells, Fargo's own resident agent, Marshall Williams, was tipping off the stage robbers.

139. *Arizona Daily Star* (Tucson), June 23, 1881.

140. *Arizona Weekly Star* (Tucson), August 25, 1881.

141. *Tombstone Nugget,* November 17, 1881.

142. Ibid.

143. Ibid.

144. Waters, pp. 157, 168.

145. Wyatt Earp is said to have used his legendary "Buntline Special" single-action Colt .45 revolver in the fight with the Clantons and McLaurys. The "Buntline" allegedly was a gift to Earp and other Dodge City peace officers, including Bat Masterson, from the famous dime novelist Ned Buntline. The revolver supposedly had a 12-inch barrel and "NED" carved

in the stock. Obviously a revolver with a 12-inch barrel would not have fit into an overcoat pocket. The Colt factory has no record of any sale to Buntline nor is there any evidence that Earp ever owned a Colt revolver with a 12-inch barrel.—James E. Serven, "The Buntline Special—Fact or Fiction?" *The American Rifleman*, 115, Number 3, 18. Colt did, however, manufacture a revolver with a 16-inch barrel in the late 1870s.

146. Ike Clanton testified that he saw Morgan Earp shoot Clanton's brother in the chest.

147. Johnny Behan testified that he saw Billy Clanton shoot Morgan Earp. Behan watched the fight from the side of C. S. Fly's boardinghouse.

148. *Tombstone Epitaph*, October 28, 1881.

149. Lloyd and Rose Hamill, *Hamill's Tombstone Picture Gallery*, p. 15.

150. *Tombstone Nugget*, October 30, 1881.

151. *Tombstone Epitaph*, October 31, 1881.

152. "Minutes of the Common Council," Records of the City of Tombstone, Arizona Territory.

153. Hamill, p. 16; Bartholomew, *Wyatt Earp: The Man and the Myth*, p. 251.

154. *Tombstone Epitaph*, November 24, 1881.

155. Waters, p. 173.

156. *Tombstone Epitaph*, March 20, 1882.

157. Ibid., March 21, 1882.

158. Waters, p. 198.

159. *Tombstone Epitaph*, March 25, 1882.

160. Waters, p. 200.

161. Bartholomew, *Wyatt Earp, The Man and the Myth*, pp. 315-16.

162. Ibid.

163. Waters, p. 199.

164. Ibid, p. 190.

165. *Arizona Weekly Star*, May 26, 1881.

166. Waters, p. 208. The papers of F. W. Pitkin at the Colorado State Archives and Public Records Center, Denver, contain nothing in regards to the extradition of Wyatt Earp or John H. Holliday.—Letter, Mrs. Velma Churchill, Principal Archivist Aide, Colorado State Archives and Public Records Center, Denver, to Dale T. Schoenberger, October 9, 1967.

167. *Arizona Enterprise* (Florence), July 7, 1888.

168. Ike Clanton was killed by J. V. Brighton near Fort Grant, Arizona, in 1887. Johnny Behan died at Tucson in 1917. Billy Claiborne, the fifth man in the Clanton-McLaury party in the famous Tombstone street fight of 1881, was killed by Frank (Buckskin) Leslie at Tombstone in 1882.

169. Miller and Snell, pp. 161-62.

170. Letters, Margaret J. Sparks, Reference Librarian, Arizona Pioneers' Historical Society, Tucson, to Dale T. Schoenberger, June 1, 1966; Mrs. Marguerite B. Cooley, Director, Arizona State Library and Archives, Phoenix, to Dale T. Schoenberger, June 21, 1966.

171. Letter, Mrs. Luisa Arps, Librarian, State Historical Society of Colorado, Denver, to the author, July 18, 1966. Frank Waters, in his book, *The Earp Brothers of Tombstone*, pages 216 and 247, states that the reference to Wyatt Earp being wounded comes from the *Arizona Gazette* (no city given) of September 14, 1884.

172. Letter, Mrs. Zelma B. Locker, Head Librarian, California Room, San Diego Public Library, to the author, July 20, 1966.

173. Ibid.

174. Waters, pp. 217-18.

175. Anton Mazzanovitch, "Wyatt Earp," *Brewery Gulch* (Arizona) *Gazette* (Bisbee), April 29, 1932.

176. *Arizona Daily Citizen* (Tucson), May 22, 1900.

177. Letter, T. F. Hobble to Dale T. Schoenberger, March 27, 1967. Alfred Williams was alleged to be alive as late as 1967, but refused to communicate with the author.

178. Letter, T. Morton, Lieutenant, Acting Commander, Public Information Division, Los Angeles Police Department, to Dale T. Schoenberger, July 28, 1966.

179. *Arizona Star* (Tucson), July 26, 1911.

180. Information given to Dale T. Schoenberger by the office of William G. Sharp, County Clerk and Clerk, Superior Court, County of Los Angeles, California.

181. Waters, p. 223. Josephine Sarah Marcus said that she had married Wyatt Earp a few years after they left Tombstone.

3. WILD BILL HICKOK

1. *Chicago* (Illinois) *Record*, December 26, 1896; William Elsey Connelley, *Wild Bill and His Era*, p. 12.

2. Years later Bill Cody said that he first met Wild Bill Hickok in September, 1857, when both were with Lewis Simpson's wagon train in the Mormon Country of Utah. Cody said that Hickok kept another teamster from manhandling him and they became friends afterwards. Cody, however, was mistaken as to where and when he met Hickok. No record exists which placed Wild Bill with the Simpson wagon train. Reliable reports place Hickok in Johnson, Kansas, at this time.

3. John Preston Arthur, *History of Watauga County, North Carolina, With Sketches of Prominent Families*.

4. Frank J. Wilstach, *Wild Bill Hickok: The Prince of Pistoleers*, pp. 67-70.

5. *Territory of Nebraska, County of Gage* vs. "*Dutch Bill, Doc, and Wellman*," July, 1861, Nebraska State Historical Society, Lincoln.

6. Connelley, p. 43.

7. *Territory of Nebraska, County of Gage* vs. "*Dutch Bill, Doc, and Wellman*," July, 1861, Nebraska State Historical Society, Lincoln.

8. Records of the War Department, Office of the Quartermaster General, "Reports of Persons and Articles Hired, 1861-1865," Old Military Records Division, National Archives, Washington, D.C.

9. If legend is correct, eight famous Western personalities were in the battle at Wilson's Creek. Wild Bill

Hickok and Major (later Brevet Major General) Samuel D. Sturgis, later the regimental commander of the famous Seventh United States Cavalry, fought with Union forces. With Confederate forces in the battle were the infamous guerrilla leader, William Clarke Quantrill, and the famous Missouri outlaw, Frank James, older brother of the legendary outlaw Jesse James. George Bent, the half-breed Cheyenne son of fur trader William Bent and later famous as a Cheyenne "squaw-man," also fought with Confederate forces. E. A. Carr, later acting regimental commander of the Indian-fighting fifth U.S. Cavalry, was also there as a Union officer. Other soon-to-be frontier personalities fighting with Union forces were Myles Moylan, later of the Seventh U.S. Cavalry, who fought at the battles of the Little Big Horn and Wounded Knee, and John Burkman, later famous as Brevet Major General George A. Custer's personal orderly.

10. Records of the War Department, Office of the Provost Marshal General, "Scouts, Guides and Spies, 1861-1866," Old Military Records Division, National Archives, Washington, D.C.
11. Joseph G. Rosa, *They Called Him Wild Bill,* p. 49.
12. Ibid.
13. *The War of the Rebellion: A Compilation of the Official Records of the Union and Confederate Armies,* Series I, Volume 48, Part I, pp. 810, 819.
14. Letter, J. B. Edwards to William Elsey Connelley, January 27, 1926, Manuscript Division, Kansas State Historical Society, Topeka.
15. *Springfield* (Missouri) *Weekly Patriot,* July 27, 1865.
16. Ibid., August 10, 1865.
17. George Ward Nichols was mustered out of the Union Army on October 23, 1865.
18. *History of Greene County, Missouri,* p. 763.
19. Letter, Elmer O. Parker, Old Military Records Division, National Archives, Washington, D.C., to Dale T. Schoenberger, November 15, 1967.
20. Lieutenant Colonel Melbourne C. Chandler, *Of Garry Owen in Glory.*
21. George A. Custer was commissioned a Major General of Volunteers to date from April 15, 1865, at age 25, making him the youngest major general in the history of the United States Army.
22. Chandler, p. 3. Thomas W. Custer was one of only two men in the history of the United States Army to be awarded two Congressional Medals of Honor.
23. Records of the War Department, Office of the Quartermaster General, "Reports of Persons and Articles Hired, 1861-1868," Old Military Records Division, National Archives, Washington, D.C.
24. Nyle H. Miller, Edgar Langsdorf, and Robert W. Richmond, *Kansas: A Pictorial History,* p. 51.
25. Organizational Returns, Seventh United States Cavalry, June 1867, Old Military Records Division, National Archives, Washington, D.C.
26. *Missouri Democrat* (St. Louis), April 4, 1867; Henry M. Stanley, *My Early Travels and Adventures in America and Africa,* pp. 5-8.
27. Ibid.
28. Nyle H. Miller and Joseph W. Snell, "Why the West Was Wild," p. 630.
29. "The Commissioner's Record Book," Volume "A," Ellsworth County, Kansas, 1867-1887, Archives Division, Kansas State Historical Society, Topeka.
30. Ibid.
31. *Leavenworth* (Kansas) *Daily Conservative,* December 14, 1867. Wild Bill Hickok had no regular commission as a deputy United States marshal (as was the custom in those days). The United States Judiciary Act of 1789 gave all United States marshals the power to appoint their own deputies. Hickok was paid on a fee basis and given travel allowances. Deputy United States marshals drew no salaries in Hickok's era.
32. *Topeka* (Kansas) *Weekly Leader,* April 2, 1868.
33. Records of the War Department, Office of the Quartermaster General, "Reports of Persons and Articles Hired, 1861-1868," Old Military Records Division, National Archives, Washington, D.C.
34. Records of the War Department, "Reports of Persons and Articles Hired, 1861-1869."
35. Miller and Snell, p. 188.
36. Records of the War Department, "Reports of Persons and Articles Hired, 1861-1869."
37. *Rocky Mountain News* (Denver), October 30, 1868.
38. Records of the War Department, "Reports of Persons and Articles Hired, 1861-1869."
39. Mary P. M. Carr, "Memoirs of Brevet Major General Eugene A. Carr," manuscript in the possession of Mrs. Virginia Carr Van Soelen, Santa Fe, New Mexico; James T. King, *War Eagle: A Life of General Eugene A. Carr,* p. 144. Buffalo Bill Cody was perhaps the greatest scout in Western history. Cody had to his credit the killing of Cheyenne Dog Soldier Chief Tall Bull (*Tatonka Haska*) in 1869 and the killing of Cheyenne War Chief Yellow Hair (*Hay-o-wei*) in 1876. He received the Congressional Medal of Honor in 1872 and had it taken away in 1916 because of his civilian status at the time he earned the medal.
40. A. T. Andreas, *History Of the State of Kansas,* p. 1291.
41. Mortality Schedule, United States census report of 1870 for Hays City, Kansas, taken on June 1, Census Division, National Archives, Washington, D.C.; Archives Division, Kansas State Historical Society, Topeka.
42. Elizabeth B. Custer, *Following the Guidon* (University of Oklahoma Press edition), p. 154.
43. Ibid., p. 27.
44. Petition of several citizens of Hays City, to Governor James M. Harvey of Kansas, July 7, 1869, "Governors' Correspondence," Archives Division, Kansas State Historical Society, Topeka.
45. *Leavenworth* (Kansas) *Times and Conservative,* September 2, 1869.
46. Letter, Major George Gibson, Fifth United States Infantry, commandiing officer at Fort Hays, Kansas, to Governor James M. Harvey of Kansas, October 3, 1869, "Governors' Correspondence," Archives Division, Kansas State Historical Society.
47. Letter, J. B. Hickok to Ellis County, Kansas, no date on letter, Manuscript Division, Kansas State Historical Society.
48. *Leavenworth Times and Conservative,* August 26, 1869.
49. Ibid., September 28, 1869; *Leavenworth* (Kansas) *Commercial,* September 28, 1869; *Lawrence* (Kansas) *Daily Tribune,* September 30, 1869; *Junction City* (Kansas) *Weekly Union,* October 2, 1869.
50. *Leavenworth Times and Conservative,* November 5, 1869.
51. Letter, Joseph W. Snell, Curator of Manuscripts, Kansas State Historical Society, to Dale T. Schoenberger, May 16, 1962.
52. *Topeka* (Kansas) *State Record,* July 26, 1871. Pete Lanihan was killed by Jim (Dog) Kelley, a saloon

owner at Hays City, later four times mayor of Dodge City.

53. Records of the War Department, Office of the Adjutant General, "Register of the Sick and Wounded at Fort Hays, Kansas, during the Month of July, 1870," Old Military Records Division, National Archives, Washington, D.C.

54. Ibid.

55. Ibid.; Muster roll, Company I, Seventh United States Cavalry, July, 1870, Old Military Records Division, National Archives; records of the War Department, Office of the Adjutant General, Final Statement of the Adjutant General of Private John Kile, Company I, Seventh U.S. Cavalry, August 6, 1870, Old Military Records Division, National Archives; records of the War Department, report of Captain Myles W. Keogh, Seventh U.S. Cavalry, August 16, 1870, to the Adjutant General's Office, Old Military Records Division, National Archives.

56. Ibid.

57. Records of the War Department, "Register of the Sick and Wounded at Fort Hays, Kansas, during the Month of August, 1870," Old Military Records Division, National Archives.

58. Chandler, pp. 34-35.

59. Tom Custer's personality did not preclude the possibility of his killing in cold blood or taking unfair advantage of his intended adversary. Acting upon orders from General George Custer, Tom and two other officers shot three unarmed deserters, one fatally, between Fort Sedgwick, Colorado, and Fort Wallace, Kansas, on or about July 7, 1867. The fatally wounded trooper, however, was not shot by Tom Custer.—Leavenworth Daily Conservative, January 10, 1868.

60. Junction City (Kansas) Union, July 23, 1870. See also the Topeka Daily Commonwealth, July 22, 1870 and the Republican Valley Empire (Clyde, Kansas), August 2, 1870, for accounts of the fight.

61. Letter, Elmer O. Parker, Old Military Records Division, National Archives, to Dale T. Schoenberger, October 28, 1966. It is of interest to note that Captain Michael V. Sheridan, Phil Sheridan's younger brother, was officially listed on the Seventh United States Cavalry's regimental roster as the commanding officer of Company L. He was, however, detached as aide-de-camp to his famous brother from 1870 to 1888.

62. George Jelinek, The Ellsworth Story—90 Years of Ellsworth and Ellsworth County History.

63. Ronald L. Davis, "Soiled Doves and Ornamental Culture," The American West Magazine, IV, Number 4, November 1967, 21.

64. Records of the City of Abilene, Kansas, "City Council Minute Book," p. 55.

65. Abilene (Kansas) Chronicle, May 18, 1871.

66. Miller and Snell, p. 201.

67. Abilene Chronicle, November 3, 1870.

68. Gard, p. 60.

69. Abilene Chronicle, July 13, 1871.

70. Records of the City of Abilene, "City Council Minute Book," p. 71.

71. Ibid., pp. 86-87.

72. Ibid., p. 71.

73. Ibid., pp. 86-87.

74. Ibid., p. 70.

75. Ibid., p. 69.

76. Abilene Chronicle, August 24, 1871.

77. Records of the City of Abilene, "Minute Book," p. 99.

78. Ibid., p. 105.

79. The Drover's Cottage was built for Joseph G. McCoy in 1867. McCoy sold the hotel in 1869. In 1872 it was dismantled and moved to Ellsworth and reconstructed.

80. Letter, Charles F. Gross, to J. B. Edwards, June 15, 1925, Manuscript Division, Kansas State Historical Society.

81. Records of the City of Abilene, "Minute Book," pp. 73, 77, 79, 81, 87, 88, 94.

82. Stuart O. Henry, Conquering Our Great American Plains, pp. 274-75.

83. Abilene Chronicle, September 14, 1871.

84. Records of the City of Abilene, "Minute Book," p. 83.

85. Topeka Daily Commonwealth, May 11, 1871.

86. Letter, Glenn R. Sanderford, Federal Records Center, Fort Worth, Texas, to the author, July 25, 1966.

87. John Wesley Hardin, The Life of John Wesley Hardin.

88. Streeter, p. 98.

89. Abilene Chronicle, August 17, 1871.

90. Ibid.

91. Letter, M. H. Dowell to J. Evetts Haley, January 12, 1939.

92. Abilene Chronicle, October 12, 1871.

93. Ibid.

94. Adolph Roenigk (editor), Pioneer Days of Kansas, p. 38.

95. Ibid.

96. Abilene Chronicle, November 30, 1871.

97. Ibid.

98. Rosa, p. 141.

99. Records of the City of Abilene, "Minute Book," pp. 107-8.

100. Letter, Charles F. Gross to J. B. Edwards, January 20, 1926, Manuscript Division, Kansas State Historical Society. The newspapers of the day, however, did not mention Wild Bill Hickok as being a member of the Grand Duke's party. Wild Bill was as famous as several members of the hunting party and more than others of the party, and he undoubtedly would have been mentioned had he actually been on the hunt. The Royal Hunt is also said to have included the celebrated scout, Charles A. (Lonesome Charlie) Reynolds, who later became General George Custer's chief of scouts and who was killed at the Little Big Horn in 1876. No contemporary record, however, has been found which would substantiate the report that Reynolds was on the hunt.

101. The Grand Duke Alexis was the uncle of Czar Nikolai Aleksandrovich Romanov II of Russia who abdicated during the Russian Revolution of 1917. Grand Duke Alexis became the Grand Admiral of the Russian Navy. He died in 1908.

102. The head of one of the bison killed on the Royal Hunt is in the possession of the Missouri Historical Society at Saint Louis. The trophy was originally presented to Brigadier General John Pope, commanding general of the Department of the Missouri. General Pope later made his home in St. Louis.

103. Niagara Falls (New York) Gazette, August 28, September 4, 1872.

104. Missouri Democrat, March 15, 1873; Mendota (Illinois) Bulletin, April 11, 1873.

105. Rochester (New York) Democrat and Chronicle, September 1, 1873.

106. Rosa, p. 179.

107. Portland (Maine) Advertiser, January 30, 1874.

108. Rochester Democrat and Chronicle, March 14, 1874.

109. Letters, Dallas Irvine, Old Military Records Division, National Archives, to Joseph G. Rosa, August 15, 1956; Charles Roos, Armed Forces Medical Library, Washington, D.C., to Joseph G. Rosa, September 11, 1956.
110. Letter, W. F. Carver to Raymond W. Thorp.
111. *Cheyenne* (Wyoming) *Daily Leader,* March 7, 1876.
112. Rosa, p. 168.
113. *Cincinnati* (Ohio) *Daily Enquirer,* March 19, 1876.
114. Gilbert S. Robinson, *Old Wagon Show Days,* p. 127. Gilbert Robinson was the son-in-law of Mrs. Agnes Lake Hickok.
115. Rosa, p. 170.
116. Letter, Joseph F. Anderson to Raymond W. Thorp. Joseph Anderson, better known as "White Eye Jack," knew both Wild Bill Hickok and Calamity Jane Cannary, and was on the Fort Laramie wagon train with them. In the spring of 1876 Calamity Jane had accompanied the military expedition of Brigadier General George Crook (who commanded the Department of the Platte) as a camp prostitute. Her sex was discovered and she was sent back to Fort Fetterman, Wyoming.
117. *Yankton* (Dakota Territory) *Press and Dakotaian,* December 5, 1876.
118. Letter, Mary A. McCall, to the United States Marshal at Yankton, Dakota Territory, February 25, 1877. Mary McCall was the sister of Jack McCall.
119. Wild Bill Hickok had known Carl and John Mann as early as 1871 when Carl ran a saloon at Abilene, Kansas.
120. *Cheyenne Daily Leader,* September 1, 1876.
121. "*The United States* vs. *John McCall,*" Trial Documents, Second Judicial Court, Territory of Dakota, at Yankton, Federal Records Center, Kansas City, Missouri.
122. Ibid.
123. *Cheyenne Daily Leader,* November 19, 1876.
124. Ibid., November 23, 1876.
125. "*The United States* vs. *John McCall.*" Trial documents, Second Judicial Court, Territory of Dakota, at Yankton, Federal Records Center, Kansas City, Missouri.
126. Ibid.
127. Ibid.
128. Ibid.
129. *Yankton Press and Dakotaian,* March 1, 1877.
130. In 1903 a sculptured figure of Wild Bill Hickok was erected over the grave. Later, authorities placed a wire enclosure around the statue to protect it from being chipped by souvenir hunters and vandals. But people managed to cut the wire enclosure and chip away at the statue. It would seem even in death people would not let Wild Bill rest.
131. Letter, Charles F. Gross to J. B. Edwards, June 15, 1925, Manuscript Division, Kansas State Historical Society.
132. Ibid.
133. Ibid.

4. DOC HOLLIDAY

1. "D.A.R. Cemetery Records from 250 Georgia Cemeteries, Volume I, Part II, Tombstone Records from Sunset Hill Cemetery, Valdosta, Georgia, Birth Dates Before 1875," Department of Archives and History, Atlanta, Georgia.
2. Pat Jahns, *The Frontier World of Doc Holliday,* p. 3; John Myers Myers, *Doc Holliday,* p. 9.
3. The United States census report of 1860 for Griffin, Spalding County, Georgia, taken on June 8.
4. Letter, Gardner P. H. Foley, Professor of Dental History, Baltimore College of Dental Surgery, University of Maryland, College Park, to Dale T. Schoenberger, August 12, 1966.
5. Ibid., October 4, 1966.
6. Letters, Harold R. Manakee, Director, Maryland Historical Society, Baltimore, to Dale T. Schoenberger, June 15, July 11, 1966.
7. Letter, Mrs. Lucille A. Boykin, Department Head, Texas History and Genealogy Department, Dallas, Texas, Public Library, to Dale T. Schoenberger, June 30, 1966.
8. Dr. David T. Carr, Mayo Clinic, Rochester, Minnesota, to Dale T. Schoenberger, October 28, 1966.
9. Ibid.
10. Letters, Harold R. Manakee, to the author, June 15, July 11, 1966.
11. Letter, Mrs. Lila M. Hawes, Director, Georgia Historical Society, Savannah, to Dale T. Schoenberger, June 21, 1966.
12. Myers, *Doc Holliday,* p. 13.
13. Ibid, p. 19.
14. Letters, Margaret J. Sparks, Reference Librarian, Arizona Pioneers' Historical Society, Tucson, to the author, July 9, 1966; Mrs. Marguerite B. Cooley, Director, Arizona State Library and Archives, Phoenix, to the author, January 16, 1967.
15. Jahns, p. 43.
16. *Dallas* (Texas) *Herald,* January 2, 1875.
17. Letter, W. W. Bill Dennis to Dale T. Schoenberger, July 9, 1966.
18. Ibid.; Bartholomew, *Wyatt Earp: The Untold Story,* p. 148.
19. Bartholomew, *Wyatt Earp: The Untold Story,* p. 148.
20. Bartholomew, *The Biographical Album of Western Gunfighters,* p. 40.
21. Various companies of both the Eleventh United States Infantry and the Tenth United States Cavalry were garrisoned at Fort Richardson, Texas, during 1876. The Tenth Cavalry was a colored regiment and Negro-hating Doc Holliday would not have sat in the same card game with a Negro.
22. Letter, W. W. Bill Dennis to the author, July 9, 1966.
23. Ibid.
24. Pat Jahns, *The Frontier World of Doc Holliday,* p. 61.

25. John D. Gilchriese, field historian at the University of Arizona, Tucson, has a deposition from Kate Elder stating that she was married to Doc Holliday at Saint Louis in 1870.—Waters, p. 44. Former United States Commissioner, Judge James C. Hancock, said that Kate Elder told him she had married Holliday at Saint Louis, where she went to school.—letter, James C. Hancock to Frank Waters, December 8, 1937; Waters, p. 44. Gilchriese, however, has told me that Kate was never married to Holliday.—letter, John D. Gilchriese to Dale T. Schoenberger, July 26, 1966. Kate was living at the Comique Theater, Fifth (now Broadway) and Biddle, Saint Louis, in 1870.—Richard Edwards' Twelfth Annual St. Louis Directory, p. 321. A search of the old marriage records of the city of Saint Louis for 1870 revealed nothing concerning the alleged marriage of Doc Holliday and Kate Elder.

26. "Miscellaneous Papers," Records of the City of Wichita, Kansas. Kate Elder was known to be alive in the early 1930s in the Los Angeles area. A Katherine O. Elder died at Long Beach, California, on March 26, 1933. Another Katherine Elder died in Santa Clara County, California, on January 24, 1937. I do not know which, if either, was the former mistress of Doc Holliday. Another report says that Kate Elder died in the Pioneers' Home at Prescott, Arizona. A search of the Arizona State vital records failed to substantiate this report.

27. Letter, W. W. Bill Dennis to Dale T. Schoenberger, July 9, 1966.

28. Bartholomew, *Wyatt Earp: The Untold Story,* p. 238.

29. Masterson, "Famous Gunfighters of the Western Frontier," *Human Life Magazine,* 1907.

30. Ibid.

31. Letter, Mrs. Alys H. Freeze, Head of the Western History Department, Denver, Colorado, Public Library, to Dale T. Schoenberger, July 14, 1966.

32. *Denver* (Colorado) *Republican,* June 22, 1887.

33. Ibid.

34. *Tombstone Nugget,* November 17, 1881.

35. Letter, Gilbert Garcia, Deputy Clerk, District Court, Las Animas County, Colorado, to the author, August 8, 1966.

36. *Dodge City Times,* February 2, 1878; *Ford County Globe,* February 5, 1878.

37. Bartholomew, *Wyatt Earp: The Man and the Myth,* pp. 6, 9-11.

38. *Tombstone Epitaph,* May 30, 1881.

39. Ibid., December 18, 1881.

40. Ibid., January 18, 1882.

41. Ibid.

42. Masterson, "Famous Gunfighters . . . ," *Human Life Magazine,* 1907.

43. Letter, Milt Hinkle to the author, January 18, 1964.

44. *Rocky Mountain News,* May 25, 1882.

45. *Denver* (Colorado) *Tribune,* May 16, 1882; *Pueblo* (Colorado) *Chieftain,* May 17, 1882.

46. *Denver Republican,* May 22, 1882.

47. Masterson, "Famous Gunfighters . . . ," *Human Life Magazine,* 1907. See footnote 166 in Chapter 2.

48. *Pueblo Chieftain,* June 1, 1882.

49. Ibid.

50. *Leadville* (Colorado) *Daily Herald,* August 20, 1884.

51. Ibid., August 26, 1884.

52. *Denver Republican,* March 27, 1885; *Denver Tribune,* March 27, 1885.

53. *Denver Republican,* March 28, 1885; *The Yuma* (Arizona) *Sentinel* carried a dispatch dated September 3, 1884, from the *Tombstone* (Arizona) *Record,* which stated that Doc Holliday had killed A. J. Kelly, a constable, at Leadville. According to the dispatch Charles Bagsby, a resident of Tombstone who was visiting in Leadville, reported the death of Kelly by Holliday. The author has found no record of Kelly's death. In contrast, the newspapers are full of the Billy Allen shooting and Holliday's subsequent trial.

5. BAT MASTERSON

1. Letter, Don W. Wilson, Archivist, Kansas State Historical Society, Topeka, to Dale T. Schoenberger, September 18, 1967.

2. Ibid.

3. It has been generally accepted that Bat Masterson's two given names were William Barclay, but on at least one occasion he signed his name as "Bartholomew" Masterson and on at least another occasion he signed his name as William Barclay Masterson. The Raymond family, especially Henry H. Raymond, Bat's companion in Illinois and Kansas, was of the opinion that Masterson's middle name was Bartholomew. In his diary of 1872-1873, Raymond recorded that Masterson was called both "Bat" and "Bart." Bat was christened Bartholomew Masterson, and in New York City during his later years he probably had his name changed to William Barclay Masterson. Bat's official will bore the latter name. The baptismal record of Bat indicates, however, that he was christened as "Bartholomew" Masterson in County Rouville, Quebec, Canada, on November 27, 1853, having been born on November 26.—Chris Penn, "A Note on Bartholomew Masterson," *Tally Book of the English Westerners Society,* April, 1967.

4. A copy of the *Diary of Henry H. Raymond, 1872-1873,* Archives Division, Kansas State Historical Society, Topeka.

5. Ibid.

6. *The American International Encyclopedia: A Comprehensive Reference Work,* Volume II. To illustrate to what extent the American bison was slaughtered in such wholesale numbers by the buffalo hunters, we have only to look at some of the records compiled by four famous hide hunters. In an eight-month period, Buffalo Bill Cody killed 4,280 buffalo. O. A. Bond killed 5,855 in a month and a half. Thomas C. Nixon, in little more than a month, killed 2,173 buffalo; 120 in a forty-minute stand. J. Wright Mooar estimated

that he had killed a total of 20,500 buffalo in his lifetime.

7. Natt N. Dodge, "Wild Life of the American West," *The Book of the American West* (Jay Monaghan, Editor-in-Chief), p. 436.

8. James D. Horan, *The Great American West: A Pictorial History from Coronado to the Last Frontier,* p. 209.

9. Robert M. Utley, "Kit Carson and the Adobe Walls Campaign," *American West Magazine,* II, Number I, Winter, 1965, 73.

10. Vestal, pp. 65-67.

11. *Leavenworth* (Kansas) *Times,* November 17, 1877, and the *Dodge City Times,* November 24, 1877, carried the names of the white participants in the Adobe Walls fight and where each was at the start of the fight except Mrs. Olds, Fred Myers, Seth Hathaway, and Henry Lease, who were obviously there. (James Carlyle and James Campbell were listed only by their nicknames.)

12. Letter, W. B. Masterson to Frederick S. Barde, October 13, 1913, Manuscript Division, Kansas State Historical Society.

13. Letter, Fred Leonard to A. C. Meyers, July 1, 1874, published in the *Leavenworth Times,* July 10, 1874.

14. *Leavenworth* (Kansas) *Daily Commercial,* July 24, 1874.

15. Records of the War Department, Office of the Quartermaster General, "Reports of Persons and Articles Hired, Indian Territory, 1874-1875," Old Military Records Division, National Archives, Washington, D.C.

16. Bat Masterson was paid $65 for his services from August 5-31. He was paid $75 for the entire month of September as per his contract, and for the period of October 1-12 he was paid $30.—Letter, Elmer O. Parker, Old Military Records Division, National Archives, Washington, D.C., to Dale T. Schoenberger, October 10, 1967.

17. Miller and Snell, p. 320.

18. Ibid.

19. Paul I. Wellman, *The Indian Wars of the West,* p. 113.

20. Miller and Snell, p. 320.

21. Ibid.

22. A copy of the report of Brevet Major General Nelson A. Miles, Fifth United States Infantry, Fort Leavenworth, Kansas, March 4, 1875, Manuscript Division, Kansas State Historical Society.

23. Miller and Snell, p. 321.

24. A copy of the March 4, 1875, report of General Miles, Kansas State Historical Society.

25. Partial diary of First Lieutenant Frank D. Baldwin, U.S.A., Manuscript Division, Kansas State Historical Society.

26. A copy of the March 4, 1875, report of General Miles, Kansas State Historical Society.

27. Records of the War Department, "Reports of Persons and Articles Hired, Indian Territory, 1874-1875," National Archives, Washington, D.C.

28. A copy of the *Diary of Henry H. Raymond, 1872-1873,* Kansas State Historical Society; letter, Elmer O. Parker, National Archives, Washington, D.C., to Dale T. Schoenberger, November 29, 1967.

29. Letter, Elmer O. Parker, National Archives, Washington, D.C., to the author, November 29, 1967.

30. Ibid.

31. Affidavit of Mrs. Catherine Cook to the Adjutant General's Office, October 16, 1877, Records of the War Department, National Archives, Washington, D.C. In her affidavit Mrs. Cook swore that "Melvin A. King" was, in reality, her son Anthony Cook.

32. Records of the War Department, Report of the Adjutant General, November 17, 1877, National Archives; Final Statement of the Adjutant General of Corporal Melvin A. King, Company H, Fourth United States Cavalry, March 4, 1876, National Archives.

33. Ibid.; Muster roll, Company H, Fourth United States Cavalry, January 1876, National Archives.

34. George G. Thompson, *Bat Masterson: The Dodge City Years,* p. 11. Thompson interviewed Thomas Masterson, Jr., the younger brother of Bat Masterson, about the King fight on November 4, 1937.

35. Letter, Elmer O. Parker, Old Military Records Division, National Archives, to Dale T. Schoenberger, October 10, 1967.

36. *Dodge City Times,* April 28, 1877.

37. Ibid., May 6, 1877.

38. Ibid., June 9, 1877.

39. Ibid., July 7, 1877.

40. Ibid., August 4, 1877.

41. Miller and Snell, p. 326.

42. Ibid.

43. *Dodge City Times,* September 29, 1877.

44. Ibid., November 3, 1877.

45. Ibid., November 10, 1877.

46. Ibid., December 8, 1877.

47. Ibid., January 12, 1878; *Ford County Globe,* January 15, 1878.

48. *Dodge City Times,* January 19, 1878.

49. Ibid., January 5, 1878.

50. Ibid., January 19, 1878.

51. Ibid., August 17, 1878.

52. Ibid., January 11, 1879.

53. Ibid., November 15, 1879.

54. Ibid.

55. Miller and Snell, p. 46.

56. Ibid., p. 644.

57. *Dodge City Times,* January 18, 1879.

58. *Ford County Globe,* March 18, 1878.

59. Ibid., February 5, 1878; *Dodge City Times,* February 9, 1878.

60. *Ford County Globe,* February 12, 1878; *Dodge City Times,* February 16, 1878.

61. *Ford County Globe,* April 23, 1878.

62. Ibid.

63. *Dodge City Times,* April 13, 1878.

64. Ibid.

65. *Ford County Globe,* April 16, 1878.

66. *Dodge City Times,* April 13, 1878.

67. Ibid.

68. *Ford County Globe,* April 16, 1878.

69. Ibid.

70. Ibid.

71. *Dodge City Times,* June 1, 1878.

72. Ibid., April 13, 1878; *Ford County Globe,* April 16, 1878.

73. *Ford County Globe,* April 16, 1878.

74. Letter, Milt Hinkle to Dale T. Schoenberger, January 18, 1964.

75. *Ford County Globe,* April 16, 1878.

76. *Dodge City Times,* April 13, 1878.

77. Thompson, p. 50. George C. Thompson interviewed Tom Masterson, Jr., on November 4, 1937. *Wichita Morning Eagle,* July 24, 1938. Tom Masterson, Jr., was interviewed by a reporter of the *Morning Eagle.*

78. *Wichita Morning Eagle,* July 24, 1938.

79. *Ford County Globe,* April 16, 1878.

80. Earle R. Forrest, "The Killing of Ed Masterson: Deputy Marshal of Old Dodge City," *Brand Book of the Los Angeles Westerners*, 1949, pp. 154-55. Earle R. Forrest interviewed George W. Reighard in 1926.
81. Thompson, p. 50. George G. Thompson interviewed Ham Bell on November 27, 1937.
82. *The Daily Journal* (Saint Louis), October 11, 1878.
83. Copies of the Dodge City, Kansas, police court dockets for the period of July to December, 1878, Walter S. Campbell Collection, Dodge City File, General Research Correspondence, Division of Manuscripts, University of Oklahoma Library, Norman.
84. Letter, Miss Fannie Garrettson to Messrs. Eshers, October 5, 1878, published in *The Daily Journal* of Saint Louis on October 11, 1878.
85. *Dodge City Times*, October 5, 1878.
86. Ibid., October 12, 1878.
87. Ibid., January 4, 1879.
88. Ibid., January 25, 1879.
89. Ibid., January 18, 1879; *Ford County Globe*, January 21, 1879.
90. *Dodge City Times*, May 22, 1880.
91. *Leavenworth Times*, February 16, 1879.
92. Miller and Snell, p. 388.
93. Ibid.
94. *Ford County Globe*, October 28, 1879.
95. Ibid., March 25, 1879.
96. *Dodge City Times*, March 29, 1879. *Ford County Globe*, in its issue of March 25, 1879, stated that Bat Masterson and his deputy Bill Duffey had recruited thirty-three men for the Santa Fe.
97. *San Antonio (Texas) Express*, March 13, 1884.
98. *Ford County Globe*, April 8, 1879.
99. Ibid., June 10, 1879.
100. *Ford County Globe*, June 14, 1879.
101. Ibid., September 16, 1879.
102. Ibid., October 28, 1879.
103. *Dodge City Times*, October 25, 1879.
104. Ibid., November 8, 1879.
105. Letter, Charles Roden to the Editor of the *Speareville* (Kansas) *News*, November 6, 1879, published in the *News* on November 8, 1879.
106. Letter, T. S. Jones to the Editor of the *Speareville News*, no date published with letter, published in the *News* on November 15, 1879.
107. Letter, W. B. Masterson to the Editor of the *Dodge City Times*, no date published with letter, published in the *Times* on November 15, 1879.
108. *Ford County Globe*, December 2, 1879; *Dodge City Times*, December 6, 1879.
109. *Dodge City Times*, January 17, 1880.
110. The United States census report of 1880 for Dodge City, Ford County, Kansas, taken on June 22, 1880.
111. Robert M. Wright, *Dodge City: The Cowboy Capitol*, pp. 301-3; Thompson, p. 36. George G. Thompson interviewed Tom Masterson, Jr., about Billy Thompson's rescue on November 4, 1937.
112. *Western Nebraskian* (North Platte), June 26, 1880.
113. Ibid.; *Dodge City Times*, June 26, 1880.
114. *Dodge City Times*, July 17, 1880.
115. *Ford County Globe*, December 7, 1880.
116. Ibid., February 15, 1881.
117. Ibid., April 19, 1881.
118. *Dodge City Times*, April 21, 1881.
119. *Caldwell* (Kansas) *Commercial*, April 21, 1881.
120. Ibid.
121. Only one copy of the *Vox Populi* seems to have survived. It is in the possession of Mrs. Merritt L. Beeson at the Beeson Museum in Dodge City, Kansas. (A reproduction of this paper is in the possession of the Kansas State Historical Society at Topeka.) The paper deals only with the local election of November, 1884, and it is doubtful if Bat Masterson, as editor, had any serious intention of embarking on a journalism career at this time in his life.
122. *Dodge City Democrat*, March 13, 1886; *Dodge City Times*, March 11, 1886; *Globe Live Stock Journal*, March 16, 1886.
123. Richard O'Connor, *Bat Masterson* (Bantam edition), p. 140.
124. *Rocky Mountain News*, September 22, 1886.
125. Ibid.
126. Ibid.
127. O'Connor, p. 178.
128. Colorado State Business Directory of 1892 and 1893, Denver Public Library.
129. Lute Johnson Scrapbook, I: 24-25, State Historical Society of Colorado, Denver.
130. Letter, Mrs. Louisa Arps, Librarian, State Historical Society of Colorado, to Dale T. Schoenberger, July 19, 1966; letter, Mrs. Alys H. Freeze, Head of the Western History Department, Denver Public Library, August 12, 1966.
131. Letter, Mrs. Velma Churchill, Principal Archivist Aide, Colorado State Archives and Public Records Center, Denver, to Dale T. Schoenberger, October 9, 1967.
132. Lute Johnson Scrapbook, I: 24-25, State Historical Society of Colorado.
133. O'Connor, pp. 142-43.
134. Ibid., p. 147.
135. Letterhead on a letter written by Bat Masterson to Henry H. Raymond, July 23, 1899, a copy of which is in the Manuscript Division, Kansas State Historical Society.
136. Ibid.
137. O'Connor, p. 150.
138. Ibid., p. 155.
139. Ibid., p. 156.
140. Ibid.
141. Ibid.
142. Letter, United States Marshal William Henkel for the State of New York to the United States Attorney General's Office, June 30, 1909, General Records of the Department of Justice, National Archives, Washington, D.C. (hereafter cited as *Gen. Rec., J. D., Nat. Arch.*)
143. The oath of the office of W. B. Masterson, Deputy U.S. Marshal for the Southern District of New York, March 28, 1905, Gen. Rec., J. D., Nat. Arch.
144. Letter, U.S. Attorney General's Office to President William Howard Taft, June 23, 1909, Gen. Rec., J. D., Nat. Arch.
145. General Records of the Department of Justice of the service of W. B. Masterson as a Deputy U.S. Marshal for the Southern District of New York, National Archives.
146. Ibid.
147. Letter, Henry A. Wise, U.S. Attorney for the Southern District of New York, to U.S. Attorney General's Office, June 16, 1909, Gen. Rec., J. D., Nat. Arch.
148. Letter, U.S. Attorney General's Office to President William Howard Taft, June 23, 1909, Gen. Rec., J. D., Nat. Arch.
149. Letter, President William Howard Taft to U.S. Attorney General's Office, June 29, 1909, Gen. Rec., J. D., Nat. Arch.

150. Letter, Alfred Henry Lewis to President William Howard Taft, July 10, 1909, Gen. Rec., J. D., Nat. Arch.
151. Letter, U.S. Attorney General's Office to U.S. Marshal William Henkel, July 12, 1909, Gen. Rec., J. D., Nat. Arch.
152. Letter, United States Marshal William Henkel to the U.S. Attorney General's Office, July 14, 1909, Gen. Rec., J. D., Nat. Arch.
153. Letter, U.S. Attorney General's Office to United States Marshal William Henkel, July 15, 1909, Gen. Rec., J. D., Nat. Arch.
154. *New York Herald*, May 17, 1907.
155. Letter, James McGurrin, County Clerk of the Su-preme Court, New York County, N.Y., to Dale T. Schoenberger, October 20, 1967.
156. O'Connor, p. 170.
157. Ibid., pp. 169-70.
158. Ibid., p. 170.
159. Information given to the author by the Office of Donald A. Harter, County Clerk, Herkimer County, Herkimer, N.Y.
160. Ibid.
161. Ibid.
162. Ibid.
163. Ibid.
164. Ibid.

6. LUKE SHORT

1. William R. Cox, *Luke Short and His Era*, p. 9.
2. Ibid., p. 16.
3. Ibid., p. 9.
4. Ibid., p. 16.
5. Ibid.
6. Ibid., p. 9.
7. Ibid., p. 30.
8. Masterson, "Famous Gunfighters of the Western Frontier," *Human Life Magazine*, 1907.
9. Letter, Garry D. Ryan, Assistant Director, Old Military Records Division, National Archives, Washington, D.C., to Dale T. Schoenberger, July 18, 1967.
10. Letter, Miss Jane F. Smith, Director, Social and Economic Records Division, National Archives, to Dale T. Schoenberger, July 24, 1967.
11. Records of the War Department, Office of the Quartermaster General, "Reports of Persons and Articles Hired at Sidney Barracks, Nebraska, October 1878," Old Military Records Division, National Archives.
12. Ibid.
13. Ibid.
14. Ibid.
15. Ibid.
16. George Whitwell Parsons, *Diary of George Whitwell Parsons*, Arizona Pioneers' Historical Society, Tucson.
17. At Leadville, Colorado, on or about September 1, 1876, Charlie Storms and John Varnes, the gambler who was implicated in the murder of Wild Bill Hickok, were involved in a gunfight.—Bartholomew, *The Biographical Album of Western Gunfighters*, p. 68.
18. Criminal Court Records, Pima County, Arizona Territory, for Tombstone, now in Cochise County Courthouse, Bisbee, Arizona. W. J. Hunsacker defended Luke Short at his hearing.—Cox, p. 80.
19. *Ford County Globe*, February 6, 1883.
20. *Dodge City Times*, April 5, 1883.
21. Ibid., April 26, 1883.
22. Ibid.
23. *Topeka Daily Commonwealth*, May 20, 1883.
24. *Topeka* (Kansas) *Daily Capital*, May 18, 1883.
25. Miller and Snell, p. 521.
26. *Ford County Globe*, May 1, 1883; Petition of Luke L. Short to Governor George W. Glick of Kansas, May 10, 1883, "Governors' Correspondence," Manuscript Division, Kansas State Historical Society, Topeka.
27. *Ford County Globe*, May 1, 1883; *Topeka Daily Commonwealth*, May 18, 1883.
28. Ibid.
29. *Dodge City Times*, May 3, 1883; Petition of Luke L. Short to Governor George W. Glick of Kansas, May 10, 1883, "Governors' Correspondence," Archives Division, Kansas State Historical Society, Topeka; *Topeka Daily Capital*, May 18, 1883.
30. Petition of Luke L. Short to Governor George W. Glick, May 10, 1883, Kansas State Historical Society; *Topeka Daily Capital*, May 18, 1883.
31. *Dodge City Times*, May 3, 1883.
32. Ibid.
33. Ibid., May 10, 1883.
34. Masterson, "Famous Gunfighters . . . ," *Human Life Life Magazine*, 1907.
35. Ibid.
36. *Kansas City* (Missouri) *Evening Star*, June 7, 1883.
37. Telegram, George T. Hinkle, Sheriff of Ford County, Kansas, to Governor George W. Glick, May 11, 1883, "Governors' Correspondence," Kansas State Historical Society.
38. Telegram, Robert M. Wright, Commissioner of Ford County, and Richard J. Hardesty to Governor Glick, May 11, 1883, Kansas State Historical Society.
39. Correspondence of Governor Glick, Kansas State Historical Society.
40. Telegram, Governor Glick to Sheriff George T. Hinkle, Ford County, May 12, 1883, Kansas State Historical Society.
41. Telegram, Sheriff George T. Hinkle to Governor Glick, May 12, 1883, Kansas State Historical Society.
42. *Topeka Daily Capital*, May 12, 1883.
43. Telegram, several citizens of Dodge City, Kansas, to Governor Glick, May 13, 1883, Kansas State Historical Society.
44. *Topeka Daily Capital*, May 16, 1883.
45. *Dodge City Times*, May 17, 1883.
46. Telegram, Thomas Moonlight, Adjutant General of Kansas, to Governor Glick, May 17, 1883, "Corre-

spondence of the Adjutant General," Kansas State Historical Society.

47. Ibid.
48. Ibid.
49. *Caldwell (Kansas) Journal,* May 24, 1883.
50. Telegram, Sheriff George T. Hinkle, to Governor Glick, May 31, 1883, Kansas State Historical Society.
51. Telegram, Thomas Moonlight, Adjutant General, Kansas, to Sheriff George T. Hinkle, June 4, 1883, Kansas State Historical Society.
52. *Topeka Daily Commonwealth,* June 5, 1883; *Kinsley (Kansas) Graphic,* June 7, 1883.
53. *Ford County Globe,* June 5, 1883.
54. Telegram, Major Harry E. Gryden of the Kansas State Militia, to Thomas Moonlight, Adjutant General of Kansas, June 5, 1883, "Correspondence of the Adjutant General," Kansas State Historical Society.
55. Telegram, several citizens of Dodge City to Governor Glick, June 6, 1883, Kansas State Historical Society.
56. Telegram, Governor Glick to the Citizens of Dodge City, June 6, 1883, Kansas State Historical Society.
57. Telegram, Thomas Moonlight to Major Harry E. Gryden of the Kansas State Militia, June 6, 1883, Kansas State Historical Society.
58. Telegram, Sheriff George T. Hinkle to Governor Glick, June 6, 1883, Kansas State Historical Society.
59. Ibid.
60. *Leavenworth Times,* June 5, 1883; *Ford County Globe,* June 12, 1883.
61. Miller and Snell, p. 561.
62. *Dodge City Times,* June 14, 1883.
63. Ibid., August 23, 1883.
64. *Ford County Globe,* November 20, 1883.
65. Ibid.
66. Ibid., January 1, 1884; *Dodge City Democrat,* December 29, 1883.
67. *Dodge City Democrat,* May 10, 1884.
68. Ibid., August 9, 1884.
69. Miller and Snell, p. 564.
70. *Fort Worth (Texas) Gazette,* February 8, 1887.
71. Ibid., February 9, 1887.
72. Ibid., February 8, 1887.
73. Ibid., February 9, 1887. Luke Short's two shots missed Jim Courtright entirely, at close range, undoubtedly because Luke was using black-powdered cartridges which filled the air with thick smoke when fired, making it difficult to see. Smokeless powder was not produced in the United States until 1893.
74. Ibid., February 10, 1887.
75. Ibid.
76. Ibid., December 24, 1890; *Dallas (Texas) News,* December 24, 1890.
77. Miller and Snell, p. 564.
78. *Geuda Springs (Kansas) Herald,* September 8, 1893.

7. BEN THOMPSON

1. Floyd Benjamin Streeter, *Ben Thompson: Man with a Gun,* p. 23.
2. Masterson, "Famous Gunfighters of the Western Frontier," *Human Life Magazine,* 1907.
3. Letter, Royal Naval Library, London, England, to Dale T. Schoenberger, December 1, 1967; letter, Michael Godfrey, Public Record Office, London, to author, December 13, 1967.
4. Streeter, *Ben Thompson: Man with a Gun,* p. 26.
5. Ibid., pp. 26-27.
6. Ibid, p. 21.
7. Ibid., p. 22.
8. Ibid.
9. Ibid.
10. "Executive Record Book," Governor Hardin R. Runnels of Texas, Number 275, 1857-1859, Texas State Library and Archives, Austin.
11. Ibid.
12. Streeter, *Ben Thompson: Man with a Gun,* p. 28.
13. Ibid., p. 30.
14. Letter, Margaret Ruckert, Head of the Louisiana Department, New Orleans Public Library, to the author, August 10, 1966.
15. Military service records of Benjamin F. Thompson, Second Regiment Texas Cavalry, Confederate States Army, Old Military Records Division, National Archives, Washington, D.C.
16. "The Old Bookaroos" [Jeff C. Dykes, Fred G. Renner, and B. W. Allred], "Western Book Roundup," *Frontier Times Magazine,* 41, Number 4, June-July, 1967, 50.
17. Information given to Dale T. Schoenberger by the National Archives, on NAR Form 331.
18. Letter, Elmer O. Parker, Old Military Records Division, National Archives, to the author, November 8, 1967.
19. Military service records of Benjamin F. Thompson, Prisoner of War Parole, Number 1817 [?], National Archives.
20. Ibid.
21. Ibid.
22. Ibid.
23. Ibid.
24. Ibid.
25. Ibid.
26. Ibid.
27. Ibid.
28. Information given to Dale T. Schoenberger by the National Archives, on NAR Form 331; letter, James M. Day, Archivist, Texas State Library and Archives, Austin, to Dale T. Schoenberger, February 13, 1967.
29. Military service records of Martino (Martin) Gonzales, 33rd Regiment Texas Cavalry, Confederate States Army, National Archives.
30. Military service records of Juan Rodriguez, Third Battalion Texas Cavalry, Confederate States Army, Archives Division, Texas State Library and Archives, Austin.
31. Letter, Eli Greer, Deputy District Court Clerk, Travis County, Texas, Austin, to Dale T. Schoenberger, August 13, 1965.

32. Letter, Garry D. Ryan, Assistant Director, Old Military Records Division, National Archives, to the author, July 11, 1967.
33. Emperor Franz Josef I of Austria was still on his throne as late as 1916, and supported his ally Germany in World War I before his death.
34. Letter, Benecio López Padilla, General of the Division, Department of Archives, Commission of History, Republic of Mexico, Mexico, D. F., to Dale T. Schoenberger, January 25, 1967.
35. Ibid.
36. *The Daily Capital* (Austin, Texas), March 13, 1884.
37. Ibid.
38. *Austin Weekly Republican,* April 8, 1868.
39. Ibid.
40. General Orders, Number 17, Headquarters, Fifth U. S. Military District, dated at Austin, Texas, October 20, 1868, National Archives.
41. Ibid.
42. Ibid.
43. Letter, Henry R. Small, Bureau of Records and Identification, Texas State Department of Corrections, Huntsville, Texas, to Dale T. Schoenberger, January 13, 1967.
44. Ibid.
45. Ibid.
46. Gard, p. 190.
47. Ibid., p. 203.
48. Streeter, *Ben Thompson: Man with a Gun,* p. 93.
49. Police Court Dockets, Records of the City of Ellsworth, Kansas, June 11, 1873.
50. Ibid.
51. Ibid.
52. Streeter, *Ben Thompson,* p. 93.
53. Police Court Dockets, Ellsworth, Kansas, July 1, 1873.
54. Ibid.
55. In September 1868, C. B. Whitney was a member of the civilian scout detachment under then Major G. A. Forsyth, acting assistant inspector-general to General P. H. Sheridan. Forsyth's detachment withstood the Cheyennes under Roman Nose (who was killed in the fight), for several days before being rescued. The battle took place on an island—later called Beecher's —in the Arickaree Fork of the Republican River in northeast Colorado. "Comanche Jack" Stilwell, brother of Frank Stilwell, and one of Forsyth's scouts, was one of the men sent by Forsyth to bring help to the besieged party. Forsyth's second-in-command, First Lieutenant Frederick H. Beecher, of the Third U.S. Infantry, who was killed in the fight, was the nephew of Henry Ward Beecher and Harriet Beecher Stowe.—lecture, "The Beecher Island Fight," by John G. Neihardt, University of Missouri, Columbia, March 30, 1966. Forsyth was one of the Indian-fighting Army's ablest officers, and was wounded three times during the engagement. He died in 1915 after a distinguished career on the frontier.
56. This shotgun is now in the possession of the Dodge City Boot Hill Museum which is owned by Mrs. Merritt L. Beeson, daughter-in-law of the late Chalk Beeson, one-time co-owner of the Long Branch Saloon. Ben Thompson had borrowed $75 from Beeson in 1877 and gave Beeson the shotgun as security on the loan. Thompson never reclaimed the gun.
57. *Ellsworth* (Kansas) *Reporter,* August 21, 1873.
58. Streeter, *Ben Thompson: Man with a Gun,* p. 99.
59. Ibid.
60. Ibid., p. 100.
61. *Ellsworth Reporter,* August 21, 1873.
62. Ibid.
63. *Rocky Mountain News,* October 23, 1898.
64. Streeter, *Ben Thompson,* p. 109.
65. Ibid., p. 113.
66. "*Testimony and Records in the Case of the State of Kansas vs. William Thompson,*" Ellsworth County, District Court, Ellsworth, September 1877.
67. Streeter, *Ben Thompson,* p. 114.
68. "*Testimony and Records in the Case of the State of Kansas vs. William Thompson,*" Ellsworth, September 1877; *Ellsworth Reporter,* September 20, 1877.
69. Streeter, *Prairie Trails and Cow Towns,* p. 166.
70. Wright, p. 267.
71. Streeter, *Ben Thompson,* p. 118.
72. William M. Walton, *The Life and Adventures of Ben Thompson, the Famous Texan,* p. 159 (1954 edition).
73. Letter, Eli Greer, Deputy District Court Clerk, Travis County, Texas, Austin, to Dale T. Schoenberger, no date on letter.
74. Letter, Ronald A. Seeliger, Newspaper Librarian, University of Texas Library, Austin, to the author, June 20, 1966.
75. Walton, pp. 160-61.
76. Ibid., p. 160.
77. Ibid., p. 161.
78. Ibid.
79. Streeter, *Ben Thompson,* p. 123.
80. Ibid.
81. "*The State of Texas* vs. *Benjamin Thompson,*" Number 5005, District Court, Travis County, Texas, Austin, May 1877.
82. Streeter, *Ben Thompson,* p. 140.
83. Ibid., p. 208.
84. *The Daily Democratic Statesman* (Austin), October 2, 1879.
85. Letter, Elsie Woosley, City Clerk, Austin, to Dale T. Schoenberger, October 31, 1967.
86. Walton, p. 154.
87. Letter, Elsie Woosley to Dale T. Schoenberger, October 31, 1967.
88. *The Daily Democratic Statesman,* December 21, 1880.
89. Letter, Elsie Woosley to Dale T. Schoenberger, November 29, 1967.
90. Ibid., October 31, 1967.
91. Streeter, *Ben Thompson,* p. 168.
92. Information given to the author by the Austin Police Department.
93. The regular Austin policemen who served under City Marshal Ben Thompson and Police Sergeant John Chenneville were: R. J. Stewart, the day clerk; John T. Bennett, the night clerk; C. H. Randolph, J. L. Watts, Del C. Lock, D. B. Withers, James Simms, Patrick Connley, J. W. LaRue, O. H. Binckley, J. C. Burchim, John Bels, and H. G. Madison.—Austin, Texas, City Directory of 1882-1883.
94. Wright, p. 267.
95. Letter, Elsie Woosley to Dale T. Schoenberger, December 11, 1967.
96. Streeter, *Ben Thompson,* p. 182.
97. Ibid., pp. 182-83.
98. Walton, p. 187.
99. Streeter, *Ben Thompson,* p. 183.
100. Ibid.
101. Ibid.
102. Ibid.
103. Ibid.

104. *"The State of Texas* vs. *Benjamin Thompson,"* Number 2118, District Court, Bexar County, Texas, San Antonio, 1882-1883.
105. Ibid.
106. Letter, Elsie Woosley to Dale T. Schoenberger, October 31, 1967.
107. Streeter, *Ben Thompson,* pp. 182-83.
108. Letter, Elsie Woosley to Dale T. Schoenberger, October 31, 1967.
109. Ibid.
110. Streeter, *Ben Thompson,* p. 190.
111. Ibid.
112. *The Daily Capital,* March 13, 1884.
113. *The Daily Statesman* (Austin), March 13, 1884.
114. Walton, pp. 221-23.
115. Streeter, *Ben Thompson,* p. 199.
116. Walton, p. 220.
117. Ibid., pp. 221-23.
118. Ibid., p. 222.
119. Streeter, *Ben Thompson,* p. 196.
120. Walton, pp. 223-26.
121. Ibid.
122. Ibid.
123. *The Daily Statesman,* March 13, 1884.
124. There is a rumor—and it is only a rumor—that Billy Thompson was killed at Laredo, Texas, circa 1888.

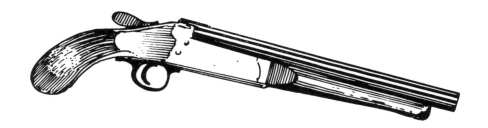

BIBLIOGRAPHY

1. PUBLIC DOCUMENTS AND RECORDS

Affidavit of Mrs. Catherine Cook to the Adjutant General's Office, October 16, 1877. Records of the War Department, Office of the Adjutant General, Old Military Records Division, National Archives, Washington, D.C.

R. A. C. Allison, Light Tennessee Artillery, Confederate States Army, military service records. Old Military Records Division, National Archives, Washington, D.C. Tennessee State Library and Archives, Nashville.

R. C. Allison, Nineteenth Regiment Tennessee Cavalry, Confederate States Army, military service records. Old Military Records Division, National Archives, Washington, D.C. Tennessee State Library and Archives, Nashville.

"City Council Minute Book," Records of the City of Abilene, Kansas.

"The Commissioner's Record Book," Volume A, Ellsworth County, Kansas, 1867-1887. Ar-chives Division, Kansas State Historical Society, Topeka.

Copies of the Dodge City, Kansas, police court dockets for the period of July 5, 1878, to December 31, 1879. Walter S. Campbell Collection, Dodge City File, General Research Correspondence, Division of Manuscripts, University of Oklahoma Library, Norman.

Copy of the Report of Brevet Major General Nelson A. Miles, Fifth United States Infantry, Fort Leavenworth, Kansas, March 4, 1875. Manuscript Division, Kansas State Historical Society, Topeka.

Criminal Court Records, Pima County, Arizona Territory, for Tombstone, now in Cochise County Courthouse, Bisbee, Arizona.

Dodge City, Kansas, Ordinance Book, Volume I. Kansas State Historical Society, Topeka.

"Executive Record Book," Governor Hardin R.

Runnels of Texas, Number 275, 1857-1859. Texas State Library and Archives, Austin.

General Orders, Number 17, Headquarters, Fifth United States Military District, dated at Austin, Texas, October 20, 1868. Old Military Records Division, National Archives, Washington, D.C.

Martino (Martin) Gonzales, 33rd Regiment Texas Cavalry, Confederate States Army, military service records. Old Military Records Division, National Archives, Washington, D.C. Texas State Library and Archives, Austin.

"List of Persons and Property Assessed for Taxation in Marion County, Arkansas, For the Year 1851." Arkansas History Commission, Little Rock.

Kansas State census report for 1875 for Dodge City, Ford County, Kansas. Archives Division, Kansas State Historical Society, Topeka.

Kansas State census report of 1875 for Wichita, Sedgwick County, Kansas, taken on March 1. Archives Division, Kansas State Historical Society, Topeka.

W. B. Masterson, deputy United States marshal, Southern District of New York, Department of Justice service records. General Records of the Department of Justice, National Archives, Washington, D.C.

Marriage Book "A," Colfax County, Courthouse, Raton, New Mexico.

"Minutes of the Common Council," Records of the City of Tombstone, Arizona Territory.

"Miscellaneous Papers," Records of the City of Wichita, Kansas.

Miscellaneous Record Book "B," Colfax County, Courthouse, Raton, New Mexico.

Mortality Schedule, United States census report of 1870 for Hays City, Kansas. Census Division, National Archives, Washington, D.C. Archives Division, Kansas State Historical Society, Topeka.

Muster roll, Company I, July, 1870, Seventh United States Cavalry. Old Military Records Division, National Archives, Washington, D.C.

Muster roll, Company H, Fourth United States Cavalry, January, 1876. Old Military Records Division, National Archives, Washington, D.C.

The oath of office of W. B. Masterson, Deputy United States marshal, Southern District of New York, March 28, 1905. General Records of the Department of Justice, National Archives, Washington, D.C.

Organizational Returns, Seventh United States Cavalry, June, 1867. Old Military Records Division, National Archives, Washington, D.C.

Petition of several citizens, Hays City, Kansas, to Governor James M. Harvey of Kansas, July 7, 1869. "Governors' Correspondence," Archives Division, Kansas State Historical Society, Topeka.

Petition of Luke L. Short to Governor George W. Glick of Kansas, May 10, 1883. "Governors' Correspondence," Archives Division, Kansas State Historical Society, Topeka.

Police court dockets, Records of the City of Ellsworth, Kansas, June and July, 1873.

"Proceedings of the Governing Body," Records of the City of Wichita, Kansas, Journal "B."

Public Health Department Records, City of Fort Worth, Texas.

Records of the War Department, Office of the Quartermaster General, "Reports of Persons and Articles Hired, 1861-1865." Old Military Records Division, National Archives, Washington, D.C.

Records of the War Department, Office of the Provost Marshal General, "Scouts, Guides and Spies, 1861-1866." Old Military Records Division, National Archives, Washington, D.C.

Records of the War Department, Office of the Quartermaster General, "Reports of Persons and Articles Hired, 1861-1868." Old Military Records Divsion, National Archives, Washington, D.C.

Records of the War Department, Office of the Quartermaster General, "Reports of Persons and Articles Hired, 1861-1869." Old Military Records Division, National Archives, Washington, D.C.

Records of the War Department, Office of the Adjutant General, "Register of the Sick and Wounded at Fort Hays, Kansas, During the Months of July and August, 1870." Old Military Records Division, National Archives, Washington, D.C.

Records of the War Department, Office of the Adjutant General, Final Statement of the Adjutant General of Private John Kile, Company I, Seventh United States Cavalry, August 6, 1870. Old Military Records Division, National Archives, Washington, D.C.

Records of the War Department, Office of the Adjutant General, Report of Captain Myles W. Keogh, Seventh United States Cavalry, to the Adjutant General's Office, August 16, 1870. Old Military Records Division, National Archives, Washington, D.C.

Records of the War Department, Office of the Quartermaster General, "Reports of Persons and Articles Hired, Indian Territory, 1874-1875." Old Military Records Division, National Archives, Washington, D.C.

Records of the War Department, Office of the Adjutant General, Final Statement of the Adjutant General of Corporal Melvin A. King, Company H, Fourth United States Cavalry, March 4, 1876. Old Military Records Division, National Archives, Washington, D.C.

Records of the War Department, Office of the Adjutant General, Report of the Adjutant General, November 17, 1877. Old Military Records Division, National Archives, Washington, D.C.

Records of the War Department, Office of the Quartermaster General, "Reports of Persons and Articles Hired at Sidney Barracks, Nebraska, October, 1878." Old Military Records Division, National Archives, Washington, D. C.

Records of Camp Rucker, Arizona Territory, for 1880. Old Military Records Division, National Archives, Washington, D.C.

Records of the County Recorder, Los Angeles, California.

William G. Ritch Papers. Henry E. Huntington Library and Art Gallery, San Marino, California. Contains some information on Clay Allison's New Mexico exploits.

Juan Rodriquez, Third Battalion Texas Cavalry, Confederate States Army, military service records. Old Military Records Division, National Archives, Washington, D.C. Texas State Library and Archives, Austin.

"The State of Texas v. Benjamin Thompson," Number 5005, District Court, Travis County, Texas, Austin, May, 1877.

"The State of Texas v. Benjamin Thompson," Number 2,118, District Court, Bexar County, Texas, San Antonio, 1882-1883.

"Strausbach v. E. Cramer," District Court, Civil Records, Ford County, Kansas, Dodge City.

Tenth United States census report, Statistics of Agriculture. Census Division, National Archives, Washington, D.C.

Territory of Nebraska, County of Gage, v. "Dutch Bill, Doc, and Wellman," July, 1861, Nebraska State Historical Society, Lincoln.

"Testimony and Records in the Case of the State of Kansas v. William Thompson," Ellsworth County, Kansas, District Court, Ellsworth, September, 1877.

Benjamin F. Thompson, Second Regiment Texas Cavalry, Confederate States Army, military service records. Old Military Records Division, National Archives, Washington, D. C.

Davis K. Tutt, Jr., 27th Regiment Arkansas Infantry, Confederate States Army, military service records. Old Military Records Division, National Archives, Washington, D.C.

United States census report of 1860 for Griffin, Spalding County, Georgia, taken on June 8. Census Division, National Archives, Washington, D.C.

United States census report of 1860 for Yellville, Marion County, Arkansas, Union Township. Census Division, National Archives, Washington, D.C. Arkansas History Commission, Little Rock.

United States census report of 1870 for Hays City, Ellis County, Kansas, taken on June 1. Census Division, National Archives, Washington, D.C. Archives Division, Kansas State Historical Society, Topeka.

United States census report of 1870 for Valdosta,

Lowndes County, Georgia, taken on June 8. Census Division, National Archives.

United States census report of 1870 for Lamar, Barton County, Missouri, Lamar Township, taken on September 3. Census Division, National Archives, Washington, D.C. State Archives, State Historical Society of Missouri, Columbia.

United States census report of 1880 for Dodge City, Ford County, Kansas, taken on June 22. Census Division, National Archives, Washington, D.C. Archives Division, Kansas State Historical Society, Topeka.

"The United States v. *John McCall,"* Trial Documents, Second Judicial Court, Territory of Dakota, at Yankton. Federal Records Center, Kansas City, Missouri.

2. MANUSCRIPTS, LETTERS, AND DIARIES

Joseph F. Anderson to Raymond W. Thorp, no date on letter.

Luke Cahill, "Recollections of A Plainsman." State Historical Society of Colorado, Denver.

Mary P. M. Carr, "Memoirs of Brevet Major General Eugene A. Carr," manuscript. In the possession of Mrs. Virginia Carr Van Soelen, Santa Fe, New Mexico.

W. F. Carver to Raymond W. Thorp, no date on letter.

Dr. Samuel J. Crumbine to Walter S. Campbell (Stanley Vestal), January 24, 1950. Walter S. Campbell Collection, Dodge City File, General Research Correspondence, Division of Manuscripts, University of Oklahoma Library, Norman.

Copy of the Diary of Henry H. Raymond, 1872-1873. Archives Division, Kansas State Historical Society, Topeka.

Partial Diary of First Lieutenant Frank D. Baldwin, U.S.A. Manuscript Division, Kansas State Historical Society, Topeka.

F. J. Dodge to Stuart N. Lake, October 8, 1928; September 15, 1929; September 18, 1930. In the possession of Carolyn Lake, San Diego, California.

M. H. Dowell to J. Evetts Haley, January 12, 1939.

Wyatt S. Earp to William S. Hart, July 3, 1925. William S. Hart Ranch and Museum, Newhall, California.

J. B. Edwards to William Elsey Connelley, January 27, 1926. Manuscript Division, Kansas State Historical Society, Topeka.

Major George Gibson, commanding officer at Fort Hays, Kansas, to Governor James M. Harvey of Kansas, October 3, 1869. "Governors' Correspondence," Archives Division, Kansas State Historical Society, Topeka.

Charles F. Gross to J. B. Edwards, June 15, 1925. Manuscript Division, Kansas State Historical Society, Topeka.

Charles F. Gross to J. B. Edwards, January 20, 1926. Manuscript Division, Kansas State Historical Society, Topeka.

James C. Hancock to Frank Waters, December 8, 1937.

J. B. Hickok to Ellis County, Kansas, no date on letter. Manuscript Division, Kansas State Historical Society, Topeka.

Milt Hinkle to "Frontier Post," *Frontier Times Magazine*, Spring, 1961.

Dallas Irvine, Old Military Records Division, National Archives, Washington, D.C., to Joseph G. Rosa, August 15, 1956.

Lute Johnson Scrapbook. Volume I. State Historical Society of Colorado, Denver.

Lonnie Lee to "Mail Roundup," *Real West Magazine*, Volume VIII, Number 39, January, 1965.

Thomas Masterson, Jr., to Floyd Benjamin Streeter, September 17, 1935. Walter S. Campbell

Collection, Dodge City File, General Research Correspondence, Division of Manuscripts, University of Oklahoma Library, Norman.

Bat Masterson to Henry H. Raymond, July 23, 1899. Copy, Archives Division, Kansas State Historical Society, Topeka.

W. B. (Bat) Masterson to Frederick S. Barde, October 13, 1913. Manuscript Division, Kansas State Historical Society, Topeka.

Mary A. McCall to the United States Marshal, Yankton, Dakota Territory, February 25, 1877.

W. R. McLaury to S. P. Green, November 8, 1881. New-York Historical Society, New York.

W. R. McLaury to D. D. Applegate, November 9, 1881. New-York Historical Society, New York.

George Whitwell Parsons, *The Private Journal of George Whitwell Parsons.* Arizona Pioneers' Historical Society, Tucson.

A. K. Richeson, "Interview with William Thatcher," January 17, 1934. State Historical Society of Colorado, Denver.

Charles Roos, Armed Forces Medical Library, Washington, D.C., to Joseph G. Rosa, September 11, 1956.

Pink Simms to Floyd Benjamin Streeter, October 27, 1935. Walter S. Campbell Collection, Dodge City File, General Research Correspondence, Division of Manuscripts, University of Oklahoma Library, Norman.

Pink Simms to Frank Waters, no date on letter.

Floyd Benjamin Streeter to Frank Waters, January 4, 1938.

Telegrams, George T. Hinkle, Sheriff of Ford County, Kansas, to Governor George W. Glick of Kansas, May 11, 1883; May 12, 1883; May 31, 1883; June 6, 1883; "Govenors' Correspondence," Archives Division, Kansas State Historical Society, Topeka.

Telegram, Robert M. Wright, Commissioner of Ford County, Kansas, and Richard J. Hardesty to Governor George W. Glick of Kansas, May 11, 1883. "Governors' Correspondence," Archives Division, Kansas State Historical Society, Topeka.

Telegram, Governor George W. Glick of Kansas,

to George T. Hinkle, Sheriff of Ford County, Kansas, May 12, 1883. "Governors' Correspondence," Archives Division, Kansas State Historical Society, Topeka.

Telegrams, Several citizens, Dodge City, Kansas, to Governor George W. Glick of Kansas, May 13, 1883; June 6, 1883; "Governors' Correspondence," Archives Division, Kansas State Historical Society, Topeka.

Telegram, Thomas Moonlight, Adjutant General of Kansas to Governor George W. Glick of Kansas, May 17, 1883. "Correspondence of the Adjutant General," Archives Division, Kansas State Historical Society, Topeka.

Telegram, Thomas Moonlight, Adjutant General of Kansas, to George T. Hinkle, Sheriff of Ford County, Kansas, June 4, 1883. "Correspondence of the Adjutant General," Archives Division, Kansas State Historical Society, Topeka.

Telegram, Major Harry E. Gryden of the Kansas State Militia, to Thomas Moonlight, Adjutant General of Kansas, June 5, 1883. "Correspondence of the Adjutant General," Archives Division, Kansas State Historical Society, Topeka.

Telegram, Governor George W. Glick of Kansas to the Citizens of Dodge City, Kansas, June 6, 1883. "Governors' Correspondence," Archives Division, Kansas State Historical Society, Topeka.

Telegram, Thomas Moonlight, Adjutant General of Kansas, to Major Harry E. Gryden of the Kansas State Militia, June 6, 1883. "Correspondence of the Adjutant General," Archives Division, Kansas State Historical Society, Topeka.

Henry A. Wise, United States Attorney, Southern District of New York, to the United States Attorney General's Office, June 16, 1909. General Records of the Department of Justice, National Archives, Washington, D.C.

United States Attorney General's Office to President William Howard Taft, June 23, 1909. General Records of the Department of Justice, National Archives, Washington, D.C.

President William Howard Taft to the United States Attorney General's Office, June 29,

1909. General Records of the Department of Justice, National Archives, Washington, D.C.

United States Marshal William Henkel, State of New York, to the United States Attorney General's Office, June 30, 1909; July 14, 1909. General Records of the Department of Justice, National Archives, Washington, D.C.

Alfred Henry Lewis to President William Howard Taft, July 10, 1909. Records of the Department of Justice, National Archives, Washington, D.C.

United States Attorney General's Office to United States Marshal William Henkel, Southern District of New York, July 12, 1909; July 15, 1909. General Records of the Department of Justice, National Archives, Washington, D.C.

3. NEWSPAPERS

Abilene (Kansas) *Chronicle*—November 3, 1870; May 18, 1871; July 13, 1871; August 17, 1871; August 24, 1871; September 14, 1871; October 12, 1871; November 30, 1871.

Arizona Daily Citizen (Tucson)—May 22, 1900.

Arizona Daily Star (Tucson)—June 23, 1881.

Arizona Enterprise (Florence)—July 7, 1888.

Arizona Star (Tucson)—July 26, 1911.

Arizona Weekly Star (Tucson)—May 26, 1881; August 25, 1881.

Associated Press wire story, March 19, 1967. (Story by John Barbour).

Austin (Texas) *Daily Capital*—March 13, 1884.

Austin (Texas) *Daily Statesman*—March 13, 1884.

Caldwell (Kansas) *Commercial*—April 21, 1881.

Caldwell (Kansas) *Journal*—May 24, 1883.

Cheyenne (Wyoming) *Daily Leader*—March 7, 1876; September 1, 1876; November 19, 1876; November 23, 1876.

Cheyenne (Wyoming) *Democratic Leader*—June 13, 1886.

Chicago (Illinois) *Record*—December 26, 1896.

Cimarron (New Mexico) *News and Press*—April 7, 1881; July 14, 1881.

Colorado Chieftain (Pueblo)—November 3, 1875; November 12, 1875; December 27, 1876; December 31, 1876; January 3, 1877; January 9, 1877; February 6, 1877.

The Daily Democratic Statesman (Austin, Tex.)— October 2, 1879; December 21, 1880.

The Daily Enquirer (Cincinnati, O.)—March 19, 1876.

The Daily Journal (St. Louis, Mo.)—October 11, 1878.

The Daily New Mexican (Santa Fe)—January 13, 1874; June 1, 1875; November 5, 1875; March 25, 1876; March 30, 1876; October 10, 1876; July 19, 1887.

Dallas (Texas) *Herald*—January 2, 1875.

Dallas (Texas) *News*—December 24, 1890.

Denver (Colorado) *Republican*—May 22, 1882; March 27, 1885; March 28, 1885; June 22, 1887; December 25, 1887.

Denver (Colorado) *Tribune*—May 16, 1882; March 27, 1885.

Dodge City (Kansas) *Democrat*—December 29, 1883; May 10, 1884; August 9, 1884; March 13, 1886.

Dodge City (Kansas) *Times*—October 14, 1876; March 31, 1877; April 28, 1877; May 6, 1877; June 9, 1877; July 7, 1877; August 4, 1877; July 21, 1877; September 29, 1877; November 3, 1877; November 10, 1877; November 24, 1877; December 8, 1877; January 5, 1878; January 12, 1878; January 19, 1878; February 2, 1878; February 9, 1878; February 16, 1878; April 13, 1878; May 11, 1878; June 1, 1878; June 8, 1878; July 6, 1878; July 26, 1878; August 10, 1878; August 17, 1878; August 24, 1878; September 7, 1878; October 5, 1878; October 12, 1878; December 7, 1878; January 4, 1879; January 11, 1879; January 18, 1879;

January 25, 1879; March 29, 1879; April 12, 1879; May 10, 1879; May 24, 1879; June 14, 1879; October 25, 1879; November 8, 1879; November 15, 1879; December 6, 1879; January 17, 1880; May 22, 1880; June 26, 1880; July 17, 1880; April 21, 1881; April 5, 1883; April 26, 1883; May 3, 1883; May 10, 1883; May 17, 1883; June 14, 1883; August 23, 1883; March 11, 1886.

Ellsworth (Kansas) *Reporter*—August 21, 1873; September 20, 1877.

Ford County (Kansas) *Globe* (Dodge City)—January 15, 1878; February 5, 1878; February 12, 1878; March 18, 1878; April 16, 1878; April 23, 1878; May 14, 1878; June 18, 1878; July 30, 1878; August 20, 1878; August 27, 1878; October 8, 1878; January 21, 1879; March 18, 1879; March 25, 1879; April 8, 1879; April 15, 1879; June 10, 1879; June 14, 1879; September 9, 1879; September 16, 1879; September 30, 1879; October 28, 1879; December 2, 1879; March 2, 1880; March 30, 1880; December 7, 1880; February 15, 1881; April 19, 1881; February 6, 1883; May 1, 1883; June 5, 1883; June 12, 1883; November 20, 1883; January 1, 1884.

Fort Worth (Texas) *Gazette*—February 10, 1884; February 8, 1887; February 9, 1887; December 24, 1890.

Geuda Herald (Geuda Springs, Kans.)—September 8, 1893.

Globe Live Stock Journal (Dodge City, Kans.)— March 16, 1886; July 26, 1887.

Jacksboro (Texas) *Frontier Echo*—February 11, 1876.

Junction City (Kansas) *Union*—July 23, 1870.

Junction City (Kansas) *Weekly Union*—October 2, 1869.

Kansas City (Missouri) *Evening Star*—June 7, 1883.

Kansas City (Missouri) *Star*—November 10, 1897.

Kinsley (Kansas) *Graphic*—June 7, 1883.

Las Animas (Colorado) *Leader*—September 24, 1875; December 22, 1876; January 5, 1877; January 12, 1877; February 9, 1877; February 16, 1877; March 30, 1877.

Las Vegas (New Mexico) *Daily Optic*—March 31, 1881; July 7, 1886.

Lawrence (Kansas) *Daily Tribune*—September 30, 1869.

Leadville (Colorado) *Daily Herald*—August 20, 1884; August 26, 1884.

Leavenworth (Kansas) *Commercial*—September 28, 1869.

Leavenworth (Kansas) *Daily Conservative*—December 14, 1867; January 10, 1868.

Leavenworth (Kansas) *Times*—July 10, 1874; November 17, 1877; February 16, 1879; June 5, 1883.

Leavenworth (Kansas) *Times and Conservative*— August 26, 1869; September 2, 1869; September 28, 1869; November 5, 1869.

Leoti (Kansas) *Standard*—March 3, 1892.

Mendota (Illinois) *Bulletin*—April 11, 1873.

Missouri Democrat (St. Louis)—April 4, 1867; March 15, 1873.

Missouri Republican (St. Louis)—July 25, 1878.

New York (New York) *Herald*—May 17, 1907.

Niagara Falls (New York) *Gazette*—August 28, 1872; September 4, 1872.

Portland (Maine) *Advertiser*—January 30, 1874.

Pueblo (Colorado) *Chieftain*—May 17, 1882; June 1, 1882.

Raton (New Mexico) *Comet*—January 21, 1887.

Raton (New Mexico) *Range*—July 22, 1887.

Republican Valley Empire (Clyde, Kans.)—August 2, 1870.

Rochester (New York) *Democrat and Chronicle*— September 1, 1873; March 14, 1874.

Rocky Mountain News (Denver, Colo.)—October 30, 1868; May 25, 1882; September 22, 1886; October 23, 1898; October 26, 1921.

San Antonio (Texas) *Express*—March 13, 1884.

San Francisco (California) *Chronicle*—December 9, 1896.

South-West Missourian (Lamar)—June 16, 1870.

Speareville (Kansas) *News*—November 8, 1879; November 15, 1879.

Springfield (Missouri) *Weekly Patriot*—July 27, 1865; August 10, 1865; January 31, 1867.

Tombstone (Arizona) *Epitaph*—October 20, 1880; October 28, 1880; May 30, 1881; October 28, 1881; October 31, 1881; November 24, 1881; December 18, 1881; January 18, 1882; March 20, 1882; March 21, 1882; March 25, 1882.

Tombstone (Arizona) *Nugget*—March 19, 1881; July 6, 1881; October 30, 1881; November 17, 1881.

Tombstone (Arizona) *Record*—September 3, 1884.

Topeka (Kansas) *Daily Capital*—May 12, 1883; May 16, 1883; May 18, 1883.

Topeka (Kansas) *Daily Commonwealth*—July 22, 1870; May 11, 1871; May 18, 1883; May 20, 1883; June 5, 1883.

Topeka (Kansas) *State Record*—July 26, 1871.

Topeka (Kansas) *Weekly Leader*—April 2, 1868.

Vox Populi (Dodge City, Kans.)—November 1, 1884.

The Weekly Austin (Texas) *Republican*—April 8, 1868.

The Weekly New Mexican (Santa Fe)—October 18, 1870.

Western Nebraskian (North Platte, Neb.)—June 26, 1880.

Wichita (Kansas) *City Eagle*—October 29, 1874; April 8, 1875; May 6, 1875; May 27, 1875.

Wichita (Kansas) *Morning Eagle*—July 24, 1938.

Wichita (Kansas) *Weekly Beacon*—April 28, 1875; May 12, 1875; May 26, 1875; December 15, 1875; January 12, 1876; April 5, 1876; May 24, 1876.

Yankton Press and Dakotaian (Dakota Territory) —December 5, 1876; March 1, 1877.

4. AUTHOR'S CORRESPONDENCE

Ernest R. Archambeau, Amarillo, Texas, no date on letter.

Mrs. Luisa Arps, Librarian, State Historical Society of Colorado, Denver, July 18, 1966; July 19, 1966.

Austin, Texas, Police Department.

Mrs. Lucile A. Boykin, Department Head, Texas History and Genealogy Department, Dallas, Texas, Public Library, June 30, 1966.

Mrs. Dorotha M. Bradley, Assistant Archivist, New Mexico State Records Center and Archives, Santa Fe, July 12, 1966.

Dr. David T. Carr, Mayo Clinic, Rochester, Minnesota, October 28, 1966.

Chamber of Commerce, Pecos, Texas.

Mrs. Velma Churchill, Principal Archivist Aide, Colorado State Archives and Public Records Center, Denver, October 9, 1967.

Mrs. Marguerite B. Cooley, Director, Arizona State Library and Archives, Phoenix, June 21, 1966; January 16, 1967.

James M. Day, Archivist, Texas State Library and Archives, Austin, February 13, 1967.

W. W. Dennis, Jacksboro, Texas, July 9, 1966.

Robert E. Eagan, Dodge City, Kansas, April 4, 1967.

Gardner P. H. Foley, Baltimore College of Dental Surgery, University of Maryland, College Park, August 12, 1966; October 4, 1966.

Mrs. Alys H. Freeze, Head of the Western History Department, Denver, Colorado, Public Library, July 14, 1966; August 12, 1966.

Gilbert Garcia, Deputy Clerk, District Court, Las Animas County, Colorado, August 8, 1966.

John D. Gilchriese, University of Arizona, Tucson, July 26, 1966.

Donald C. Gisick, Deputy City Clerk, Wichita, Kansas, March 15, 1967.

Michael Godfrey, Public Record Office, London, England, December 13, 1967.

Eli Greer, Deputy District Court Clerk, Travis

County, Texas, Austin, no date on letter; also letter dated August 13, 1965.

Mrs. Katherine Halverson, Chief, Historical Division, Wyoming State Archives and Historical Department, Cheyenne, September 24, 1965.

Mrs. Lilla M. Hawes, Director, Georgia Historical Society, Savannah, June 21, 1966.

George R. Henrichs, Executive Director, Dodge City, Kansas, Boot Hill Museum, July 12, 1963.

Tom Hill, County and District Court Clerk, Hemphill County, Texas, no date on letter.

Milt Hinkle, Kissimmee, Florida, no date on letter; also letters dated January 18, 1964; March 6, 1964; March 17, 1964.

T. F. Hobble, Needles, California, March 27, 1967.

Waldo E. Koop, Wichita, Kansas, June 26, 1962; July 1, 1962.

Lonnie Lee, Iowa Park, Texas, December 10, 1964.

Mrs. Zelma B. Locker, Head Librarian, California Room, San Diego, California, Public Library, July 20, 1966.

Harold R. Manakee, Director, Maryland Historical Society, Baltimore, June 15, 1966; July 11, 1966.

James McGurrin, County Clerk and Clerk of the Supreme Court, New York County, New York, October 20, 1967.

T. Morton, Acting Commander, Public Information Division, Los Angeles, California, Police Department, July 28, 1966.

NAR form 331. Old Military Records Division, National Archives, Washington, D.C.

Office of Ted R. Carpenter, County Recorder, San Bernardino County, San Bernardino, California, December 1, 1967.

Office of Donald A. Harter, County Clerk, Herkimer County, Herkimer, New York.

Office of William G. Sharp, County Clerk and Clerk, Superior Court, County of Los Angeles, Los Angeles, California.

Benecio López Padilla, General of the Division, Department of Archives, Commission of History, Republic of Mexico, Mexico, D. F., January 25, 1967.

Elmer O. Parker, Assistant Director, Old Military Records Division, National Archives, Washington, D. C., October 28, 1966; October 10, 1967; November 8, 1967; November 14, 1967; November 15, 1967; November 29, 1967; August 13, 1970.

Royal Naval Library, London, England, December 1, 1967.

Margaret Ruckert, Head of the Louisiana Department, New Orleans, Louisiana, Public Library, August 10, 1966.

Mrs. Virginia Rust, Assistant in Manuscripts, Henry E. Huntington Library and Art Gallery, San Marino, California, June 29, 1966.

Garry R. Ryan, Assistant Director, Old Military Records Division, National Archives, Washington, D. C., July 11, 1967; July 18, 1967.

Glenn R. Sanderford, Federal Records Center, Fort Worth, Texas, July 25, 1966.

Ronald A. Seeliger, Newspaper Librarian, University of Texas Library, Austin, June 20, 1966.

Stanley J. Sierson, Jr., Chief of Detectives, East Saint Louis, Illinois, Police Department, August 24, 1965.

Henry R. Small, Bureau of Records and Identification, Texas State Department of Corrections, Huntsville, Texas, January 13, 1967.

Miss Jane F. Smith, Director, Social and Economic Records Division, National Archives, Washington, D.C., July 24, 1967.

Joseph W. Snell, Curator of Manuscripts, Kansas State Historical Society, Topeka, May 16, 1962.

Margaret J. Sparks, Reference Librarian, Arizona Pioneers' Historical Society, Tucson, July 9, 1966; July 27, 1966.

F. Stanley, Pep, Texas, July 25, 1965; July 26, 1965.

Stewart P. Verckler, Abilene, Kansas, August 7, 1967.

Don W. Wilson, Archivist, Kansas State Historical Society, Topeka, September 18, 1967.

Ben L. Witherspoon, Deputy City Clerk, Wichita, Kansas, July 16, 1962; July 24, 1962.

Elsie Woosley, City Clerk, Austin, Texas, October 31, 1967; November 29, 1967; December 11, 1967.

5. BOOKS AND PAMPHLETS

The American International Encyclopedia: A Comprehensive Reference Work. Volume II. New York: J. J. Little and Ives Company, Inc., 1954.

Andreas, A. T. *History of the State of Kansas.* Chicago, A. T. Andreas, 1883.

Arthur, John Preston. *History of Watauga County, North Carolina, With Sketches of Prominent Families.* Richmond, Virginia: Everett Waddey Company, 1915.

Bartholomew, Ed. *The Biographical Album of Western Gunfighters.* Houston: The Frontier Press of Texas, 1958.

———. *Wyatt Earp: The Untold Story.* Toyahvale, Texas: The Frontier Book Company, 1963.

———. *Wyatt Earp: The Man and the Myth.* Toyahvale, Texas: The Frontier Book Company, 1964.

Burns, Walter Noble. *Tombstone: An Iliad of the West.* Garden City, N.Y.: Doubleday, Page and Company, 1927.

Chandler, Lieutenant Colonel Melbourne C., U.S.A. *Of Garry Owen in Glory.* Annandale, Va.; The Turnpike Press, Inc., 1960.

City Directory, Austin, Texas, 1882-1883.

Clark, O. S. *Clay Allison of the Washita.* Attica, Ind.: G. M. Williams, 1920.

Cleaveland, Agnes Morley. *No Life For A Lady.* Boston: Houghton Mifflin Company, 1941.

Colorado State Business Directory of 1892 and 1893. Denver, Colo., Public Library.

Connelley, William Elsey. *Wild Bill and His Era.* New York: The Press of the Pioneers, 1933.

Cox, William R. *Luke Short and His Era.* Garden City, N.Y.: Doubleday and Company, Inc., 1961.

Custer, Elizabeth B. *Following the Guidon.* Norman: University of Oklahoma Press, 1966. Originally published 1890 in New York.

"Daughters of the American Revolution Cemetery Records from 250 Georgia Cemeteries, Volume I, Part II, Tombstone Records from Sunset Hill Cemetery, Valdosta, Georgia, Birth Dates Before 1875." W.P.A. Project Number 4341, Atlanta, Ga., 1937.

Dixon, Olive K. *The Life of "Billy" Dixon.* Dallas, Tex.: P. L. Turner Company, 1914.

Dodge, Natt N. "Wild Life of the American West." In *The Book of the American West* (Jay Monaghan, Editor-in-Chief). New York: Julian Messner, Inc., 1963.

Drago, Harry Sinclair. *Wild, Woolly and Wicked.* New York: Clarkson N. Potter, Inc., Publisher, 1960.

Edwards, J. B. *Early Days in Abilene.* Abilene, Kans.: C. W. Wheeler, *Abilene Chronicle,* 1896. Published in the *Abilene Daily Chronicle* in 1938 with added material from the papers of Edwards.

Edwards, Richard. *Richard Edwards' Twelfth Annual St. Louis Directory.* St. Louis, Missouri: Edwards Company, 1870.

Fisher, O. C. (with J. C. Dykes). *King Fisher: His Life and Times.* Norman: University of Oklahoma Press, 1966.

Foy, Eddie and Harlow, Alvin F. *Clowning Through Life.* New York: E. P. Dutton and Company, 1928.

Gard, Wayne. *The Chisholm Trail.* Norman: University of Oklahoma Press, 1954.

Hamill, Lloyd and Rose. *Hamill's Tombstone Picture Gallery.* Glendale, Cal.: Western Americana Press of Glendale, 1960.

Hardin, John Wesley. *The Life of John Wesley Hardin.* Seguin, Tex.: Smith and Moore, 1896.

Hays (Kansas) Chamber of Commerce, *The Story of the Early Life of Fort Hays and of Hays City.* Hays, Kansas, Old Fort Hays Historical Association, 1959.

Henry, Stuart O. *Conquering Our Great American Plains.* New York: E. P. Dutton and Company, Inc., 1930.

History of Greene County, Mo., n. p., 1883.

Horan, James D. *The Great American West: A Pictorial History From Coronado to the Last*

Frontier. New York: Crown Publishers, Inc., 1959.

Jahns, Pat. *The Frontier World of Doc Holliday.* New York: Hastings House Publishers, Inc., 1957.

Jelinek, George. *The Ellsworth Story—90 Years of Ellsworth and Ellsworth County History.* Ellsworth, Kans.: n. d.

———. *Ellsworth, Kansas, 1867-1947.* Salina, Kans.: Consolidated, 1947.

King, James T. *War Eagle: A Life of General Eugene A. Carr.* Lincoln: University of Nebraska Press, 1963.

Lake, Stuart N. *Wyatt Earp: Frontier Marshal.* Boston and New York, Houghton Mifflin Company, 1931.

Leckie, William H. *The Buffalo Soldiers.* Norman: University of Oklahoma Press, 1967.

Miller, Nyle H., Langsdorf, Edgar, and Richmond, Robert W. *Kansas: A Pictorial History.* Topeka: the Kansas Centennial Commission and the State Historical Society, 1961.

——— and Joseph W. Snell. *Why the West Was Wild.* Topeka: Kansas State Historical Society, 1963.

Myers, John Myers. *Doc Holliday.* Boston: Little, Brown and Company, 1955.

O'Connor, Richard. *Bat Masterson.* New York: Bantam Books, 1958. Originally published in Garden City, N.Y., by Doubleday and Company, Inc., in 1957.

Otero, Miguel Antonio. *My Life on the Frontier.* Volume I, (1864-1882). New York: the Press of the Pioneers, 1935.

Pearson, Jim Berry. *The Maxwell Land Grant.* Norman: University of Oklahoma Press, 1961.

Robinson, Gilbert S. *Old Wagon Show Days.* Cincinnati, O.: Brockwell Company, 1925.

Roenigk, Adolph (editor). *Pioneer Days of Kansas.* Lincoln, Kans.: The Author, 1933.

Rosa, Joseph G. *They Called Him Wild Bill.* Norman: University of Oklahoma Press, 1964.

Russell, Don. *The Lives and Legends of Buffalo Bill.* Norman: University of Oklahoma Press, 1960.

———. "Indians and Soldiers of the American West." In *The Book of the American West* (Jay Monaghan, Editor-in-chief). New York: Julian Messner, Inc., 1963.

Settle, William A., Jr. *Jesse James Was His Name.* Columbia: University of Missouri Press, 1966.

Siringo, Charles A. *A Lone Star Cowboy.* Santa Fe, N.M., The Author, 1919.

———. *Riata and Spurs.* Boston and New York: Houghton Mifflin, 1927.

Stanley, F. *The Grant That Maxwell Bought.* Denver: World Press, Inc., 1952.

———. *Desperadoes of New Mexico.* Denver: World Press, Inc., 1953.

———. *Fort Union* (New Mexico). n. p., 1953.

———. *Clay Allison.* Denver: World Press, Inc., 1956.

Stanley, Henry M. *My Early Travels and Adventures in America and Asia.* London, 1895.

Streeter, Floyd Benjamin. *Prairie Trails and Cow Towns.* Boston: Chapman and Grimes, 1936.

———. *Ben Thompson: Man with a Gun.* New York: Frederick Fell, Inc., Publisher, 1957.

Thompson, George G. *Bat Masterson: The Dodge City Years.* Topeka, Kans.: Fort Hays Kansas State College Studies, Language and Literature Series Number I, 1943.

Thorp, Raymond W. *Spirit Gun of the West: The Story of Doc W. F. Carver.* Glendale, Calif.: Arthur H. Clark Company, 1957.

Tilghman, Zoe A. *Spotlight: Bat Masterson and Wyatt Earp as U.S. Deputy Marshals.* San Antonio, Tex.: The Naylor Company, 1960.

United States Government, *The War of the Rebellion: A Compilation of the Official Records of the Union and Confederate Armies.* Series I, Volume 48, Part I. Washington, D.C.: The United States Government Printing Office, 1880-1901.

Vestal, Stanley. *Dodge City: Queen of Cowtowns.* New York: Bantam Books edition, 1957. Originally published as *Queen of Cowtowns: Dodge City,* in 1952 by Harper and Brothers, New York.

Walton, William M. *The Life and Adventures of*

Ben Thompson, the Famous Texan. Houston: Frontier Press of Texas, 1954. Originally published by the author in 1884.

Waters, Frank. *The Earp Brothers of Tombstone.* New York: Clarkson N. Potter, Inc., Publisher, 1960.

Webb, Walter Prescott. *The Great Plains.* New York: Grosset and Dunlap, n. d. Originally published in 1931 by Ginn and Company in Boston.

Wellman, Paul I. *The Indian Wars of the West.* Garden City, N.Y.: Doubleday and Company, Inc., 1954. Previously published as *Death on Horseback* in 1947. Originally published as *Death on the Prairie* in 1934 and *Death in the Desert* in 1935.

Wilstach, Frank J. *Wild Bill Hickok: The Prince of Pistoleers.* Garden City, N.Y.: Doubleday, Page and Company, 1926.

Wright, Robert M. *Dodge City: The Cowboy Capital.* Wichita, Kans.: Wichita Eagle Press, 1913.

6. MAGAZINE ARTICLES

Davis, Ronald L. "Soiled Doves and Ornamental Culture." *The American West Magazine,* Volume IV, Number 4, November, 1967.

Dykes, Jeff C., Renner, Fred G., and Allred, B. W. "The Old Bookaroos, Western Book Round-up." *Frontier Times Magazine,* Volume 41, Number 4, June-July, 1967.

Forrest, Earle R. "The Killing of Ed Masterson: Deputy Marshal of Old Dodge City." *Brand Book of the Los Angeles Westerners,* 1949.

Kelsey, Harry E., Jr. "Clay Allison: Western Gunman." *Brand Book of the Denver Westerners.* Boulder, Colo.: Johnson Publishing Company, 1957.

Masterson, W. B. (Bat). "Famous Gunfighters of the Western Frontier." *Human Life Magazine,* January-May, 1907.

Mazzanovitch, Anton. "Wyatt Earp." *Brewery Gulch Gazette,* Bisbee, Ariz., April 29, 1932.

Nebraska History Magazine, Volume 10, Number 2, April-June, 1927. Library, Nebraska State Historical Society, Lincoln.

Penn, Chris. "A Note on Bartholomew Masterson." *Tally Book of the English Westerners Society,* London, April, 1967.

Schoenberger, Dale T. "Clay Allison: The Cowboy Gunfighter." *Frontier Times Magazine,* Volume 40, Number 6, New Series Number 44, October-November, 1966.

Serven, James E. "The Buntline Special—Fact or Fiction?" *The American Rifleman,* Volume 115, Number 3, March, 1967.

Streeter, Floyd Benjamin. "Tragedies of a Cow Town." *The Aerend: A Kansas Quarterly,* Volume V, Numbers 2 and 3, Spring and Summer, 1934.

Utley, Robert M. "Kit Carson and the Adobe Walls Campaign." *The American West Magazine,* Volume II, Number I, Winter, 1965.

7. MISCELLANEOUS

The Dale T. Schoenberger Western History Files.

The Dale T. Schoenberger lecture notebook on the Sioux Indians. Lectures by Dr. John G. Neihardt, University of Missouri, Columbia, February-May, 1966.

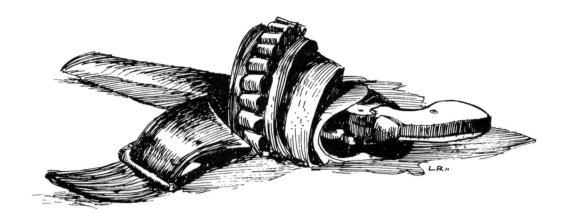

INDEX

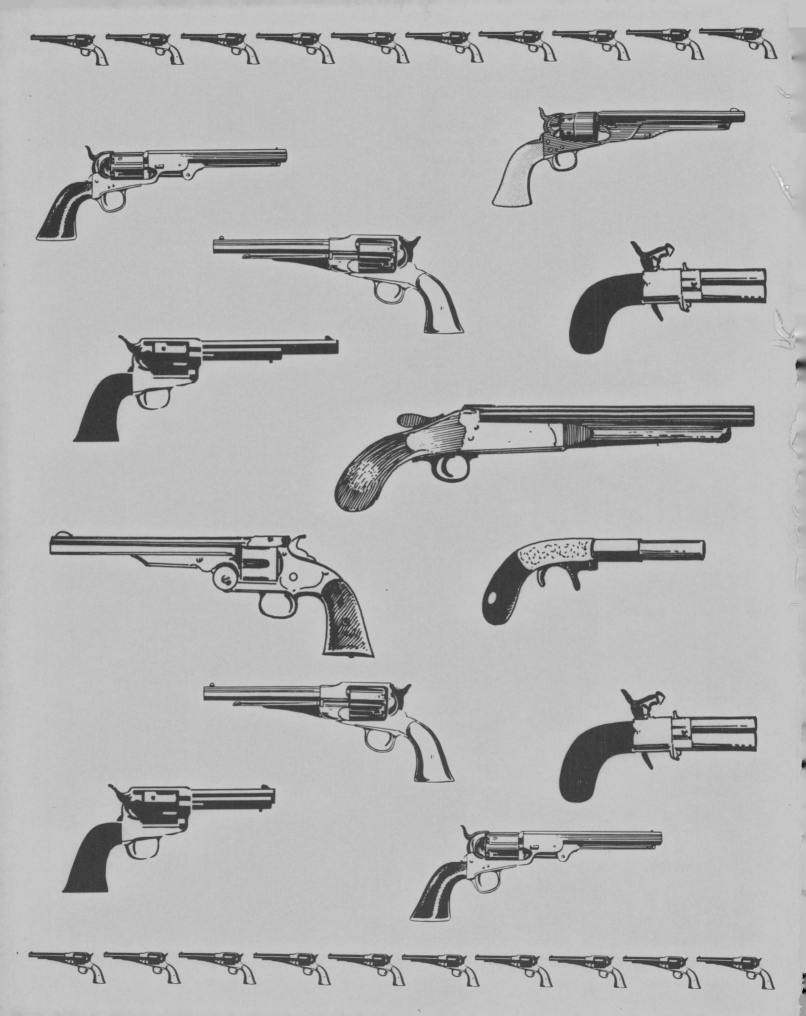